Dictionary of Business Biography

Supplement
Indexes, Contributors, Errata

edited by

David J Jeremy

Research Fellow, Business History Unit
London School of Economics and Political Science

London
Butterworths
1986

United Kingdom   Butterworth & Co (Publishers) Ltd, 88 Kingsway, LONDON WC2B 6AB and 61A North Castle Street, EDINBURGH EH2 3LT.
Australia   Butterworth Pty Ltd, SYDNEY, MELBOURNE, BRISBANE, ADELAIDE, PERTH, CANBERRA and HOBART
Canada   Butterworths. A division of Reed Inc, TORONTO and VANCOUVER
New Zealand   Butterworths of New Zealand Ltd, WELLINGTON and AUCKLAND
Singapore   Butterworth & Co (Asia) Pte Ltd, SINGAPORE
South Africa   Butterworth Publishers (Pty) Ltd, DURBAN
USA   Mason Publishing Co, ST PAUL, Minnesota
                  Butterworth Legal Publishers, Minnesota, SEATTLE, Washington, BOSTON, Massachusetts, AUSTIN, Texas and D & S Publishers, CLEARWATER, Florida

ISBN for the complete set of volumes: 0 406 27340 5
        for this volume: 0 406 27346 4

Typeset by Kerrypress Ltd, Luton
Printed by Whitefriars Press Ltd, Tonbridge

Editorial note

This final part of the *Dictionary of Business Biography* is intended to extend the usefulness of the *DBB*. Of especial utility will be the three indexes and the list of errata. The first two indexes, listing industries and companies represented by the businessmen's (and women's) biographies, have been compiled by Dr Geoffrey Tweedale and are self-explanatory. The index of business people, compiled by Mr Francis Goodall, spans all the subject entries in the five volumes of the *DBB* together with those people who appear in the entries as secondary but major figures. It should be emphasised, however, that these indexes are designed to be preliminary finding aids. Unlike a concordance, they do not claim to contain every name or topic in the *DBB*. The bibliographical resources of the *DBB* will soon be amplified by Mr Goodall's *Bibliography of British Business History*.

The list of errata, jointly compiled by the editorial team and various sharp-eyed readers and contributors (most substantially, Mr Michael Robbins and Mr T A B Corley), to whom we are most grateful, will improve the accuracy of the *DBB* as a reference tool.

With the *DBB* project now completed (though this does not preclude the appearance of further supplements, if sufficient funding is ever forthcoming from private sources), we can round off the work with lists of members of industry advisory committees and of all authors, showing their contributions. While reiterated thanks may seem superfluous, I must conclude by expressing sincere gratitude to everyone who has in any way been involved in this collective effort to move forward the frontiers of business history.

David J Jeremy

Contents

Editorial note   iii

Index of industries, with subject entry   1

Index of companies and trade associations, with subject entry   17

Index of business people, of subjects and of major business figures in entries   39

List of members of industry advisory committees   94

List of contributors, showing their entries   95

List of errata   114

Index of industries, with subject entry

Compiled by Dr Geoffrey Tweedale

I — MINING AND QUARRYING

Coal Mining

BAINBRIDGE, Emerson Muschamp
BERRY, Henry Seymour
BLUNDELL, Henry Blundell-Hollinshead
BOWES, John
BOWMAN, Sir James
BRIGGS, Henry Currer
BURR, Arthur
CHARLESWORTH, John Charlesworth Dodgson
CHILDE, Rowland
DAVIES, David
DEWRANCE, Sir John
FITZWILLIAM, William Thomas Spencer Wentworth
GARFORTH, Sir William Edward
GUÉRET, Louis Jean Baptiste
HARRISON, Robert
HARRISON, William Edward
HEATH II, Robert
HEATH III, Robert
HEATH, Arthur Howard
HEATH, Sir James
HEWITT, Sir Joseph
HEWLETT, Alfred
HICKMAN, Sir Alfred
HINDLEY, John Scott
HOULDSWORTH, Sir Hubert Stanley
INSTONE, Sir Samuel
JOICEY, James
JOLLY, James Hornby
LEGGE, William Heneage
LEWIS, William Thomas
LINDSAY, David Alexander Edward

I — MINING AND QUARRYING

Coal Mining

LLEWELLYN, Sir David Richard
MCLAREN, Charles Benjamin Bright
MCLAREN, Henry Duncan
MARKHAM, Charles Paxton
NIXON, John
PALMER, Sir Charles Mark
PEASE, Joseph Albert
PERCY, Alan Ian
PRIESTMAN, Francis
RITSON, Utrick Alexander
SIMPSON, John Bell
SMITH, George Samuel Fereday
SMITH, Richard Tilden
STEPHENSON, Sir William Haswell
THOMAS, David Alfred
TURNER, Sir John
WARD, William
WARD, William Humble Eric
WILLIAMS, Sir Evan
WOOD, Sir Lindsay

Petroleum

BRIDGEMAN, Sir Maurice Richard
CADMAN, John
CARGILL, Sir John Traill
D'ARCY, William Knox
DOWN, Sir Alastair Frederick
DRAKE, Sir Arthur Eric Courtney
FRASER, William Milligan
GODBER, Frederick
GREENWAY, Charles
LANE, Frederick
PEARSON, Weetman Dickinson

I — MINING AND QUARRYING

Petroleum

PLATT, James Westlake
REDWOOD, Sir Thomas Boverton
SAMUEL, Marcus
WALLACE, Charles William
WATSON, Robert Irving
WILLIAMSON, Archibald

Other Mining and Quarrying

BAILLIEU, Clive Latham
BEATTY, Sir Alfred Chester
BEIT, Alfred
BOLITHO, Thomas Bedford
BUDD, Sir Cecil Lindsay
DOUGLAS-PENNANT, George Sholto Gordon
DUNCAN, Sir John Norman Valette
FALK, Herman Eugen
FARLEY, Reuben
FIELDING, Charles William Ewing
GEDDES, Auckland Campbell
HADFIELD, John
HORNE, Robert Stevenson
KEAY, Sir John
LLYTELTON, Oliver
MCLAREN, Henry Duncan
MALCOLM, George William
MATHESON, Hugh Mackay
MOREING, Charles Algernon
SMITH, Richard Tilden
STOCKER, Thomas Medland
TURNER, Sir Ronald Mark Cunliffe
WERNHER, Sir Julius Carl

II — FOOD, DRINK AND TOBACCO

Food

BERRY, Albert Eustace
BIBBY, Joseph
BIRD, Sir Alfred Frederick
CADBURY, George
CADBURY, Laurence John
CARR, Arthur
CARR, Jonathan Dodgson
CHIVERS, John
COLMAN, Jeremiah James
FRY, Joseph Storrs
GLUCKSTEIN, Montague
HARRIS, George James
HARTLEY, Sir William Pickles
HEYWORTH, Geoffrey
HORLICK, Sir James
JOHNSTON, George Lawson
JOHNSTON, John Lawson
LEVER, William Hesketh
LYLE, Charles Ernest Leonard
LYONS, Sir Joseph Nathaniel
MACKINTOSH, Harold Vincent
MACKINTOSH, John
PALMER, George
RANK, James Voase
RANK, Joseph
RANK, Joseph Arthur
ROWNTREE, Benjamin Seebohm
ROWNTREE, Joseph
SALMON, Harry
SHELDON, Oliver
SHIPPAM, Alfred Ernest Cooper
STEWART, Sir Halley
TATE, Sir Henry
VAN DEN BERGH, Jacob
VAN DEN BERGH, Henry
WATSON, Sir James Angus
WESTON, Willard Garfield
WOODGER, John

Drink

BARHAM, Arthur Saxby

II — FOOD, DRINK AND TOBACCO

Drink

BARHAM, Sir George
BARHAM, George Titus
BEAVER, Sir Hugh Eyre Campbell
BONSOR, Sir Henry Cosmo Orme
BUTLER, Sir Robert Reginald Frederick
BUTLER, Sir William Waters
COCHRANE, Sir Henry
COMBE, Simon Harvey
DEUCHAR, James
DEWAR, Thomas Robert
EVANS, William
GARTON, Sir Richard Charles
GREENE, Edward
GRETTON, John
GUINNESS, Edward Cecil
HOOPER, Sir Frederic Collins
HORLICK, Sir James
MAGGS, Joseph Hebert
MAGGS, Leonard
NEVILE, Sir Sydney Oswald
PRICE, Sir William
SIMONDS, Frederick Adolphus
STEVENSON, James
TISDALL, Edmund Charles
WHITBREAD, Francis Pelham
WHITE, Edwin

Tobacco

BARON, Bernhard
CUNLIFFE-OWEN, Sir Hugo Von Reitzenstein
GALLAHER, Thomas
PLAYER, John
PLAYER, John Dane
PLAYER, William Goodacre
WILLS, Sir George Alfred
WILLS, William Henry

III — CHEMICAL AND ALLIED INDUSTRIES

General Chemicals

ALLHUSEN, Christian Augustus Henry
BADER, Ernest
BRUNNER, Sir John Tomlinson
BRYANT, Wilberforce
CASTNER, Hamilton Young
CHAMBERS, Sir Stanley Paul
COATES, Sir William Henry
CRONSHAW, Cecil John Turrell
DREYFUS, Henry
FERENS, Thomas Robinson
FLECK, Alexander
GAMBLE, Sir David
GASKELL, Holbrook
HAYMAN, Sir Cecil George Graham
LEVINSTEIN, Ivan
MCGOWAN, Sir Harry Duncan
MOND, Alfred Moritz
MOND, Henry Ludwig
MOND, Sir Robert Ludwig
MUSPRATT, Sir Max
NEWALL, Robert Stirling
RECKITT, Sir James
STAMP, Josiah Charles
STEVENSON, James Cochran

Photographic Chemicals (Film)

BLAKE, Ernest Edgar
HARMAN, Alfred Hugh
KNOBEL, Edward Ball
MATTISON, Francis Charles
PHILIPPS, Sir Ivor

Pharmaceuticals and Toiletries

BEECHAM, Sir Joseph
BEECHAM, Thomas
BOOT, Jesse

III — CHEMICAL AND ALLIED INDUSTRIES

Pharmaceuticals and Toiletries

COLLINS, Douglas Raymond
ENO, James Crossley
HOLLOWAY, Thomas
JEPHCOTT, Sir Harry
LAZELL, Henry George Leslie
MORSON, Thomas
PERRIN, Sir Michael Willcox
SMITH, Horatio Nelson
WELLCOME, Sir Henry Solomon
WHIFFEN, Thomas

Soap

CROSFIELD, John
GOSSAGE, William
HEDLEY, Thomas
HEYWORTH, Geoffrey
LEVER, William Hesketh
PEARS, Andrew
WATSON, Joseph

Dyestuffs

CRONSHAW, Cecil John Turrell
COATES, John Bernard Maurice
LEVINSTEIN, Ivan
PERKIN, Sir William Henry

Fertilisers

FISON, Sir Frank Guy Clavering

IV — METAL MANUFACTURE

Iron and Steel

ADAMSON, Daniel
ARMSTRONG, William George
BAGNALL, John Nock
BALDWIN, Alfred

IV — METAL MANUFACTURE

Iron and Steel

BALFOUR, Arthur
BELL, Sir Isaac Lowthian
BELL, Sir Thomas Hugh
BERRY, Henry Seymour
BESSEMER, Sir Henry
BOLCKOW, Henry William Ferdinand
BROOKES, Raymond Percival
BROWN, Sir John
CAMMELL, Charles
CLARK, George Thomas
CRAWSHAY, George
DALE, Sir David
DORMAN, Sir Arthur John
DUNCAN, Sir Andrew Rae
ELLIS, John Devonshire
ELLIS, Sir William Henry
FARLEY, Reuben
FIRTH, Mark
FOSTER, William Orme
FURNESS, Christopher
FURNESS, Marmaduke
GARDNER, Sir Charles Bruce
GILBERTSON, Francis William
GILCHRIST, Percy Carlisle
HADFIELD, Sir Robert Abbott
HANDYSIDE, Andrew
HARMOOD-BANNER, Sir John Sutherland
HEATH II, Robert
HEATH III, Robert
HEATH, Arthur H
HEATH, Sir James
HICHENS, William Lionel
HICKMAN, Sir Alfred
HILTON, Sir Robert Stuart
HINGLEY, Sir Benjamin
HOULDSWORTH, Sir William Henry
HUNTER, Sir Ellis
JENKINS, William
JOLLY, James Hornby
JONES, Sir Walter Benton
JUDGE, Edward Thomas

IV — METAL MANUFACTURE

Iron and Steel

KEEN, Arthur
KITSON, James
LYSAGHT, John
LYSAGHT, William Royse
MCLAREN, Charles Benjamin Bright
MARKHAM, Charles Paxton
MENELAUS, William
MENSFORTH, Sir Holberry
MOND, Julian Edward Alfred
PALMER, Sir Charles Mark
PLOWDEN, Edwin Noel August
RICHARDS, Edward Windsor
SAMUELSON, Sir Bernhard
SANKEY, John William
SHONE, Sir Robert Minshull
SIEMENS, Sir Charles William
STEEL, Gerald
STEEL, Henry
TALBOT, Benjamin
THOMAS, Richard
THOMAS, Sidney Gilchrist
VICKERS, Albert
VICKERS, Thomas Edward
WARD, William
WARD, William Humble Eric
WILLIAMS, Edward
WRIGHT, Sir John Roper
WRIGHT, Sir William Charles

Non-ferrous Metals

ALLEN, Samuel
BALL, Charles James Prior
COOKSON, Clive
COOKSON, Norman Charles
COOKSON, Roland Antony
COUSSMAKER, Arthur Blakeney
FOSTER, Alfred James
GRIFFITHS, Sir William Thomas
LANCASTER, Arthur Henry
LEATHART, James

IV — METAL MANUFACTURE
Non-ferrous Metals
MATHESON, Hugh Mackay
MATTHEY, George
MOND, Sir Robert Ludwig
WALLIS, Frederick

V — MECHANICAL ENGINEERING

Agricultural Machinery

AVELING, Thomas Lake
BARFORD, Edward James
BURRELL, Charles
CLAYTON, Nathaniel
FERGUSON, Henry George
FOWLER, Robert Henry
HOWARD, James
PERKINS, Frank Arthur
RANSOME, James Edward
RANSOME, Robert Charles
RUSTON, Joseph
SAMUELSON, Sir Bernhard
SHUTTLEWORTH, Joseph

Machine Tools

GABRIEL, John Beresford
  Stuart
GREENWOOD, Arthur
GREENWOOD, Thomas
HERBERT, Sir Alfred
  Edward
ROGERS, Sir Hallewell
TANGYE, Sir Richard
WESTON, Harry
WHITWORTH, Sir Joseph

Textile Machinery

BULLOUGH, Sir George
BULLOUGH, John
DOBSON, Sir Benjamin
  Alfred
FAIRBAIRN, Sir Andrew
HATTERSLEY, Richard
  Longden
HOLLINS, Denis Machell
LISTER, Samuel Cunliffe
MACKIE, James
PLATT, John

V — MECHANICAL ENGINEERING
Textile Machinery
PLATT, Samuel Radcliffe
SMITH, Sir Prince

General and Office Machinery

AVERY, Thomas
DAVIDSON, Sir Samuel
  Clement
GESTETNER, David
GILPIN, Sir Edmund Henry
HASLAM, Sir Alfred Seale
KLABER, Augustus David
LAWRENCE, Sir Joseph
WOOD, Hugh Nicholas

Industrial Plant

DEWRANCE, Sir John
GALLOWAY, John
HICK, John
KEMNAL, Sir James
LISTER, Sir Charles Percy
MORRIS, Herbert
PARSONS, The Honourable
  Sir Charles Algernon
SIMON, Ernest Emil Darwin
SIMON, Henry

Armaments

ANDERSON, Sir John
ANDERSON, Sir William
BIRCH, Sir James Frederick
  Noel
BRINDLEY, Harry Samuel
  Bickerton
CAILLARD, Sir Vincent
  Henry Penalver
CHAMBERLAIN, Arthur
DAWSON, Sir Arthur Trevor
DYER, Henry Clement
  Swinnerton
GIROUARD, Sir Edouard
  Percy Cranwill
HICHENS, William Lionel
KYNOCH, George
NOBLE, Sir Andrew
POLLEN, Arthur Joseph
  Hungerford

V — MECHANICAL ENGINEERING
Armaments
ROGERS, Sir Hallewell
WEST, Sir Glynn Hamilton

General Mechanical Engineering

ANGUS, Edmund Graham
ARMSTRONG, William
  George
BARFORD, Edward James
BENNION, Charles
BURMAN, Sir Stephen
  France
CHAMBERLAIN, Arthur
COLES, Henry James
CROSSLEY, Francis William
CROSSLEY, Sir William
  John
CRUDDAS, William
  Donaldson
DOCKER, Sir Bernard
  Dudley Frank
DOCKER, Frank Dudley
HAYWARD, Sir Charles
  William
LOCKWOOD, Sir Joseph
  Flawith
MUSGRAVE, John
OWEN, Sir Alfred George
  Beech
PERKINS, Frank Arthur
STOTHERT, John Lum
THWAITES, Leslie Basil
WEST, John

VI — INSTRUMENT ENGINEERING

Photographic Equipment

MATTISON, Francis Charles

Watches and Clocks

DENNISON, Aaron Lufkin
GORDON-SMITH, Sir Allan
HEWITT, Thomas Peter
KULLBERG, Victor
MERCER, Thomas

VI — INSTRUMENT ENGINEERING

Scientific Instruments

DARWIN, Sir Horace
GRIFFIN, John Ross
PYE, Harold John
PYE, William George
STANLEY, William Ford
Robinson
TWYMAN, Frank
ZEAL, Giles Henry

VII — ELECTRICAL ENGINEERING

Electrical Machinery

BROWN, Sidney George
CROMPTON, Rookes Evelyn
Bell
DE FERRANTI, Sir Gerard
Vincent Sebastian
DE FERRANTI, Sebastian
Ziana
GHALIB, Selchouk Ahmed
GIBB, Sir Claude Dixon
HIRST, Hugo
KAPP, Gisbert
LYTTELTON, Oliver
MANN, Reginald William
MATHER, Sir William
MENSFORTH, Sir Holberry
MUIRHEAD, Alexander
NELSON, George Horatio
NELSON, Henry George
PARSONS, The Honourable
Sir Charles Algernon
PYBUS, Sir John Percy
RAILING, Max John
RAILING, Sir Harry
REYROLLE, Alphonse
Constant
SIEMENS, Alexander
SIEMENS, Sir Charles
William

Insulated Wires and Cables

CALLENDER, Sir Thomas
Octavius

VII — ELECTRICAL ENGINEERING

Insulated Wires and Cables

MCFADZEAN, William
Hunter
NEWALL, Robert Stirling
PENDER, Sir John

Telegraph and Telephone Apparatus

CREED, Frederick George

Radio and Electronic Components

CLARK, Sir Allen George
COLE, Eric Kirkham
COSSOR, Alfred Charles
ERIKS, Sierd Sint
MULLARD, Stanley Robert
MURPHY, Frank
PYE, Harold John
PYE, William George

Broadcast and Sound Reproducing Equipment

CLARK, Alfred Corning
ISAACS, Godfrey Charles
LEWIS, Sir Edward Robert
LOCKWOOD, Sir Joseph
Flawith
OWEN, William Barry
SAMUEL, Frank

Electrical Appliances (Domestic) and Electrical Goods

BELLING, Charles Reginald
BEST, Robert Hall
COLSTON, Sir Charles
Blampied
LUCAS, Joseph
MORPHY, Donal William
RICHARDS, Charles
Frederick Paul
SWAN, Sir Joseph Wilson
THORN, Sir Jules

VII — ELECTRICAL ENGINEERING

Electrical Appliances (Domestic) and Electrical Goods

WARING, Sir Arthur
Bertram

VIII — SHIPBUILDING AND MARINE ENGINEERING

ADAMS, William
BARTRAM, Sir Robert
Appleby
BATEY, John Thomas
BOYD, William
BROWNE, Sir Benjamin
Chapman
CLARK, George
CLARK, Sir George Smith
DIXON, Sir Raylton
DOXFORD, Sir William
Theodore
FURNESS, Marmaduke
GRAY, Sir William
HARLAND, Sir Edward
James
HICHENS, William Lionel
HUNTER, Sir Ernest John
HUNTER, Sir George Burton
ISHERWOOD, Sir Joseph
William
LAING, Sir James
LESLIE, Andrew
MCLAREN, Charles
Benjamin Bright
MCLAREN, Henry Duncan
MARR, Sir James
MARSHALL, Francis Carr
MENSFORTH, Sir Holberry
PALMER, Sir Charles Mark
PARSONS, The Honourable
Sir Charles Algernon
PICKERSGILL, William
PIRRIE, William James
PRIESTMAN, Sir John
REBBECK, Sir Frederick
Ernest
RICHARDSON, John
Wigham

VIII — SHIPBUILDING AND MARINE ENGINEERING

ROPNER, Sir Robert
ROWELL, Sir Herbert Babington
SHORT, John Young
THOMPSON, Robert
THORNYCROFT, Sir John Isaac
TURNBULL, Thomas
WEIR, William Douglas
WOLFF, Gustav Wilhelm
WORKMAN, Francis

IX — VEHICLES

Motor Vehicles, Motor Cycles and Cycles

AUSTIN, Herbert
BARTLETT, Sir Charles John
BETTMANN, Siegfried
BOWDEN, Sir Harold
BULLOCK, William Edward
CROSSLEY, Sir William John
CURRY, Henry
DENNIS, John Cawsey
DENNIS, Sir Herbert Raymond
DOCKER, Sir Bernard Dudley Frank
DICK, Alick Sydney
EADIE, Albert
EDGE, Selwyn Francis
ENGELBACH, Charles Richard Fox
FERGUSON, Henry George
FODEN, William
FODEN, Edwin Richard
FRISWELL, Sir Charles Ernest Hain
HARRIMAN, Sir George William
HENNESSY, Sir Patrick
HILLMAN, William
JOHNSON, Claude Goodman
KIMBER, Cecil

IX — VEHICLES

Motor Vehicles, Motor Cycles and Cycles

LAWSON, Henry John
LORD, Leonard Percy
LYONS, Sir William
MANVILLE, Sir Edward
MARKLAND, Stanley
MARTIN, Percy
MAUDSLAY, Reginald Walter
MORRIS, William Richard
NAPIER, Montagu Stanley
PEARSON, Sir James Reginald
PERRY, Percival Lee Dewhurst
POLLEN, Arthur Joseph Hungerford
PUGH, Charles Vernon
ROLLS, The Honourable Charles Stewart
ROOTES, Sir Reginald Claud
ROOTES, William Edward
ROYCE, Sir Frederick Henry
SANGSTER, John Young
SIDDELEY, John Davenport
SIDGREAVES, Sir Arthur Frederick
SIMMS, Frederick Richard
SPURRIER, Sir Henry
STARLEY, John Kemp
STOKES, Donald Gresham
THOMAS, William Miles Webster
THORNYCROFT, Sir John Isaac
THURGOOD, Walter Leonard
TURNER, Edward
TURNER, Eric
WILKS, Spencer Bernau
WOOLLARD, Frank George

Aerospace

BIRD, Sir James
BLACKBURN, Robert
BURNEY, Sir Charles Dennistoun

IX — VEHICLES

Aerospace

CAMM, Sir Sydney
DE HAVILLAND, Sir Geoffrey
DOBSON, Sir Roy Hardy
DOWTY, Sir George Herbert
EDWARDS, Sir George Robert
FAIREY, Sir Charles Richard
FEDDEN, Sir Alfred Hubert Roy
HALFORD, Frank Bernard
HEARLE, Frank Trounson
HIVES, Ernest Walter
HUNTING, Sir Percy Llewellyn
JOHNSON, Claude Goodman
KILNER, Sir Hew Ross
MCLEAN, Sir Robert
MARTIN, Sir James
MILES, Frederick George
NAPIER, Montague Stanley
NELSON, George Horatio
NELSON, Henry George
NORTH, John Dudley
PAGE, Sir Frederick Handley
PETTER, Sir Ernest Willoughby
PETTER, Percival Waddams
PORTAL, Charles Frederick Algernon
ROYCE, Sir Frederick Henry
SCOTT-PAINE, Charles Hubert
SHORT, Hugh Oswald
SIDDELEY, John Davenport
SIDGREAVES, Sir Arthur Frederick
SOPWITH, Sir Thomas Octave Murdoch
SPRIGGS, Sir Frank Spencer
THOMAS, George Holt
THOMAS, Herbert John
VERDON-ROE, Sir Edwin Alliott Verdon
WEEKS, Ronald Morce
WHITE-SMITH, Sir Henry
WHITE, Sir George

IX — VEHICLES
Locomotives, Railway Carriages and Railway Track Equipment
ADAMS, William
DALZIEL, Davison Alexander
DOCKER, Sir Bernard Frank Dudley
DOCKER, Frank Dudley
DRUMMOND, Dugald
GOOCH, Sir Daniel
GRESLEY, Sir Herbert Nigel
KITSON, James
SAXBY, John
SPENCER, George
STIRLING, Patrick
STROUDLEY, William
SYKES, William Robert

X — METAL GOODS NOT ELSEWHERE SPECIFIED

Tools, Cutlery and Ironmongery

BENHAM, James
FLAVEL, Sidney Smith
KENRICK, William Edmund
MAPPIN, Sir Frederick Thorpe
MASON, Sir Josiah
WOSTENHOLM, George

Bolts, Nuts, Screws

BROOKES, Raymond Percival
CHAMBERLAIN, Joseph
KEEN, Arthur
NETTLEFOLD, Joseph Henry

Wire

RYLANDS, Sir William Peter

X — METAL GOODS NOT ELSEWHERE SPECIFIED
Cans
BARLOW, Sir Robert

General Metal Industries

CRITTALL, Francis Henry
HINGLEY, Sir Benjamin
OWEN, Sir Alfred George Beech
PEACOCK, Sir Kenneth Swift
RENOLD, Sir Charles Garonne
SANKEY, Joseph

XI — TEXTILES

Cotton

BROADHURST, Sir Edward Tootal
BUNTING, John
CASH, John
CROSS, Herbert Shepherd
DIXON, Sir Alfred Herbert
GARTSIDE, Thomas Edward
GREG, Henry Philips
HARRISON, Sir Cyril Ernest
HARWOOD, Harold Marsh
HOLLAND, William Henry
HOLLINS, Sir Frank
HOLLINS, Henry Ernest
HOULDSWORTH, Sir William Henry
JOHNSON, Henry
LATHAM, Sir Thomas Paul
LEE, Henry
LEE, Sir Henry Cocksey
LEE, Lennox Bertram
LEES, Sir William Clare
MACARA, Sir Charles Wright
MARCROFT, William
MASON, Hugh
MORTON, Sir James
NELSON, Sir Amos
PLATT, Sir Frank
RYLANDS, John
TATTERSALL, John Brown

XI — TEXTILES
Flax
BARBOUR, Sir John Milne
CRAWFORD, Sir William
EWART, Sir William
MULHOLLAND, John
RICHARDSON, James Nicholson

Silk

CASH, John
CASH, Joseph
COURTAULD III, Samuel
WARDLE, Sir Thomas
WARNER, Sir Frank

Man-made Fibres

COURTAULD IV, Samuel
DREYFUS, Henry
HANBURY-WILLIAMS, Sir John Coldbrook
HARRISON, Sir Cyril Ernest
JOHNSON, Henry
KEARTON, Christopher Frank
KNIGHT, Sir Arthur William
LATHAM, Sir Thomas Paul
NELSON, Sir Amos
TETLEY, Henry Greenwood

Woollen and Worsted

AMBLER, Geoffrey Hill
DOUGLAS, George
FOSTER, William
GATES, Ernest Henry
HOLDEN, Sir Isaac
ILLINGWORTH, Alfred
JOWITT, John
LAVERTON, Abraham
LISTER, Samuel Cunliffe
MITCHELL, Sir Henry
OLDROYD, Sir Mark
RAPER, George Frederick
SALT, Sir Titus
WILLEY, Francis Vernon

Hosiery

MORLEY, Samuel

XI — TEXTILES

Hosiery
MUNDELLA, Anthony John
PASOLD, Eric Walter

Carpets

ADAM, William
CROSSLEY, Sir Francis
LORD, Cyril
TOMKINSON, Michael

Other Textile Industries and Textile Finishing

SMILES, William Holmes
SYKES, Sir Alan John
WARDLE, Sir Thomas
WHITTAKER, Croyden
   Meredith

XII — LEATHER

ANGUS, George
BRIGGS, Francis Henry
JACKSON, William Lawies
ODEY, George William
PATERSON, John Craig
PITTARD, Wreford John
   Charles
POSNETT, Robert Harold

XIII — CLOTHING AND FOOTWEAR

Clothing

ALLCROFT, John Derby
ATHERTON, Giles
BARRAN, Sir John
BURTON, Sir Montague
   Maurice
HEPWORTH, Joseph
HOLLINS, Henry Ernest
PASOLD, Eric Walter
SIMPSON, Samuel Leonard

Footwear

BARRATT, Arthur William

XIII — CLOTHING AND FOOTWEAR

Footwear
BOSTOCK, Henry John
CLARK, William Stephens
CLORE, Sir Charles William
COLMAN, Cecil
GEE, Henry Simpson
MANFIELD, Sir Moses
   Philip
NORTH, Sir Jonathan
SEARS, John George
SOMERVELL, Sir Arnold
   Colin
TRICKETT, Sir Henry
   Whittaker
WOOD, Sir Edward

XIV — BRICKS, POTTERY, GLASS, CEMENT, ETC

Bricks and Refractories

EDWARDS, James Coster
HILL, John Cathles
LOWOOD, John Grayson
STEWART, Sir Halley
STEWART, Sir Percy
   Malcolm

Pottery

CAMPBELL, Colin Minton
COPELAND, Richard Ronald
   John
DOULTON, Sir Henry
JOHNSON, Sir Ernest James
WEDGWOOD, Josiah
WOODALL, William

Glass

CANDLISH, John
CHANCE, Sir James
   Timmins
HARTLEY, James
JOBLING-PURSER, Ernest
   Joseph
PILKINGTON, Sir Lionel
   Alexander Bethune

XIV — BRICKS, POTTERY, GLASS, CEMENT, ETC

Glass
PILKINGTON, William
   Henry
SWINBURNE, Robert Walter

Cement and Building Materials

MARRIOTT, Thomas
   Geoffrey
MARTIN, Cecil
REDDISH, Sir Halford
   Walter Lupton
STEWART, Sir Percy
   Malcolm
WILKINSON, William
   Boutland
YOUNG, Alexander Frederick
   Farquhar

XV — TIMBER, FURNITURE, ETC

Timber

BAMBERGER, Louis
GLIKSTEN, Albert Arnold
LATHAM, Edward Bryan
MALLINSON, Sir Stuart
   Sidney
MALLINSON, Sir William
   James

Furniture

ERCOLANI, Lucian
   Randolph
GOMME, Ebenezer
LEBUS, Harris
LEBUS, Sir Hermann
   Andrew
RUSSELL, Sir Sydney
   Gordon

XVI — PAPER, PRINTING AND PUBLISHING

Paper and Packaging

BAKER, Arthur

XVI — PAPER, PRINTING AND PUBLISHING
Paper and Packaging
BALSTON, Charles Henry
BOWATER, Sir Eric (Frederic) Vansittart
CHANCELLOR, Sir Christopher John Howard
COCKSHUT, John
EVANS, Sir John
LING, Reuben Herbert
LLOYD, Edward
LLOYD, Frank
REED, Albert Edwin
REED, Sir Albert Ralph
ROUTLEDGE, Thomas
SHELDON, Clifford Dommett
SPICER, Sir Albert
WATSON, Victor Hugo

Publishing and Printing

AITKEN, William Maxwell
ALLEN, William Edward
BENN, Sir Ernest John Pickstone
BERRY, William Ewert
BERRY, James Gomer
BLACKWELL, Richard
BOND, Stanley Shaw
CHANCELLOR, Sir Christopher John Howard
CROWTHER, Geoffrey
DE LA RUE, Warren
DENT, Joseph Malaby
GOLLANCZ, Sir Victor
HARMSWORTH, Alfred Charles William
HARMSWORTH, Harold Sidney
HULTON, Sir Edward
ILIFFE, Edward Mauger
LANE, Sir Allen
LAWSON, Edward Levy
LETTS, Charles John
LITTLETON, Henry
LLOYD, Edward
LLOYD, Frank
LONGMAN, Charles James
MACMILLAN, Sir Frederick

XVII — PAPER, PRINTING AND PUBLISHING
Publishing and Printing
MARKS, Harry Hananel
METHUEN, Sir Algernon Methuen Marshall
MILFORD, Sir Humphrey Sumner
NEWNES, Sir George
PEARSON, Sir Cyril Arthur
PERCY, Sir Alan Ian
PITMAN, Sir Isaac
RIDDELL, George Allardice
STOREY, Samuel
UNWIN, Sir Stanley
WALTER III, John
WATSON, Victor Hugo
WATT, Alexander Pollock

XVII — OTHER MANUFACTURING INDUSTRIES

Rubber

DU CROS, Sir Arthur Philip
DU CROS, William Harvey
DUNLOP, John Boyd
FULLER, George Pargiter
GEDDES, Sir Eric Campbell
MOULTON, Stephen

Toys, Pianos, Ink Manufacture, Linoleum

BRINSMEAD, John
BROADWOOD, Henry Fowler
HORNBY, Frank
KNIGHT, Alfred Edward
STEPHENS, Henry Charles
WATSON, Victor Hugo
WILLIAMSON, James

XVIII — CONSTRUCTION

AIRD, Sir John
AIREY, Sir Edwin
BARTLETT, Sir Herbert Henry
BURT, Sir George Mowlem

XVIII — CONSTRUCTION
CARMICHAEL, Sir James
COLLS, John Howard
COSTAIN, Sir Richard Rylandes
COWLIN, Sir Francis Nicholas
DAVIES, David
DAW, William Adams
DOVE, Frederick John
FIELD, William
FREAKE, Sir Charles James
GIBB, Sir Alexander
GRIFFITHS, Sir John Norton
HANDYSIDE, Andrew
HIGGS, William
HILL, John Cathles
JACKSON, Sir John
LAING, Sir John William
LASCELLES, William Henry
LONGLEY, Sir Norman
MCALPINE, Sir Alfred David
MCALPINE, Sir Thomas Malcolm
MITCHELL, Sir Godfrey Way
PARKINSON, Sir Albert Lindsay
PEARSON, Weetman Dickinson
PETO, Sir Samuel Morton
RADFORD, Francis
TAYLOR, Francis
WALMSLEY, William
WALMSLEY, Benjamin
WATES, Norman Edward
WILKINSON, William Boutland
WILLETT, William
YATES, Edward

XIX — GAS, ELECTRICITY AND ATOMIC ENERGY

Gas

COLSON, Alfred

XIX — GAS, ELECTRICITY AND ATOMIC ENERGY

Gas

DUCKHAM, Sir Arthur McDougall
HETHERINGTON, Sir Arthur Ford
JONES, Sir Henry Frank Harding
LIVESEY, Sir George Thomas
MAPPIN, Sir Frederick Thorpe
MILNE-WATSON, Sir David
STEPHENSON, Sir William Haswell
WEST, John
WOODALL, Sir Corbet

Electricity

BALFOUR, George
BELLAMY, Dennis
BRAITHWAITE, Joseph Bevan
BROWN, Sir Frederick Herbert Stanley
CITRINE, Walter McLennan
ECCLES, Sir Josiah
ELLIOTT, Sir Norman Randall
FORBES, James Staats
GARCKE, Emile Oscar

Water

BATEMAN, Sir John Frederic La Trobe
BINNIE, Geoffrey Morse
HAWKSLEY, Thomas
STEPHENSON, Sir William Haswell

Atomic Energy

GROVE, Walter Patrick
HINTON, Christopher

XIX — GAS, ELECTRICITY AND ATOMIC ENERGY

Atomic Energy

PLOWDEN, Edwin Noel August
PORTAL, Charles Frederick Algernon

XX — TRANSPORT AND COMMUNICATION

Railways

ALLPORT, Sir James Joseph
ASPINALL, John Audley Frederick
BANBURY, Frederick George
BELL, John
BUTTERWORTH, Sir Alexander Kaye
DALE, Sir David
DENT, Sir Francis Henry
DRUMMOND, Dugald
ELLIOT, Sir John
FAY, Sir Samuel
FENTON, Sir Myles
FINDLAY, Sir George
FORBES, James Staats
FORBES, Sir William de Guise
GEDDES, Sir Eric Campbell
GIBB, Sir George Stegmann
GOOCH, Sir Daniel
GRANET, Sir William Guy
HAMILTON, Lord Claud John
HARTLEY, Sir Harold Brewer
HENDERSON, Alexander
HORNE, Robert Stevenson
HURCOMB, Cyril William
INGLIS, Sir James Charles
MCLEAN, Sir Robert
MILNE, Sir James
MISSENDEN, Sir Eustace James
MOON, Sir Richard
OAKLEY, Sir Henry
PERKS, Sir Robert William
PETO, Sir Samuel Morton

XX — TRANSPORT AND COMMUNICATION

Railways

PICK, Frank
POLE, Sir Felix John Clewett
RAMSBOTTOM, John
RAMSDEN, Sir James
RAVEN, Sir Vincent Litchfield
SARLE, Sir Allen Lanyon
SELBIE, Robert Hope
SPAGNOLETTI, Charles Ernest Paolo della Diana
STAMP, Josiah Charles
STANLEY, Albert Henry
STEPHENS, Holman Frederick
STIRLING, Patrick
TENNANT, Henry
THORNTON, Sir Henry Worth
TYLER, Sir Henry Whatley
WALKER, Sir Herbert Ashcombe
WATKIN, Sir Edward William
WEDGWOOD, Sir Ralph Lewis

Road Passenger

DRAYTON, Harold Charles Gilbert
GARCKE, Sidney Emile
HEATON, Sir John Frederick
HILLMAN, Edward Henry
HOWLEY, Richard Joseph
HURCOMB, Cyril William
PICK, Frank

Road Haulage

BAXENDALE, Lloyd Henry
HENMAN, Philip Sydney
HILTON, Ralph
HURCOMB, Cyril William
WHITE, Sir George

Sea and Water Transport

ADAMSON, Daniel

XX — TRANSPORT AND COMMUNICATION
Sea and Water Transport
ANDERSON, Sir Alan Garrett
ANDERSON, Sir Donald Forsyth
ANDERSON, James
BOOTH, Alfred
BOWRING, Charles Tricks
BROCKLEBANK, Ralph
BYTHELL, John Kenworthy
CURRIE, Sir Donald
ELLERMAN, Sir John Reeves
ELLERMAN, Sir John Reeves
FORWOOD, Sir William Bower
FURNESS, Christopher
FURNESS, Marmaduke
GRAY, Sir William
HAIN, Sir Edward
HARRISON, Thomas
HARRISON, James
HOLT, Alfred
HOULDER, Edwin Savory
HOUSTON, Sir Robert Paterson
HUGHES, John William
HUNTING, Sir Percy Llewellyn
INMAN, William
INSTONE, Sir Samuel
ISMAY, Thomas Henry
JONES, Sir Alfred Lewis
KEARLEY, Hudson Ewbanke
KNOTT, Sir James
LEWIS, Frederick William
MACKAY, James Lyle
MURRANT, Sir Ernest Henry
PHILIPPS, Laurence Richard
PHILIPPS, Owen Cosby
PIRRIE, William James
RADCLIFFE, Henry
RANKIN, John
ROPNER, Sir Robert
RUNCIMAN, Walter
SHORT, John Young
SMALLPEICE, Sir Basil

XX — TRANSPORT AND COMMUNICATION
Sea and Water Transport
SMITH, George Samuel Fereday
SMITH, Sir William Reardon
STOKER, Robert Burdon
SUTHERLAND, Sir Arthur Munro
TYRER, Henry
WEIR, Andrew
WILSON, Arthur
WILSON, Charles Henry

Air Transport
BRACKLEY, Herbert George
COBHAM, Sir Alan John
D'ERLANGER, Sir Gerard John Regis Leo
D'ERLANGER, Leo Frederic Alfred
DOUGLAS, William Sholto
GEDDES, Sir Eric Campbell
GUTHRIE, Sir Giles
HARTLEY, Sir Harold Brewer
HILLMAN, Edward Henry
INSTONE, Sir Samuel
KNOLLYS, Edward George William Tyrwhitt
MCRINDLE, John Ronald
MASEFIELD, Sir Peter Gordon
MILWARD, Sir Anthony Horace
SCOTT-PAINE, Charles Hubert
SMALLPEICE, Sir Basil
STRAIGHT, Whitney Willard
THOMAS, George Holt
THOMAS, William Miles Webster
THURGOOD, Walter Leonard
WOODS-HUMPHERY, George Edward
WYATT, Sir Myles Dermot Norris

XX — TRANSPORT AND COMMUNICATION
Postal Services & Telecommunications
BLACKWOOD, Sir Stevenson Arthur
MURRAY, Sir George Evelyn Pemberton
SCUDAMORE, Frank Ives
TILLEY, Sir John

XXI — DISTRIBUTIVE TRADES
Wholesaling
BALFOUR, Alexander
BARHAM, Arthur Saxby
BARHAM, Sir George
BARHAM, George Titus
BARROW, Harrison
BEHRENS, Sir Jacob
BELLINGER, Sir Robert Ian
BORTHWICK, Sir Thomas
BROOKE, Arthur
BROUGH, Edward
BUDD, Sir Cecil Lindsay
BUTLER, Sir Robert Reginald Frederick
CAMPBELL, John Middleton
COPEMAN, Henry John
CZARNIKOW, Julius Caesar
FORWOOD, Sir William Bower
FYFFE, Edward Wathen
GIBBS, Henry Hucks
GLUCKSTEIN, Montague
GOLDIE, Sir Henry Dashwood Taubman-
GOODMAN, Frederick Buck
GUERET, Louis Jean Baptiste
IRVIN, Richard
JACQUES, John Henry
KEEVIL, Sir Ambrose
LIDDERDALE, William
LIPMAN, Michael Isaac
LYONS, Sir Joseph Nathaniel
LYTTELTON, Oliver
MAGGS, Joseph Herbert
MAGGS, Leonard

XX — TRANSPORT AND COMMUNICATION
Wholesaling
MANFIELD, Sir Moses Philip
MATHESON, Hugh Mackay
MITCHELL, Sir Henry
MITCHELL, John Thomas Whitehead
MORLEY, Samuel
NEALE, Edward Vansittart
PATON, Alexander Allan
PEACOCK, John Atkins
PEDDIE, James Mortimer
PRICE, Sir William
RANK, James Voase
RANK, Joseph
RANK, Joseph Arthur
RATHBONE, William Benson
SALMON, Harry
SAMUEL, Frank
SPICER, Sir Albert
SUGDEN, Sir Arthur
SWIRE, John Samuel
TISDALL, Edmund Charles
TWINING III, Richard
VESTEY, Sir Edmund Hoyle
VESTEY, William
WEBB, Weston Fulford Marriott
WESTON, Willard Garfield
WHITE, Edwin
WILLEY, Francis Vernon
WILLIAMS, Sir George
WILLIAMSON, Archibald
WILSON, Peter Cecil
WINN, Rowland
WOOLF, Charles Moss

Retailing (Including Multiples)

BARRATT, Arthur William
BARROW, Harrison
BEALE, George
BEDFORD, John
BOOT, Jesse
BROUGH, Joseph William
COHEN, Sir John Edward
CURRY, Henry
DREW, Julius Charles

XXI — DISTRIBUTIVE TRADES
Retailing (Including Multiples)
EVANS, William
GEE, Henry Simpson
GIBBONS, Edward Stanley
GLUCKSTEIN, Montague
HALFORD, Frederick William
JACQUES, John Henry
KEARLEY, Hudson Ewbanke
KEEVIL, Sir Ambrose
LEWIS, David
LEWIS, John
LEWIS, John Spedan
LIPTON, Sir Thomas Johnstone
LYONS, Sir Joseph Nathaniel
MANFIELD, Sir Moses Philip
MARKS, Michael
MARKS, Simon
MARQUIS, Frederick James
MITCHELL, John Thomas Whitehead
MOORES, Sir John
MOSS, Harry Neville
NEALE, Edward Vansittart
NORTH, Sir Jonathan
PEDDIE, James Mortimer
REED, Austin Leonard
RUSHBROOKE, Frederick William
SAINSBURY, Alan John
SAINSBURY, John Benjamin
SAINSBURY, John James
SAINSBURY, Sir Robert
SALMON, Harry
SEARS, John George
SIEFF, Israel Moses
SIMPSON, Samuel Leonard
SLAUGHTER, Sir William Capel
SOMERVELL, Sir Arnold Colin
STEPHENSON, William Lawrence
SUGDEN, Sir Arthur
TWINING III, Richard
VESTEY, Sir Edmund Hoyle

XXI — DISTRIBUTIVE TRADES
Retailing (Including Multiples)
VESTEY, William
WESTON, Willard Garfield
WHITE, Edwin
WILLIAMS, Sir George
WILSON, Peter Cecil
WOOD, Sir Edward

Department Stores

BAINBRIDGE, Emerson Muschamp
BARKER, Sir John
BEALE, John Elmes
BEDFORD, John
BENTALL, Leonard Hugh
BURBIDGE, Sir Richard
FENWICK, John James
GAMAGE, Albert Walter
LEWIS, David
LEWIS, John
LEWIS, John Spedan
LIBERTY, Sir Arthur Lasenby
MARQUIS, Frederick James
MORGAN, David
OLIVER, Frederick Scott
OWEN, Owen
SELFRIDGE, Harry Gordon
STEWART-LIBERTY, Arthur
WHITELEY, William

Miscellaneous Distribution

DUVEEN, Joseph
FRISWELL, Sir Charles Ernest Hain
GIBBONS, Edward Stanley
KENNING, Sir George
LETTS, Sir William Malesbury
MANN, Gerard Noel Cornwallis
MUDIE, Charles Edward

XXII — INSURANCE, BANKING, FINANCE AND BUSINESS SERVICES

Insurance

BAIN, Albert Wellesley
BOULT, Swinton
BOWRING, Charles Tricks
DEUCHAR, John James Walker
ELDERTON, Sir William Palin
FOLEY, Patrick James
HARBEN, Sir Henry
HEATH, Cuthbert Eden
KEYNES, John Maynard
LAYBORN, Thomas Alec Edwin
LONGRIDGE, Robert Bewick
LOWNDES, Noble Frank
MARKS, Geoffrey
MAY, George Ernest
MOUNTAIN, Sir Edward Mortimer
PIPKIN, Samuel Jones
PYBUS, Sir Percy John
RUTTER, Sir Frederick William Pascoe
SHORT, John Young
SPRAGUE, Thomas Bond

Banking

ADDIS, Sir Charles Stewart
BANBURY, Frederick George
BARING, John
BECKETT, Rupert Evelyn
BEVAN, Francis Augustus
BOLITHO, Thomas Bedford
BOLTON, Sir George Lewis French
BRAND, Robert Henry
CAMPBELL, Colin Frederick
CASSEL, Sir Ernest Joseph
CATTO, Thomas Sivewright
COBBOLD, Cameron Fromanteel
CUNLIFFE, Walter

XXII — INSURANCE, BANKING, FINANCE AND BUSINESS SERVICES

Banking

DAWNAY, Guy Payan
D'ERLANGER, Leo Frederic Alfred
DUNN, Sir James Hamet
ELLERTON, Sir Frederick Cecil
FRASER, William Lionel
FRESHFIELD, Edwin
GARDNER, Sir Charles Bruce
GIBBS, Henry Hucks
GIBBS, Henry Cokayne
GOODENOUGH, Frederick Crauford
GOODENOUGH, Sir William Macnamara
GRENFELL, Edward Charles
HAMBRO, Sir Everard Alexander
HODGE, Sir Julian Stephen Alfred
HOLDEN, Sir Edward Hopkinson
KINDERSLEY, Robert Molesworth
KLEINWORT, Sir Alexander Drake
KLEINWORT, Ernest Greverus
LAWRENCE, Sir Herbert Alexander
LEAF, Walter
LIDBURY, Sir Charles
LIDDERDALE, William
LLOYD, Howard
LOYD, Samuel Jones
LUBBOCK, John
MCKENNA, Reginald
MARTIN, Sir Richard Biddulph
MONTAGU, Samuel
MORRISON, Charles
NORMAN, Montagu Collet
PAM, Albert Samuel
PEACOCK, Sir Edward Robert

XXII — INSURANCE, BANKING, FINANCE AND BUSINESS SERVICES

Banking

PEASE, John William Beaumont
PHILLIPS, John Spencer
RAE, George
ROTHSCHILD, Nathan Meyer
SALT, Sir Thomas
SCHRÖDER, Baron Rudolph Bruno
SCHUSTER, Sir Felix Otto
SECCOMBE, Lawrence Henry
SIKES, Sir Charles William
SMITH, Vivian Hugh
STERN, Sir Edward David
TIARKS, Frank Cyril
TRINDER, Arthur William
TRITTON, Joseph Herbert
TUKE, Anthony William
TURNER, Sir Ronald Mark Cunliffe
VASSAR-SMITH, Sir Richard Vassar

Other Financial Institutions – Including Stock Exchange

BEGG, Ferdinand Faithfull
BEVAN, Gerard Lee
BOOTH, George Macaulay
BRAITHWAITE, Sir John Bevan
BRAITHWAITE, Joseph Bevan
GILLETT, Ronald Brodie
GORDON, Harry Panmure
HUME, Sir Hubert Nutcombe
NICKALLS, Thomas
PIERCY, William Stuckey
RAE, Edward
SZARVASY, Frederick Alexander
TAIT, Andrew Wilson
WHEELER, Sir Arthur

XXII — INSURANCE, BANKING, FINANCE AND BUSINESS SERVICES

Building Societies

BALFOUR, Jabez Spencer
BELLMAN, Sir Charles Harold
COHEN, Lewis Coleman
HIGHAM, James
HILL, Sir Enoch
STARR, Richard Benjamin
WEBB, Arthur
WOOD, Edward
WYCHERLEY, Sir Robert Bruce

Property Owning and Managing

BALFOUR, Jabez Spencer
CLORE, Sir Charles
COTTON, Jack
FREAKE, Sir Charles James
HILL, Philip Ernest
MALLABY-DEELEY, Sir Harry C
O'HAGAN, Henry Osborne
STEVENS, Marshall
WARD, William
WARD, William Humble Eric

Advertising

BARRATT, Thomas James
BENSON, Samuel Herbert
CRAWFORD, Sir William Smith
HIGHAM, Sir Charles Frederick
RUSSELL, Thomas Baron
STREET, George

Other Business and Financial Services

BEIT, Alfred
BIGELOW, Arthur Perkins
BOOTH, Sir Robert Camm
BOWIE, James Alexander

XXII — INSURANCE, BANKING, FINANCE AND BUSINESS SERVICES

Other Business and Financial Services

BUNTING, John
CAVENDISH, William
CHADWICK, David
CRISP, Charles Birch
CZARNIKOW, Julius Caesar
DRAYTON, Harold Charles Gilbert
DUNN, Sir James Hamet
DYER, Henry Clement Swinnerton
EDWARDS, Sir Ronald
FFRENCH, Charles Austin Thomas Robert John Joseph
GLYN-JONES, Sir William Samuel
GRENFELL, Arthur Morton
HENDERSON, Alexander
HOOPER, Sir Frederic Collins
HOZIER, Sir Henry Montague
KEYNES, John Maynard
LOCOCK, Sir Guy Harold
MURPHY, William Martin
PHILIPPS, Sir Ivor
PHILIPPS, John Wynford
PHILIPPS, Laurence Richard
PIERCY, William Stuckey
REUTER, Paul Julius
ROGER, Sir Alexander Forbes Proctor
TAYLOR, James Frater
WERNHER, Sir Julius Carl

Company Promotion

BOTTOMLEY, Horatio William
DALZIEL, Davison Alexander
DAVIS, Sir Edmund Gabriel
FORBES, James Staats
GRANT (GOTTHEIMER), Albert (Abraham) Zachariah
HATRY, Clarence Charles

XXII — INSURANCE, BANKING, FINANCE AND BUSINESS SERVICES

Company Promotion

HENDERSON, Alexander
HOOLEY, Ernest Terah
LAWSON, Henry John
MORRIS, John
O'HAGAN, Henry Osborne
RAMSDEN, Sir James
STARR, Richard Benjamin
WHITE, James
WRIGHT, Whitaker

XXIII — PROFESSIONAL AND SCIENTIFIC SERVICES

Accountancy

BARTON, Sir Harold Montague
BENSON, Henry Alexander
COOPER, Arthur
COOPER, Ernest
COOPER, Sir Francis D'Arcy
DELOITTE, William Welch
DE PAULA, Frederic Rudolf Mackley
DICKINSON, Sir Arthur Lowes
EDWARDS, Sir Ronald
FELLS, John Manger
GARCKE, Emile Oscar
GARNSEY, Sir Gilbert Francis
GUTHRIE, Edwin
HARDING, Sir Robert Palmer
HARMOOD-BANNER, Sir John Sutherland
JENKINSON, Sir Mark Webster
JONES, Theodore Brooke
MCLINTOCK, Sir William
MAYHEW, Sir Basil Edgar
PEAT, Sir William Barclay
PLENDER, William
QUILTER, William
SMALLPEICE, Sir Basil

XXIII — PROFESSIONAL AND SCIENTIFIC SERVICES

Accountancy

STAMP, Josiah Charles
TOUCHE, Sir George Alexander
WATERHOUSE, Edwin
WHINNEY, Frederick

Legal

CLIFFORD-TURNER, Harry
FRESHFIELD, Edwin
HYDE, Sir Robert Robertson
LEESE, Sir William Hargreaves
MORRIS, John
MORTIMER, John
PEPPIATT, Sir Leslie Ernest
PERKS, Sir Robert William
SLAUGHTER, Sir William Capel

Consultancy in Business and Engineering

BAKER, Sir Benjamin
BALFOUR, George
BARLOW, William Henry
BARRY, Sir John Wolfe
BATEMAN, John Frederic La Trobe
BINNIE, Geoffrey Morse
CHILDE, Rowland
DRUMMOND, Dugald
FOWLER, Sir John
GIBB, Sir Alexander
GREATHEAD, James Henry
HACKING, Sir John
HAMMOND, Robert
HARRISON, Thomas Elliot
HAWKSHAW, Sir John
HAWKSLEY, Thomas
HOPKINSON, John
INGLIS, Sir James Charles
JACKSON, Sir John
KAPP, Gisbert
LIVESEY, James
MERZ, Charles Hesterman

XXIII — PROFESSIONAL AND SCIENTIFIC SERVICES

Consultancy in Business and Engineering

MOTT, Sir Basil
NUGENT, Sir Roland Thomas
PREECE, Sir William Henry
RAMSBOTTOM, John
RAVEN, Sir Vincent Litchfield
REDWOOD, Sir Thomas Boverton
SPAGNOLETTI, Charles Ernest Paolo della Diana

Research and Development

BROWN, Sidney George
BURNEY, Sir Charles Dennistoun
FLEMING, Sir Arthur Percy Morris
GILCHRIST, Percy Carlisle
GRIFFITHS, Sir William Thomas
HALFORD, Frank Bernard
HINTON, Christopher
JACKSON, Willis
POLLEN, Arthur Joseph Hungerford
SALOMONS, Sir David Lionel Goldsmid-Stern-
THOMAS, Sidney Gilchrist

Miscellaneous Professional Services, Including Management Education

CLUTTON, John
ELLIS, Richard Adam
HYDE, Sir Robert Robinson
LUTYENS, Sir Edwin Landseer
MORRIS, William
PLATT, James Westlake
PUCKEY, Sir Walter Charles
ROWNTREE, Benjamin Seebohm
SCOTT, Sir George Gilbert
SCOTT, Sir Giles Gilbert

XXIII — PROFESSIONAL AND SCIENTIFIC SERVICES

Miscellaneous Professional Services, Including Management Education

SHELDON, Oliver
SMITH, Sir Allan MacGregor
STOTT, Sir Philip Sidney
STREAT, Sir Edward Raymond
URWICK, Lyndall Fownes
WARD, Harry
WATERHOUSE, Alfred
WATT, Alexander Pollock
YOUNG, Arthur Primrose

XXIV — MISCELLANEOUS SERVICES

Cinemas, Theatres, Radio and Entertainment

ALEXANDER, Sir George
BALCON, Sir Michael Elias
BANCROFT, Sir Squire
BAYLIS, Lilian Mary
BLAKE, Ernest Edgar
COCHRAN, Sir Charles Blake
DEUTSCH, Oscar
HARWOOD, Harold Marsh
IRVING, Sir Henry
KORDA, Sir Alexander
MAXWELL, John
MILLS, Bertram Wagstaff
OSTRER, Isidore
RANK, Joseph Arthur
REITH, John Charles Walsham
SANGER, George
STOLL, Sir Oswald
TREE, Sir Herbert Beerbohm
WOOLF, Charles Moss
WYNDHAM, Sir Charles

Sport and Leisure

BUTLIN, Sir William Heygate Edmund Colbourne
COOK, John Mason

Index of companies and trade associations, with subject entry

Compiled by Dr Geoffrey Tweedale

A

Abbey Road Building Society
  BELLMAN, Sir Charles Harold
Adamson, Daniel & Co
  ADAMSON, Daniel
Agricultural & General Engineers Ltd
  AVELING, Thomas Lake
  PERKINS, Frank Arthur
Air Holdings Group
  WYATT, Sir Myles Dermot Norris
Airco
  THOMAS, George Holt
Aird, John & Co
  AIRD, Sir John
Allan, Cockshut & Co
  COCKSHUT, John
Allen, David & Sons
  ALLEN, William Edward
Allen & Unwin
  UNWIN, Sir Stanley
Algoma Steel Corporation
  DUNN, Sir James Hamet
Allied Newspapers
  BERRY, William Ewert
  BERRY, James Gomer
Angus, George & Co
  ANGUS, Edmund Graham
  ANGUS, George
Ariel Motors
  SANGSTER, John Young
Armstrong Whitworth
  ARMSTRONG, William George
  CRUDDAS, William Donaldson
  DAWNAY, Guy Payan
  DYER, Henry Clement Swinnerton
  GIROUARD, Sir Edouard Percy Cranwill
  NOBLE, Sir Andrew
  TAYLOR, James Frater
  WEST, Sir Glynn Hamilton
  WHITWORTH, Sir Joseph
Associated British Foods
  WESTON, Willard Garfield
Associated British Picture Corporation Ltd
  MAXWELL, Joseph

Associated Electrical Industries (AEI)
  LYTTELTON, Oliver
Associated Iliffe Press
  ILIFFE, Edward Mauger
Associated Lead Manufacturers Ltd
  COOKSON, Clive
  FOSTER, Alfred James
  LANCASTER, Arthur Henry
Associated Newspapers
  HARMSWORTH, Alfred Charles William
  HARMSWORTH, Harold Sidney
Atlas Assurance Co
  PIPKIN, Samuel James
Atherton & Co
  ATHERTON, Giles
Austin Friars Trust Ltd
  HATRY, Clarence Charles
Austin Motor Co
  AUSTIN, Herbert
  ENGELBACH, Charles Richard Fox
Aveling-Barford Ltd
  BARFORD, Edward James
Aveling & Porter Ltd
  AVELING, Thomas Lake
Avery, W & T
  AVERY, Thomas
Avon Rubber Co
  FULLER, George Pargiter

B

Babcock & Wilcox
  DEWRANCE, Sir John
  FRASER, William Lionel
  KEMNAL, Sir James
Bagnall, John & Sons
  BAGNALL, John Nock
Bain, A W & Sons
  BAIN, Albert Wellesley
Bainbridge & Co
  BAINBRIDGE, Emerson Muschamp
Baker Perkins
  GILPIN, Sir Edmund Henry

Baldwins Ltd
  BALDWIN, Alfred
  WRIGHT, Sir John Roper
Balfour Williamson
  BALFOUR, Alexander
  WILLIAMSON, Archibald
Balfour, Arthur & Co
  BALFOUR, Arthur
Balfour Beatty
  BALFOUR, George
Balston, W & R
  BALSTON, Charles Henry
Bank of England
  ADDIS, Sir Charles Stewart
  BOLTON, Sir George Lewis French
  CATTO, Thomas Sivewright
  COBBOLD, Cameron Fromanteel
  CUNLIFFE, Walter
  FRESHFIELD, Edwin
  GARDNER, Sir Charles Bruce
  GIBBS, Henry Hucks
  KINDERSLEY, Robert Molesworth
  LEESE, Sir William Hargreaves
  LIDDERDALE, William
  PEACOCK, Sir Edward Robert
  PEPPIATT, Sir Leslie Ernest
  NORMAN, Montagu Collet
  SECCOMBE, Lawrence Henry
Bank of London & South America
  BOLTON, Sir George Lewis French
Bannerman, Henry & Sons
  MACARA, Sir Charles Wright
Barber, Walker & Co
  HARRISON, Robert
Barclays Bank
  BEVAN, Francis Augustus
  ELLERTON, Sir Frederick Cecil
  GOODENOUGH, Frederick Crauford
  GOODENOUGH, Sir William Macnamara
  TRITTON, Joseph Herbert
  TUKE, Anthony William
Baring Bros
  BARING, John
  PEACOCK, Sir Edward Robert
Barker & Allen
  ALLEN, Samuel
Barker, John & Co
  BARKER, Sir John
Barnett Samuel
  SAMUEL, Frank
Barran, John & Sons
  BARRAN, Sir John

Barratts
  BARRATT, Arthur William
Barrow, Hepburn & Gale
  ODEY, George William
Barrow's Stores
  BARROW, Harrison
Barry Co
  DAVIES, David
Barton, Mayhew & Co
  BARTON, Sir Harold Montague
Bartram & Sons
  BARTRAM, Sir Robert Appleby
Basic & Dephosphorising Patents Co
  GILCHRIST, Percy Carlisle
  THOMAS, Sidney Gilchrist
Bass Brewery
  GRETTON, John
Beales
  BEALE, John Elmes
Beecham Group
  BEECHAM, Sir Joseph
  BEECHAM, Thomas
  EDWARDS, Sir Ronald
  HILL, Philip Ernest
  LAZELL, Henry George Leslie
Behrens
  BEHRENS, Sir Jacob
Belfast Ropework Co
  SMILES, William Holmes
Bell Bros
  BELL, Sir Isaac Lowthian
Belling & Co
  BELLING, Charles Reginald
Benham & Sons
  BENHAM, James
Benn, Ernest Ltd
  BENN, Sir Ernest John Pickstone
Bentalls
  BENTALL, Leonard Hugh
Bessbrook Spinning Co
  RICHARDSON,
  James Nicholson
Bessemer Steel Co
  BESSEMER, Sir Henry
Best & Lloyd
  BEST, Robert Hall
Bibby, J & Sons
  BIBBY, Joseph
Biddulph Valley Colliery/Ironworks
  HEATH II, Robert
Bird, Alfred & Sons
  BIRD, Sir Alfred Frederick

Birmingham Plate Glass Works
  HARTLEY, James
Birmingham Small Arms (BSA)
  DOCKER, Sir Bernard Dudley Frank
  DOCKER, Frank Dudley
  EADIE, Albert
  MANVILLE, Sir Edward
  MARTIN, Percy
  POLLEN, Arthur Joseph Hungerford
  ROGER, Sir Alexander Forbes Proctor
  ROGERS, Sir Hallewell
  SANGSTER, John Young
  TURNER, Edward
  TURNER, Eric
Birmingham Trust Ltd
  CHAMBERLAIN, Arthur
Black Dyke Mills
  FOSTER, William
Blackburn Aircraft Ltd
  BLACKBURN, Robert
Blackwell Ltd
  BLACKWELL, Richard
Bleachers' Association Ltd
  CROSS, Herbert Shepherd
  LEES, Sir William Clare
  SYKES, Sir Alan John
Blue Circle Industries
  STEWART, Sir Percy Malcolm
Blundell, J & Son
  BLUNDELL, Henry Blundell-Hollinshead
Bolckow, Vaughan
  BOLCKOW, Henry William Ferdinand
  MENSFORTH, Sir Holberry
  RICHARDS, Edward Windsor
  WILLIAMS, Edward
Booker McConnell
  CAMPBELL, John Middleton
Booth, Alfred & Co
  BOOTH, Alfred
Boots
  BOOT, Jesse
Borthwick, Thomas & Sons
  BORTHWICK, Sir Thomas
Boulton & Paul
  NORTH, John Dudley
Bovril
  JOHNSTON, George Lawson
  JOHNSTON, John Lawson
Bowaters
  BOWATER, Sir Eric (Frederic)Vansittart
  BAKER, Arthur

  CHANCELLOR, Sir Christopher John
    Howard
Bowring, C T & Co
  BOWRING, Charles Tricks
Bradford Dyers' Association
  DOUGLAS, George
Bridgewater Trust
  SMITH, George Samuel Fereday
Briggs, H & Son
  BRIGGS, Henry Currer
Briggs (Tanners) Ltd
  BRIGGS, Francis Henry
Brighton & Sussex Building Society
  COHEN, Lewis Coleman
Brinsmeads
  BRINSMEAD, John
Bristol Aeroplane Co
  FEDDEN, Sir Alfred Hubert Roy
  THOMAS, Herbert John
  WHITE-SMITH, Sir Henry
  WHITE, Sir George
British Aircraft Corporation (BAC)
  EDWARDS, Sir George Robert
  KNOLLYS, Edward George William
    Tyrwhitt
  PORTAL, Charles Frederick Algernon
British Airways
  D'ERLANGER, Leo Frederic Alfred
British American Tobacco Co
  CUNLIFFE-OWEN, Sir Hugo Von
    Reitzenstein
British Bank for Foreign Trade
  CRISP, Charles Birch
British Broadcasting Corporation (BBC)
  REITH, John Charles Walsham
British Celanese
  DREYFUS, Henry
British Electric Traction
  DRAYTON, Harold Charles Gilbert
  GARCKE, Emile Oscar
  GARCKE, Sidney Emile
  HEATON, Sir John Frederick
  HOWLEY, Richard Joseph
British Electricity Authority
  ECCLES, Sir Josiah
British Engine Insurance Ltd
  LONGRIDGE, Robert Bewick
British European Airways (BEA)
  D'ERLANGER, Sir Gerard John Regis Leo
  DOUGLAS, William Sholto
  HARTLEY, Sir Harold Brewer

MASEFIELD, Sir Peter
MILWARD, Sir Anthony Horace
British Foreign & Colonial Corporation
SZARVASY, Frederick Alexander
British Gas Corporation
HETHERINGTON, Sir Arthur Ford
British Insulated Cables
ROGER, Sir Alexander Forbes Proctor
British Iron & Steel Federation
DUNCAN, Sir Andrew Rae
HONE, Sir Robert Minshull
British Leather
PATERSON, John Craig
British Leyland
MARKLAND, Stanley
British Metal Corporation
BUDD, Sir Cecil Lindsay
LYTTELTON, Oliver
British Marine Air
Navigation Co
SCOTT-PAINE, Charles Hubert
British Motor Corporation (BMC)
HARRIMAN, Sir George William
LORD, Leonard Percy
British Motor Syndicate
LAWSON, Henry John
British Northrop Ltd
HOLLINS, Denis Machell
British Overseas Airways Corporation (BOAC)
BRACKLEY, Herbert George
D'ERLANGER, Sir Gerard John Regis Leo
GUTHRIE, Sir Giles
HARTLEY, Sir Harold Brewer
MCCRINDLE, John Ronald
SMALLPEICE, Sir Basil
STRAIGHT, Sir Whitney Willard
THOMAS, William Miles Webster
British Petroleum (BP)
BRIDGEMAN, Sir Maurice Richard
CADMAN, John
D'ARCY, William Knox
DRAKE, Sir Arthur Eric Courtney
FRASER, William Milligan
GREENWAY, Charles
British Power Boat Co
SCOTT-PAINE, Charles Hubert
British Pullman Palace Car Co
DALZIEL, Davison Alexander
British Rail
MISSENDEN, Sir Eustace James

British South Africa Co
DAVIS, Sir Edmund Gabriel
British Steel Corporation (BSC)
MOND, Julian Edward Alfred
British Stockbrokers' Trust
FFRENCH, Charles Austin Thomas Robert
John Joseph
British Thomson-Houston
YOUNG, Arthur Primrose
British Trade Corporation
HENDERSON, Alexander
British Transport Commission
HURCOMB, Cyril William
British United Shoe Machinery Co
BENNION, Charles
Broadwood, J & Sons
BROADWOOD, Henry Fowler
Brocklebanks
BROCKLEBANK, Ralph
Broughs Ltd
BROUGH, Edward
BROUGH, Joseph William
Brown, John Ltd
BROWN, Sir John
ELLIS, John Devonshire
ELLIS, Sir William Henry
MCLAREN, Charles Benjamin Bright
MCLAREN, Henry Duncan
MENSFORTH, Sir Holberry
Brown, S G
BROWN, Sidney George
Brunner Mond (cf also ICI)
BRUNNER, Sir John Tomlinson
MOND, Ludwig
Bryant & May
BRYANT, Wilberforce
Bulmers
BULMER, Edward Frederick
Burmah Corporation
SMITH, Richard Tilden
Burmah Oil Co
CARGILL, Sir John Traill
DOWN, Sir Alastair Frederick
GREENWAY, Charles
WALLACE, Charles William
WATSON, Robert Irving
Burrell, C & Son
BURRELL, Charles
Burtons
BURTON, Sir Montague Maurice

Bute Estates
  LEWIS, William Thomas
Butlins
  BUTLIN, Sir William Heygate Edmund
    Colbourne
Butterworths
  BOND, Stanley Shaw

C

Cadburys
  CADBURY, George
  CADBURY, Laurence John
Caledonian Railway
  DRUMMOND, Dugald
Calico Printers' Association
  LEE, Lennox Bertram
Callenders Cable & Construction Co
  CALLENDER, Sir Thomas Octavius
  MCFADZEAN, William Hunter
Cambrian Combine
  LLEWELLYN, Sir David Richard
  THOMAS, David Alfred
Cambridge Scientific Instruments
  DARWIN, Sir Horace
Cammell-Laird
  CAMMELL, Charles
  HICHENS, Lionel
Cantrell & Cochrane
  COCHRANE, Sir Henry
Carmichael (Contractors) Ltd
  CARMICHAEL, Sir James
Carnegie-Storey Newspaper Syndicate
  STOREY, Samuel
Carr & Co
  CARR, Jonathan Dodgson
Carreras Ltd
  BARON, Bernhard
Cash, J & J
  CASH, John
  CASH, Joseph
Castle Mail Packets Co Ltd
  CURRIE, Sir Donald
Castner-Kellner Alkali Co
  CASTNER, Hamilton Young
Central Electricity Generating Board
  BROWN, Sir Frederick Herbert Stanley
  CITRINE, Walter
  DUNCAN, Sir Andrew Rae
  HINTON, Christopher

  HOSKING, John
Chadwick & Co
  CHADWICK, David
Chamberlain & Hookham
  CHAMBERLAIN, Arthur
Chance Bros
  CHANCE, Sir James Timmins
Channel Tunnel Co
  D'ERLANGER, Leo Frederic Alfred
Charlesworths
  CHARLESWORTH, John Charlesworth
    Dodgson
Charterhouse Group
  HUME, Sir Hubert Nutcombe
Chinese Engineering & Mining Co
  DAVIS, Sir Edmund Gabriel
Chivers & Son
  CHIVERS, John
Churchill-Redman
  GABRIEL, John Beresford Stuart
City & Central Investments Ltd
  CLORE, Sir Charles
City Centre Properties
  COTTON, Jack
City Equitable Fire Insurance Co
  BEVAN, Gerard Lee
City of London Electric Lighting Co
  SALOMONS, Sir David Lionel
    Goldsmid-Stern-
Clark, C & J
  CLARK, William Stephens
Clark, George Ltd
  CLARK, George
Clayton & Shuttleworth
  CLAYTON, Nathaniel
  SHUTTLEWORTH, Joseph
Clifford-Turner
  CLIFFORD-TURNER, Henry
Cluttons
  CLUTTON, John
Coalowners' Association
  LEWIS, William Thomas
Coates Bros
  COATES, John Bernard Maurice
Cole, E K Ltd (ECKO)
  COLE, Eric Kirkham
Coles Ltd
  Cole, Henry James
Colman, J & J
  COLMAN, Jeremiah James
  MAYHEW, Sir Basil Edgar

Coliseum Theatre
  STOLL, Sir Oswald
Coltness Iron Co
  HOULDSWORTH, Sir William Henry
Commercial Bank of Wales
  HODGE, Sir Julian Stephen Alfred
Consett Iron Co
  DALE, Sir David
  JENKINS, William
Consolidated African Selection Trust
  BEATTY, Sir Alfred Chester
Consolidated Bank of Cornwall Ltd
  BOLITHO, Thomas Edward
Consolidated Nyassa Co
  DAVIS, Sir Edmund Gabriel
Cook, Thomas & Son
  COOK, John Mason
  COOK, Thomas
Cooper Bros
  BENSON, Henry Alexander
  COOPER, Arthur
  COOPER, Ernest
  COOPER, Sir Francis D'Arcy
Co-operative Building Society
  WEBB, Arthur
Co-operative Wholesale Society (CWS)
  JACQUES, John Henry
  MITCHELL, John Thomas Whitehead
  NEALE, Edward Vansittart
  PEDDIE, James Mortimer
  SUGDEN, Sir Arthur
Copemans
  COPEMAN, Henry John
Cornish Consolidated Tin Smelting Co
  BOLITHO, Thomas Bedford
Cossor, A C Ltd
  COSSOR, Alfred Charles
Costain, R Ltd
  COSTAIN, Sir Richard Rylandes
Cotton Board
  STREAT, Sir Edward Raymond
Council of Associated Stock Exchanges
  RAE, Edward
Court Line Ltd
  PHILIPPS, Laurence Richard
Courtaulds
  COURTAULD III, Samuel
  COURTAULD IV, Samuel
  HANBURY-WILLIAMS, Sir John
    Coldbrook
  JOHNSON, Henry

  KEARTON, Christopher Frank
  KNIGHT, Sir Arthur William
  LATHAM, Sir Thomas Paul
  TETLEY, Henry Greenwood
  WHITTAKER, Croyden Meredith
Cowlin, W & Son
  COWLIN, Sir Francis Nicholas
Credit Foncier & Mobilier
  GRANT (GOTTHEIMER), Albert
    (Abraham) Zachariah
Creed & Co
  CREED, Frederick George
Crittall Co
  CRITTALL, Francis Henry
Crompton & Co
  CROMPTON, Rookes Evelyn Bell
Crosfield, J & Sons
  CROSFIELD, John
Crossley Bros
  CROSSLEY, Francis William
  CROSSLEY, Sir William John
Crossley, J & Sons
  CROSSLEY, Sir Francis
Cunard
  SMALLPEICE, Sir Basil
Currie, D & Co
  CURRIE, Sir Donald
Currys Ltd
  CURRY, Henry
Czarnikow & Co
  CZARNIKOW, Julius Caesar

D

Daily Telegraph
  LAWSON, Edward Levy
Daimler Motor Cars
  MANVILLE, Sir Edward
  MARTIN, Percy
  POLLEN, Arthur Joseph Hungerford
Davidson & Co Ltd
  DAVIDSON, Sir Samuel Clement
Daw, C A & Son Ltd
  DAW, William Adams
Dawnay Day (DD)
  DAWNAY, Guy Payan
Debenhams
  BEDFORD, John
  OLIVER, Frederick Scott
Decca
  LEWIS, Sir Edward Roberts

SAMUEL, Frank
De Havilland
  DE HAVILLAND, Sir Geoffrey
  HALFORD, Frank Bernard
  HEARLE, Francis Trounson
De La Rue Co
  DE LA RUE, Warren
Deloitte, Plender & Co
  DELOITTE, William Welch
  PLENDER, William
Dennis Bros
  DENNIS, John Cawsey
  DENNIS, Sir Herbert Raymond
Dennis Watch Case Co
  DENNISON, Aaron Lufkin
Dent, Allcroft & Co
  ALLCROFT, John Derby
Dent, J M & Sons
  DENT, Joseph Malaby
Derby Pure Ice & Cold Storage Co
  HASLAM, Sir Alfred Seale
Derbyshire Stone Ltd
  HADFIELD, John
Deuchar, J Ltd
  DEUCHAR, James
Dewar, J & Sons Ltd
  DEWAR, Thomas Robert
Dickinson, John & Co
  EVANS, Sir John
  LING, Reuben Herbert
Distillers Co Ltd (DCL)
  BALL, Charles Prior James
  DEWAR, Thomas Robert
  HAYMAN, Sir Cecil George Graham
  STEVENSON, James
Dixons
  DIXON, Sir Raylton
Dobson & Barlow
  DOBSON, Sir Benjamin Alfred
Dorman, Long
  BELL, Sir Isaac Lowthian
  DORMAN, Sir Arthur John
  HUNTER, Sir Ellis
  JUDGE, Edward Thomas
Doulton & Co
  DOULTON, Sir Henry
Dove Bros
  DOVE, Frederick John
Dowlais Iron Co
  CLARK, George Thomas
  MENELAUS, William

WILLIAMS, Edward
Dowty Group
  DOWTY, Sir George Herbert
Doxford, W & Sons
  DOXFORD, Sir William Theodore
Dublin United Tramway Co
  MURPHY, William Martin
Dudley Estate
  WARD, William
  WARD, William Eric Humble
Dunlop
  DE PAULA, Frederic Rudolf Mackley
  DU CROS, Sir Arthur Philip
  DU CROS, William Harvey
  DUNLOP, John Boyd
  GEDDES, Sir Eric Campbell
Duveen Bros
  DUVEEN, Joseph

E

Eagle Star Group
  MOUNTAIN, Sir Edward Mortimer
Ealing Studios
  BALCON, Sir Michael Elias
Eastern Telegraph Co
  PENDER, Sir John
Edison & Swan Electric Light Co
  SWAN, Sir Joseph Wilson
Edwards, J C
  EDWARDS, James Coster
Elder Dempster
  JONES, Sir Alfred Lewis
Electric & General Industrial Trusts Ltd
  HAYWARD, Sir Charles William
Electric & Musical Industries (EMI)
  CLARK, Alfred Corning
  LOCKWOOD, Sir Joseph Flawith
Electricity Council
  EDWARDS, Sir Ronald
  ELLIOTT, Sir Norman Randall
Ellerman Lines
  ELLERMAN, Sir John Reeves (1862–1933)
  ELLERMAN, Sir John Reeves (1909–1973)
Ellis, Richard
  ELLIS, Richard Adam
Enfield Armory
  ANDERSON, Sir John
Engineering Employers' Federation
  DYER, Henry Clement Swinnerton
  SMITH, Sir Allan MacGregor

English Clays Lovering Pochin
  KEAY, Sir John
  MCLAREN, Henry Duncan
  STOCKER, Thomas Medland
English Electric (EE Co)
  MENSFORTH, Sir Holberry
  NELSON, George Horatio
  NELSON, Henry George
  PYBUS, Sir Percy John
English Sewing Cotton Co
  HARRISON, Sir Cyril Ernest
Eno, J C Ltd
  ENO, James Crossley
Equitable Life Assurance Society
  ELDERTON, Sir William Palin
Ernst & Whinney
  HARDING, Sir Robert Palmer
  WHINNEY, Frederick
Ethelburga Syndicate
  PAM, Albert Samuel
Express Dairy Co
  BARHAM, Sir George
  BARHAM, George Titus

F

Fairbairn, Naylor & Macpherson
  FAIRBAIRN, Sir Andrew
Fairey Aviation Co
  FAIREY, Sir Charles Richard
Faithfull Begg & Co
  BEGG, Ferdinand Faithfull
Federation of British Industries (FBI)
  BAILLIEU, Clive Latham
  LOCOCK, Sir Guy Harold
  NUGENT, Sir Roland Thomas
Federation of Master Cotton Spinners'
    Associations
  MACARA, Sir Charles Wright
  TATTERSALL, John Brown
Fenwicks
  FENWICK, John James
Ferguson Ltd
  FERGUSON, Henry George
Ferranti Engineering
  DE FERRANTI, Sir Gerard Vincent
    Sebastian
  DE FERRANTI, Sebastian Ziani
  FIELD, William
Financial News Ltd
  MARKS, Harry Hananel

Financial Newspaper Group
  DAWNAY, Guy Payan
Fine Cotton Spinners' & Doublers' Association
  DIXON, Sir Alfred Herbert
  HARWOOD, Harold Marsh
  HOLLAND, William Henry
  HOULDSWORTH, Sir William Henry
Firth Cleveland Ltd
  HAYWARD, Sir Charles William
Firth, Thomas & Sons
  FIRTH, Mark
Fisons Ltd
  FISON, Sir Frank Guy Clavering
Fitch Lovell
  KEEVIL, Sir Ambrose
Flavel, S & Co
  FLAVEL, Sidney Smith
Flight Refuelling Ltd
  COBHAM, Sir Alan John
Fodens
  FODEN, William
  FODEN, Henry Richard
Ford Motor Co
  HENNESSY, Sir Patrick
  PERRY, Percival Lee Dewhurst
Forwoods
  FORWOOD, Sir William Bower
Foster & Braithwaite
  BRAITHWAITE, Sir John Bevan
  BRAITHWAITE, Joseph Bevan
Foundation of Management Education
  PLATT, James Westlake
Fourth City Mutual Building and Investment
    Society
  HIGHAM, James
Fowler, J & Co
  FOWLER, Robert Henry
Fowler, Perks & Co
  PERKS, Sir Robert William
Freeman, Hardy & Willis
  WOOD, Sir Edward
Freshfields
  FRESHFIELD, Edwin
  LEESE, Sir William Hargreaves
  PEPPIATT, Sir Leslie Ernest
Fry, J S & Son
  FRY, Joseph Storrs
Furness Railway
  CAVENDISH, William
Furness, Withy
  FURNESS, Christopher

FURNESS, Marmaduke
LEWIS, Frederick William
MURRANT, Sir Ernest Henry
STOKER, Robert Burdon
TALBOT, Benjamin
Furniture Industries Ltd
ERCOLANI, Lucian Randolph
Fyffe, E W & Son
FYFFE, Edward Wathen

G

Gallaher Ltd
GALLAHER, Thomas
Galloway, W & J
GALLOWAY, John
Gamages
GAMAGE, Albert Walter
Gamble, J C & Son
GAMBLE, Sir David
Gas Council
JONES, Sir Henry Frank Harding
Gas Light & Coke Co
MILNE-WATSON, Sir David
WOODALL, Sir Corbet
Gaskell Deacon & Co
GASKELL, Holbrook
Gates, E H & Co
GATES, Ernest Henry
Gaumont British Picture Corporation
BALCON, Sir Michael Elias
OSTRER, Isidore
General Electric Co (GEC)
HIRST, Hugo
NELSON, Henry George
RAILING, Max John
RAILING, Sir Harry
General Film Distributors
WOOLF, Charles Moss
Gestetner Holdings
GESTETNER, David
Gibb, Alexander & Partners
GIBB, Sir Alexander
Gibbs, Antony & Sons
GIBBS, Henry Hucks
GIBBS, Herbert Cokayne
Gilbertson & Co
GILBERTSON, Francis William
Gillett Bros
GILLETT, Ronald Brodie

Glaxo
JEPHCOTT, Sir Harry
Gliksten, J & Son
GLIKSTEN, Albert Arnold
Glynwed Tubes
WALLIS, Frederick
Gollancz, V Ltd
GOLLANCZ, Sir Victor
Gomme, E Ltd
GOMME, Ebenezer
Gordon Hotels
DAWNAY, Guy Payan
Gordon, Panmure
GORDON, Harry Panmure
Gossage, W & Sons Ltd
GOSSAGE, William
Goya
COLLINS, Douglas Raymond
Gramophone Co
CLARK, Alfred Corning
OWEN, William Barry
Grand Metropolitan
JOSEPH, Sir Maxwell
Grand Trunk Railway of Canada
TYLER, Sir Henry Whatley
Gray, W & Co
GRAY, Sir William
Great Central Railway
FAY, Sir Samuel
Great Eastern Railway
ADAMS, William
HAMILTON, Lord Claud John
THORNTON, Sir Henry Worth
Great Northern Railway
OAKLEY, Sir Henry
STIRLING, Patrick
Great Western Railway
GOOCH, Sir Daniel
HORNE, Robert Stevenson
INGLIS, Sir James Charles
MILNE, Sir James
POLE, Sir Felix John Clewett
SPAGNOLETTI, Charles Ernest Paulo della
   Diana
Greene, John & Sons
HEDLEY, Thomas
Greene, King & Sons
GREENE, Edward
Greenwood & Batley
GREENWOOD, Arthur

GREENWOOD, Thomas
Greg, R & Co Ltd
  GREG, Henry Philips
Greyhound Racing Association
  CRITCHLEY, Alfred Cecil
Griffin & George Ltd
  GRIFFIN, John Ross
Griffiths, J Norton Ltd
  GRIFFITHS, Sir John Norton
Guéret, L Ltd
  GUÉRET, Louis Jean Baptiste
Guernsey Airways
  THURGOOD, Walter Leonard
Guest, Keen, Baldwins
  WRIGHT, Sir Charles William
Guest, Keen, Nettlefolds (GKN)
  BERRY, Henry Seymour
  BROOKES, Raymond Percival
  HAYWARD, Sir Charles William
  JOLLY, James Hornby
  KEEN, Arthur
  LLEWELLYN, Sir David Richard
  LYSAGHT, William Royse
  MARKLAND, Stanley
  PEACOCK, Sir Kenneth Swift
Guinness
  BEAVER, Sir Hugh Eyre Campbell
  GUINNESS, Edward Cecil
Guthrie, E & Co
  GUTHRIE, Edwin

H

Hadfields Ltd
  HADFIELD, Sir Robert Abbott
Hain Steamship Co
  HAIN, Sir Edward
Haldin & Co
  PHILIPPS, Laurence Richard
Halfords
  RUSHBROOKE, Frederick William
Halifax Building Society
  HILL, Sir Enoch
Hall, English & Co
  ENGLISH, John
Hambros Bank
  HAMBRO, Sir Everard Alexander
Handley-Page Ltd
  PAGE, Sir Frederick Handley
Handyside, A & Co
  HANDYSIDE, Andrew

Harland & Wolff
  PIRRIE, William James
  HARLAND, Sir Edward James
  REBBECK, Sir Frederick Ernest
  WOOLFF, Gustav Wilhelm
Harrison Colleries
  HARRISON, William Edward
Harrison, T & J
  HARRISON, James
  HARRISON, Thomas
  HUGHES, John William
Harrods
  BURBIDGE, Sir Richard
Hartley Glass Works
  HARTLEY, James
Hartley, W P
  HARTLEY, Sir William Pickles
Harton Coal Co
  WOOD, Sir Lindsay
Hattersley, G & Sons
  HATTERSLEY, Richard Longden
Hawker Siddeley Group
  CAMM, Sir Sydney
  DOBSON, Sir Roy Hardy
  SIDDELEY, John Davenport
  SOPWITH, Sir Thomas Octave Murdoch
  SPRIGGS, Sir Frank Spencer
Hawthorn-Leslie
  BATEY, John Thomas
  BROWNE, Sir Benjamin Chapman
  LESLIE, Andrew
  MARSHALL, Francis Carr
  ROWELL, Sir Herbert Babington
Hedley, T & Co
  HEDLEY, Thomas
Hepworth, J & Sons
  HEPWORTH, Joseph
Henry, A & S
  MITCHELL, Sir Henry
Her Majesty's Theatre
  TREE, Sir Herbert Beerbohm
Herbert, Alfred
  HERBERT, Sir Alfred Edward
Hick, B & Son
  HICK, John
Hickman, A Ltd
  HICKMAN, Sir Alfred
Higgs & Hill Ltd
  HIGGS, William
Highfield Tanning Co
  POSNETT, Robert Harold

Hilger & Watts
TWYMAN, Frank
Hill, Sir James & Sons
AMBLER, Geoffrey Hill
Hill Organisation, William
HILL, William
Hillman's Airways
HILLMAN, Edward Henry
Hillman Car Co
HILLMAN, William
Hilton Transport Service
HILTON, Ralph
Hine & Mundella
MUNDELLA, Anthony John
Hingley Ltd
HINGLEY, Sir Benjamin
Hitchcock, Williams & Co
WILLIAMS, Sir George
Hodge Group
HODGE, Sir Julian Stephen Alfred
Holden, Isaac & Sons
HOLDEN, Isaac
RAPER, George Frederick
Holland & Webb
WEBB, Weston Fulford Marriott
Hollins, W & Co Ltd
HOLLINS, Ernest Henry
Holloway Patent Medicine Co
HOLLOWAY, Thomas
Holt, Alfred & Co
HOLT, Alfred
Home & Colonial Stores
DREW, Julius Charles
SLAUGHTER, Sir William Capel
Hoover Ltd
COLSTON, Sir Charles Blampied
PUCKEY, Sir Walter Charles
Horlicks Food Co
HORLICK, Sir James
Horrockses, Crewdson & Co
HOLLINS, Sir Frank
Horrockses, Miller & Co
HERMON, Edward
Houlder Bros
HOULDER, Edwin Savory
Houldsworth, T & Co
HOULDSWORTH, Sir William Henry
House to House Electric Lighting Co
HAMMOND, Robert
Houston Line Ltd
HOUSTON, Sir Robert Paterson

Howard & Bullough
BULLOUGH, Sir George
BULLOUGH, John
Howard, J & Son
HOWARD, James
Huddersfield Banking Co
SIKES, Sir Charles William
Hulton, E & Co Ltd
HULTON, Sir Edward
Humber & Pneumatic Tyre Co
LAWSON, Henry John
Hunting Group
HUNTING, Sir Percy Llewellyn
Huntley & Palmers
PALMER, George
Huwood Mining Machinery Co
WOOD, Hugh Nicholas

I

Ilford Ltd
HARMAN, Alfred Hugh
KNOBEL, Edward Ball
PHILIPPS, Sir Ivor
Illingworth, D & Sons
ILLINGWORTH, Alfred
Imperial Airways
BRACKLEY, Herbert George
GEDDES, Sir Eric Campbell
SCOTT-PAINE, Charles Hubert
WOODS-HUMPHERY, George Edward
Imperial Chemical Industries (ICI)
CHAMBERS, Sir Stanley Paul
COATES, Sir William Henry
CRONSHAW, Cecil John Turrell
FLECK, Alexander
MCGOWAN, Sir Harry Duncan
MOND, Alfred Moritz
MOND, Henry Ludwig
PERRIN, Sir Michael Willcox
Imperial Tobacco
WILLS, Sir George Alfred
WILLS, William Henry
Inchcape Group
MACKAY, James Lyle
Industrial & Commercial Finance Corporation
PIERCY, William Stuckey
Industrial Welfare Society
HYDE, Sir Robert Robertson
Initial Carrier Co
BIGELOW, Arthur Perkins

Inman Line
  INMAN, William
Instone Group
  INSTONE, Sir Samuel
Intercontinental Trust
  SMITH, Richard Tilden
International Nickel Co
  MOND, Sir Robert Ludwig
International Tea Co
  KEARLEY, Hudson Ewbanke
International Telephone & Telegraph
    Corporation
  CREED, Frederick George
Internationale des Wagons-Lits, Cie
  DALZIEL, Davison Alexander
Irrigation Investment Co
  CASSEL, Sir Ernest Joseph
Irvin, R & Sons
  IRVIN, Richard
Isherwood, J W & Co Ltd
  ISHERWOOD, Sir Joseph William
Ismay, T H & Co
  ISMAY, Thomas Henry

J

Jaguar Cars
  Lyons, Sir William
Japhet, S & Co
  CASSEL, Sir Ernest Joseph
Jardine Matheson
  MATHESON, Hugh Mackay
Jarrott & Letts
  LETTS, Sir William Malesbury
Jarrow Chemical Co
  STEVENSON, James Cochran
Jobling, J A & Co
  JOBLING-PURSER, Ernest Joseph
John Lewis Partnership
  LEWIS, John Spedan
Johnson Matthey
  COUSSMAKER, Arthur Blakeney
  MATTHEY, George
Joicey, J & Co
  JOICEY, James
Jones, Loyd & Co
  LOYD, Samuel Jones
Jones, T B & Co
  JONES, Theodore Brooke
Jowitt, R & Sons
  JOWITT, John

K

K Shoes Ltd
  SOMERVELL, Sir Arnold Colin
Kenning Motor Group
  KENNING, Sir George
Kenricks
  KENRICK, William Edmund
Kent Coal Concessions Group
  BURR, Arthur
  DEWRANCE, Sir John
Kinloch Ltd
  BELLINGER, Sir Robert Ian
Kitsons
  KITSON, James
Kleinwort Benson
  KLEINWORT, Sir Alexander Drake
  KLEINWORT, Ernest Greverus
  TURNER, Sir Robert Mark Cunliffe
Knight Piano Co
  KNIGHT, Alfred Edward
Kodak Ltd
  BLAKE, Ernest Edgar
  MATTISON, Francis Charles
Kullbergs
  KULLBERG, Victor
Kynoch Ltd
  CHAMBERLAIN, Arthur
  KYNOCH, George

L

Laing, J & Son
  LAING, Sir John William
Laings
  LAING, Sir James
Lancashire Cotton Corporation
  PLATT, Sir Frank
Lancashire & Yorkshire Railway
  ASPINALL, John Audley Frederick
Lancashire Watch Co
  HEWITT, Thomas Peter
Lascelles, W H
  LASCELLES, William Henry
Latham, J Ltd
  LATHAM, Edward Bryan
Lavertons
  LAVERTON, Abraham
Lazard Bros
  BRAND, Robert Henry
  KINDERSLEY, Robert Molesworth

Lead Industries Group
   COOKSON, Roland Antony
Leavesley & North
   NORTH, Sir Jonathan
Lebus, H Ltd
   LEBUS, Harris
   LEBUS, Sir Hermann Andrew
Legal & General Assurance
   LAYBORN, Thomas Alec Edwin
Leicester Gas Corporation
   COLSON, Alfred
Letts, C & Co Ltd
   LETTS, Charles John
Levinstein & Co Ltd
   LEVINSTEIN, Ivan
Lewis, John
   LEWIS, John
   LEWIS, John Spedan
Lewis's
   LEWIS, David
   MARQUIS, Frederick James
Leyland Motors
   SPURRIER, Sir Henry
   STOKES, Donald Gresham
Liberator Building Society
   BALFOUR, Jabez Spencer
Liberty & Co
   LIBERTY, Sir Arthur Lasenby
   STEWART-LIBERTY, Arthur
Limmer & Trinidad Lake Asphalt Co
   MARRIOTT, Thomas Geoffrey
Linen Thread Co
   BARBOUR, Sir John Milne
Linotype Co
   LAWRENCE, Sir Joseph
   POLLEN, Arthur Joseph Hungerford
Lipton, T J Ltd
   LIPTON, Sir Thomas Johnstone
Listers
   LISTER, Samuel Cunliffe
Littlewoods Organisation
   MOORES, Sir John
Liverpool & London Fire & Life Insurance Co
   BOULT, Swinton
Livesey & Son
   LIVESEY, James
Lloyd, E Ltd
   LLOYD, Frank
Lloyds Bank
   LLOYD, Howard
   PEASE, John William Beaumont

PHILLIPS, John Spencer
   SALT, Sir Thomas
   VASSAR-SMITH, Sir Richard Vassar
Lloyds Register
   HOZIER, Sir Henry Montague
Locke, Blackett & Co
   LEATHART, James
London Brick Co
   HILL, John Cathles
   STEWART, Sir Halley
   STEWART, Sir Percy Malcolm
London, Brighton & South Coast Railway
   FORBES, Sir William de Guise
   SARLE, Sir Allen Lanyon
   STROUDLEY, William
London Chatham & Dover Railway
   FORBES, James Staats
London Express Newspapers
   AITKEN, William Maxwell
London Film Production
   KORDA, Sir Alexander
London & Lancashire Insurance Co
   RUTTER, Sir Frederick William
      Pascoe
London Metal Exchange
   BUDD, Sir Cecil Lindsay
London, Midland & Scottish Railway
   STAMP, Josiah Charles
London & North Eastern Railway
   GRESLEY, Sir Hebert Nigel
London & North Western Railway
   RAMSBOTTOM, John
   WEDGWOOD, Sir Ralph Lewis
London & South Western Railway
   ADAMS, William
   DRUMMOND, Dugald
   WALKER, Sir Herbert Ashcombe
London Transport
   ELLIOT, Sir John
   PICK, Frank
   STANLEY, Albert Henry
Londonderry Bottle Works
   CANDLISH, John
Longleys
   LONGLEY, Sir Norman
Longmans, House of
   LONGMAN, Charles James
Lord, Cyril Ltd
   LORD, Cyril
Lotus Ltd
   BOSTOCK, Henry John

Lowood, J G & Co
    LOWOOD, John Grayson
Lubbock, Foster & Co
    LUBBOCK, John
Lucas Industries
    LUCAS, Joseph
    WARING, Sir Arthur Bertram
Lyceum
    IRVING, Sir Henry
Lyons, J & C
    GLUCKSTEIN, Montague
    LYONS, Sir Joseph Nathaniel
    SALMON, Harry
Lysaght, J Ltd
    LYSAGHT, John
    LYSAGHT, William Royse

M

McAlpine Group
    MCALPINE, Sir Alfred David
McAlpine, Sir Robert & Sons
    MCALPINE, Sir Thomas Malcolm
Mcintyre's Pottery
    WOODALL, William
Mackie, J & Sons
    MACKIE, James
McLintock, T & Co
    MCLINTOCK, Sir William
Macmillan Ltd
    MACMILLAN, Sir Frederick
Mallinson & Denny Mott Ltd
    MALLINSON, Sir Stuart Sidney
    MALLINSON, Sir William James
Management Research Groups
    ROWNTREE, Benjamin Seebohm
    WARD, Harry
Magnesium Elektron Ltd
    BALL, Charles James Prior
Management Selection Ltd
    PUCKEY, Sir Walter Charles
Manbré & Garton
    BERRY, Albert Eustace
    GARTON, Sir Richard Charles
Manchester Chamber of Commerce
    STREAT, Sir Edward Raymond
Manchester, Sheffield & Lincolnshire Railway
    WATKIN, Sir Edward William
Manchester Ship Canal
    BYTHELL, John Kenworthy

Manfield & Sons Ltd
    MANFIELD, Sir Moses Philip
Mann Egerton & Co Ltd
    MANN, Gerard Noel Cornwallis
Mappin & Webb Ltd
    MAPPIN, Sir Frederick Thorpe
Marks & Spencer
    MARKS, Michael
    MARKS, Simon
    SIEFF, Israel Moses
Marconi Wireless Telegraph Co
    ISAACS, Godfrey Charles
Marley Hill Coking Co
    BOWES, John
    PALMER, Sir Charles Mark
Martin-Baker Aircraft Co
    MARTIN, Sir James
Martin's Bank
    MARTIN, Sir Richard Biddulph
Masons
    MASON, Hugh
Mather & Platt
    MATHER, Sir William
Meadow Dairy Co
    BEALE, George
Meccano Ltd
    HORNBY, Frank
Merz & McLellan
    MERZ, Charles Hesterman
Metal Box
    BARLOW, Sir Robert
Methuen & Co
    METHUEN, Sir Algernon Methuen Marshall
Metropolitan Carriage, Wagon & Finance Co
    DOCKER, Sir Bernard Dudley Frank
    DOCKER, Frank Dudley
Metropolitan Railway
    BELL, John
    FENTON, Sir Myles
    PERKS, Sir Robert William
    SELBIE, Robert Hope
Metropolitan-Vickers
    FLEMING, Sir Arthur Percy Morris
    JACKSON, Willis
    MENSFORTH, Sir Holberry
Midland Bank
    HOLDEN, Sir Edward Hopkinson
    MCKENNA, Reginald
Midland Counties Dairy
    WHITE, Edwin

Midland News Association
  STOREY, Samuel
Midland Railway
  ALLPORT, Sir James Joseph
  GRANET, Sir Guy
Miles Aircraft Ltd
  MILES, Frederick George
Mills, Bertram Circus
  MILLS, Bertram Wagstaff
Minton Pottery
  CAMPBELL, Colin Minton
Mitchell & Butlers
  BUTLER, Sir William Waters
Modern Machine Tools
  WESTON, Harry
Moira Collieries
  TURNER, Sir John
Mond Nickel Co
  GRIFFITHS, Sir William Thomas
Moor Line Ltd
  RUNCIMAN, Walter
Morgan, D Ltd
  MORGAN, David
Morgan Grenfell
  GRENFELL, Edward Charles
  SMITH, Vivian Hugh
Morley, I & R
  MORLEY, Samuel
Morphy-Richards
  MORPHY, Donal William
Morris Garages (MG)
  KIMBER, Cecil
Morris, H Ltd
  MORRIS, Herbert
Morris Motors
  MORRIS, William Richard
  THOMAS, William Miles Webster
  WOOLLARD, Frank George
Morrison, Sons & Co
  MORRISON, Charles
Morsons
  MORSON, Thomas
Morton, A & Co
  MORTON, Sir James
Moss Bros
  MOSS, Harry Neville
Mowlem, John & Co
  BURT, Sir George Mowlem
Mudie's Select Library
  MUDIE, Charles Edward

Muirhead & Co
  MUIRHEAD, Alexander
Mullard Co
  ERIKS, Sierd Sint
  MULLARD, Stanley Robert
Municipal & General Securities
  BOOTH, George Macaulay
Murphy Radio Ltd
  MURPHY, Frank
Musgrave, J & Sons
  MUSGRAVE, John

N

Napier, D & Son
  EDGE, Selwyn Francis
  HALFORD, Frank Bernard
  NAPIER, Montague Stanley
National Bank of Egypt
  CASSEL, Sir Ernest Joseph
National Building Society
  WYCHERLEY, Sir Robert Bruce
National Coal Board (NCB)
  BOWMAN, Sir James
  HINDLEY, John Scott
  HOULDSWORTH, Sir Hubert Stanley
National Council for Technological Awards
  PUCKEY, Sir Walter Charles
National Economic Development Council
  SHONE, Sir Robert Minshull
National Exhibition Centre
  BOOTH, Sir Robert Camm
National Mutual Life Assurance Co
  MARKS, Geoffrey
National Provincial Bank
  CAMPBELL, Colin Frederick
  SCHUSTER, Sir Felix Otto
National Smelting Co
  HORNE, Robert Stevenson
  SMITH, Richard Tilden
Nelson, J & Sons
  NELSON, Sir Amos
Nettlefold & Chamberlain
  CHAMBERLAIN, Joseph
  NETTLEFOLD, Joseph Henry
Newcastle & Gateshead Gas Co
  STEPHENSON, Sir William Haswell
Newcastle & Gateshead Water Co
  STEPHENSON, Sir William Haswell

Newcastle Chemical Works
  ALLHUSEN, Christian Augustus Henry
Newnes Ltd
  NEWNES, Sir George
Newnes & Pearson
  PEARSON, Sir Cyril Arthur
  RIDDELL, George Allardice
Nixon's Navigation Co Ltd
  NIXON, John
Nobel Industries
  STAMP, Josiah Charles
Noble Lowndes & Partners
  LOWNDES, Noble Frank
North Eastern Railway
  BUTTERWORTH, Sir Alexander Kaye
  GEDDES, Sir Eric Campbell
  GIBB, Sir George Stegmann
  HARRISON, Thomas Elliot
  RAVEN, Sir Vincent Litchfield
  TENNANT, Henry
Norvic Shoe Co
  COLMAN, Cecil
Norwich Union Life Insurance Co
  DEUCHAR, John James Walker
Novello & Co
  LITTLETON, Henry
Nunnery Colliery Co Ltd
  BAINBRIDGE, Emerson Muschamp
Nurdin & Peacock
  PEACOCK, John Atkins

O

Odeon Cinemas
  DEUTSCH, Oscar
Odhams
  CHANCELLOR, Sir Christopher John
    Howard
Old Vic Theatre
  BAYLIS, Lilian Mary
Oldham Master Cotton Spinners' Association
  TATTERSALL, John Brown
Oldroyd, Messrs M & Sons
  OLDROYD, Sir Mark
Oxford University Press
  MILFORD, Sir Humphrey Sumner
Orient Steam Navigation Co
  ANDERSON, James
Overseas Containers Ltd
  ANDERSON, Sir Donald Forsyth

Owen Owen
  OWEN, Owen

P

Palmer's Iron & Shipbuilding Co
  PALMER, Sir Charles Mark
Parkinson, Lindsay & Co
  PARKINSON, Sir Albert Lindsay
Parsons, C A & Co
  GIBB, Sir Claude Dixon
  PARSONS, The Honourable Sir Charles
    Algernon
Pasolds Ltd
  PASOLDS, Eric W
Paton McLaren & Co
  PATON, Alexander Allan
Pearson, S & Son
  PEARSON, Weetman Dickinson
Pearl Life Assurance Co
  FOLEY, Patrick James
Pears Soap
  BARRATT, Thomas James
  PEARS, Andrew
Pearson & Knowles
  HARMOOD-BANNER, Sir John Sutherland
Pease & Partners
  PEASE, Joseph Albert
Peat, Marwick, Mitchell & Co
  PEAT, Sir William Barclay
Peek Frean
  CARR, Arthur
Penguin Books
  LANE, Sir Allen
Peninsular & Oriental Steamship Co
  ANDERSON, Sir Alan Garrett
  ANDERSON, Sir Donald Forsyth
Penrhyn Quarry
  DOUGLAS-PENNANT, George Sholto
    Gordon
People's Motor Services Ltd
  THURGOOD, Walter Leonard
Perkin & Sons
  PERKIN, Sir William Henry
Perkins Engine Co
  PERKINS, Frank Arthur
Perry & Co
  BARTLETT, Sir Herbert Henry
Perry & Co
  MASON, Sir Josiah

Peto & Co
  PETO, Sir Samuel Morton
Petters Ltd
  PETTER, Sir Ernest Willoughby
  PETTER, Percival Waddams
Philips
  ERIKS, Sierd Sint
Phoenix Assurance
  PYBUS, Sir Percy John
Pickersgill Ltd
  PICKERSGILL, William
Pickfords
  BAXENDALE, Lloyd Henry
Pilkington Bros
  PILKINGTON, Sir Lionel Alexander
    Bethune
  PILKINGTON, William Henry
Pitman Ltd
  PITMAN, Sir Isaac
Pittards
  PITTARD, Wreford John Charles
Platt Bros
  PLATT, John
  PLATT, Samuel Radcliffe
Plessey
  CLARK, Sir Allen George
Pope & Pearson
  GARFORTH, Sir William Edward
Port of London Authority
  KEARLEY, Hudson Ewbanke
Post Office
  BLACKWOOD, Sir Stevenson Arthur
  MURRAY, Sir George Evelyn Pemberton
  SCUDAMORE, Frank Ives
  TILLEY, Sir John
Power Securities Ltd
  BALFOUR, George
Pressed Steel Co
  PAM, Albert Samuel
Price, Waterhouse
  DICKINSON, Sir Arthur Lowes
  GARNSEY, Sir Gilbert Francis
  WATERHOUSE, Edwin
Priestman Collieries
  PRIESTMAN, Francis
Prince Line Ltd
  KNOTT, Sir James
Prince of Wales Theatre
  BANCROFT, Sir Squire
Proprietary Articles Trade Association (PATA)
  GLYN-JONES, Sir William Samuel

Prudential Assurance Co
  HARBEN, Sir Henry
  MAY, George Ernest
Pye Ltd
  PYE, Harold John
  PYE, William George

Q

Quilter, Ball
  QUILTER, William

R

Radcliffe, Evan Thomas & Co
  RADCLIFFE, Henry
Raleigh Cycle Co
  BOWDEN, Sir Harold
Rank, J Ltd
  RANK, James Voase
  RANK, Joseph
  RANK, Joseph Arthur
Rankin, Gilmour & Co
  RANKIN, John
Ransomes, Simms & Jefferies
  RANSOME, James Edward
  RANSOME, Robert Charles
Rathbones
  LIDDERDALE, William
  RATHBONE, William Benson
Reckitt & Sons Ltd
  FERENS, Thomas Robinson
  RECKITT, Sir James
Redland Holdings
  YOUNG, Alexander Frederick Farquhar
Reed, A E & Co
  REED, Albert Edwin
  REED, Sir Albert Ralph
  SHELDON, Clifford Dommett
Reed, Austin
  REED, Austin Leonard
Rees Roturbo Manufacturing
  BRINDLEY, Harry Samuel Bickerton
Renold Chains Ltd
  RENOLD, Sir Charles Garonne
Reuters
  CHANCELLOR, Sir Christopher John
    Howard
  REUTER, Paul Julius
Reynolds Metal
  PORTAL, Charles Frederick Algernon

Reyrolle & Co
  REYROLLE, Alphonse Constant
Rhondda Valley Coalfield
  DAVIES, David
Richardson, E & J Ltd
  RICHARDSON, John Wigham
Rio Tinto Zinc
  BAILLIEU, Clive Latham
  DUNCAN, Sir John Norman Valette
  FIELDING, Charles William Ewing
  GEDDES, Auckland Campbell
  MATHESON, Hugh Mackay
  TURNER, Sir Ronald Mark Cunliffe
Ripley, Edward & Son
  DOUGLAS, George
Roe, A V
  VERDON-ROE, Sir Edwin Alliott Verdon
Rolls Razor
  COLSTON, Sir Charles
Rolls Royce
  HIVES, Ernest Walter
  JOHNSON, Claude Goodman
  ROLLS, The Honourable Charles Stewart
  ROYCE, Sir Frederick Henry
  SIDGREAVES, Sir Arthur Frederick
Roneo Ltd
  KLABER, Augustus David
Rootes Group
  ROOTES, Sir Reginald Claud
  ROOTES, William Edward
Rothschilds
  ROTHSCHILD, Nathan Meyer
Routledge & Co
  ROUTLEDGE, Thomas
Rover Cycle Co
  STARLEY, John Kemp
Rover Car Co
  WILKS, Spencer Bernau
Rowntree Mackintosh
  HARRIS, George James
  MACKINTOSH, Harold Vincent
  MACKINTOSH, John
  ROWNTREE, Benjamin Seebohm
  ROWNTREE, Joseph
  SHELDON, Oliver
Royal Mail Group
  MCLINTOCK, Sir William
  PHILIPPS, Owen Cosby
Royal Niger Co
  GOLDIE, Sir George Dashwood Taubman-

Rubery Owen Group
  OWEN, Sir Alfred George Beech
Rudge Whitworth
  PUGH, Charles Vernon
Rugby Portland Cement
  REDDISH, Sir Halford Walter Lupton
Russell, Gordon Ltd
  RUSSELL, Sir Sydney Gordon
Ruston, Proctor & Co
  RUSTON, Joseph
Rylands & Son
  RYLANDS, John
Rylands Bros
  RYLANDS, Sir William Peter

S

Sainsburys
  SAINSBURY, Alan John
  SAINSBURY, John Benjamin
  SAINSBURY, John James
  SAINSBURY, Sir Robert
St Davids Group
  PHILIPPS, John Wynford
  ROGER, Sir Alexander Forbes Proctor
St James Theatre
  ALEXANDER, Sir George
Salt Union Ltd
  FALK, Herman Eugen
  MALCOLM, George William
Salts (Saltaire) Ltd
  GATES, Ernest Henry
  SALT, Sir Titus
Samuel & Montagu
  MONTAGU, Samuel
Samuelson & Co
  SAMUELSON, Sir Bernhard
Sankey, Joseph & Sons
  SANKEY, John William
  SANKEY, Joseph
Saxby & Farmer
  SAXBY, John
Scholefield & Goodman
  GOODMAN, Frederick Buck
Schröder, J Henry
  PAM, Albert Samuel
  SCHRÖDER, Baron Rudolph Bruno
  TIARKS, Frank Cyril
Schweppes
  HOOPER, Sir Frederic Collins

PHILIPPS, Sir Ivor
Scott Bader Ltd
  BADER, Ernest
Scottish Equitable Assurance Society
  SPRAGUE, Thomas Bond
Sears Holdings
  CLORE, Sir Charles
Sears (True Form Boot Co)
  SEARS, John George
Seccombe, Marshall & Campion
  SECCOMBE, Lawrence Henry
Selfridge & Co
  SELFRIDGE, Harry Gordon
Share Guarantee Trust
  SMITH, Richard Tilden
Sheffield Gas & Light Co
  MAPPIN, Sir Frederick Thorpe
Shell Group
  GODBER, Frederick
  LANE, Frederick
  PLATT, James Westlake
Shiloh Spinning Co Ltd
  GARTSIDE, Thomas Edmund
Shippams
  SHIPPAM, Alfred Ernest Cooper
Short Bros
  SHORT, Hugh Oswald
Short Bros
  SHORT, John Young
Siemens Bros
  SIEMENS, Alexander
  SIEMENS, Sir Charles William
Simms Motor Units Ltd
  SIMMS, Frederick Richard
Simon Engineering Group
  LOCKWOOD, Sir Joseph Flawith
  SIMON, Ernest Emil Darwin
  SIMON, Henry
Simonds, H & G
  SIMONDS, Frederick Adolphus
Simpson, S Ltd
  SIMPSON, Samuel Leonard
Singer Motors Ltd
  BULLOCK, William Edward
Slaughter & May
  MORTIMER, William Egerton
  SLAUGHTER, Sir William Capel
Smith & Nephew
  SMITH, Horatio Nelson
Smith, Prince & Son
  SMITH, Sir Prince

Smith, Sir W R & Sons
  SMITH, Sir William Reardon
Smiths Industries
  GORDON-SMITH, Sir Allan
Somervell Bros
  SOMERVELL, Sir Arnold Colin
Sothebys
  WILSON, Peter Cecil
South Eastern & Chatham Railway
  DENT, Sir Francis Henry
  SALOMONS, Sir David Lionel
    Goldsmid-Stern-
South Metropolitan Gas Co
  LIVESEY, Sir George Thomas
Spencer-Moulton
  MOULTON, Stephen
  SPENCER, George
Spicers Ltd
  SPICER, Sir Albert
Spode Pottery
  COPELAND, Richard Ronald John
Standard Motor Co
  DICK, Alick Sydney
  FRISWELL, Sir Charles Ernest Hain
  MAUDSLAY, Reginald Walter
Stanley Gibbons
  GIBBONS, Edward Stanley
Stanley, W F
  STANLEY, William Ford Robinson
Stanton & Staveley
  MARKHAM, Charles Paxton
Starr Bowkett Building Societies
  STARR, Richard Benjamin
Stead & Simpson
  GEE, Henry Simpson
Stella Coal Co
  SIMPSON, John Bell
Stephens, H
  STEPHENS, Henry Charles
Stephens' Railways
  STEPHENS, Holman Frederick
Stern Bros
  STERN, Sir Edward David
Stewart Bros
  STEWART, Sir Halley
Stock Exchange
  BEGG, Ferdinand Faithfull
  BRAITHWAITE, Sir John Bevan
  BRAITHWAITE, Joseph Bevan
  NICKALLS, Thomas
  RAE, Edward

Stockport Ring Spinning Co
  ATHERTON, Giles
Stoll Picture Productions
  STOLL, Sir Oswald
Stothert & Pitt
  STOTHERT, John Lumm
Street, G & Co
  STREET, George
Stourbridge Ironworks
  FOSTER, William Orme
Summers, John & Son
  GARDNER, Sir Charles Bruce
Sun Mill Co
  MARCROFT, William
Supermarine Aviation
  BIRD, Sir James
Sutherland, B J & Co
  SUTHERLAND, Sir Arthur Munro
Swan Hunter
  HUNTER, Sir Ernest John
  HUNTER, Sir George Burton
Swire, J & Sons
  SWIRE, John Samuel
Sykes & Co
  SYKES, Sir Alan John
Sykes Interlocking Signal Co
  SYKES, William Robert

T

Tangyes Ltd
  TANGYE, Sir Richard
Tarmac Ltd
  MARTIN, Cecil
Tate & Lyle
  LYLE, Charles Ernest Leonard
  TATE, Sir Henry
Taylor & Farley
  FARLEY, Reuben
Taylor Woodrow
  TAYLOR, Francis
Telegraph Condenser Co
  BROWN, Sidney George
Temperance Building Society
  WOOD, Edward
Tesco Stores Ltd
  COHEN, Sir John Edward
The Nuclear Power Group (TNPG)
  GHALIB, Selchouk Ahmed
Thomas & Evans
  EVANS, William

Thomas, R & Co
  THOMAS, Richard
Thompson, J L & Sons
  MARR, Sir James
  THOMPSON, Robert (1819–1910)
  THOMPSON, Robert (1850–1908)
Thorn Electrical Industries
  THORN, Sir Jules
Thornycrofts
  THORNCROFT, Sir John Isaac
Throckley Coal Co
  STEPHENSON, Sir William Haswell
Thwaites Ltd
  THWAITES, Leslie Basil
Tillings
  FRASER, William Lionel
  GARCKE, Sidney Emile
  HEATON, Sir John Frederick
Tilmanstone (Kent) Collieries
  SMITH, Richard Tilden
Times Newspapers
  WALTER III, John
Tomkinson & Adam
  ADAM, William
  TOMKINSON, Michael
Tootal Group
  BROADHURST, Sir Edward Tootal
  LEE, Henry
  LEE, Sir Joseph Cocksey
Touche Ross
  TAIT, Andrew Wilson
  TOUCHE, Sir George Alexander
Trafford Park Estates
  STEVENS, Marshall
Trafalgar House
  CROWTHER, Geoffrey
Transport Development Group
  HENMAN, Philip Sydney
Tredegar Iron & Coal Co
  MCLAREN, Charles Benjamin
  Bright
  MCLAREN, Henry Duncan
Trickett, H W Ltd
  TRICKETT, Sir Henry Whittaker
Triumph Engineering
  BETTMANN, Siegfried
  SANGSTER, John Young
Trollope & Colls Ltd
  COLLS, John Howard
Trust Houses
  CROWTHER, Geoffrey

Tube Investments
  PLOWDEN, Edwin Noel August
Tunks & Tisdall
  TISDALL, Edmund Charles
Turnbull Shipping Co
  TURNBULL, Thomas
Turner & Newall
  NEWALL, Robert Stirling
Twinings
  TWINING III, Richard
Tyne Plate Glass Co
  SWINBURNE, Robert Walter
Tyrer, H & Co
  TYRER, Henry

U

Unigate Ltd
  MAGGS, Leonard
Unilever
  COOPER, Sir Francis D'Arcy
  HEYWORTH, Geoffrey
  LEVER, William Hesketh
  SAMUEL, Frank
  VAN DEN BERGH, Jacob
  VAN DEN BERGH, Henry
Union Bank of London
  SCHUSTER, Sir Felix Otto
Union Cold Storage Co
  VESTEY, Sir Edmund Hoyle
  VESTEY, William
Union Discount
  TRINDER, Arthur William
United Africa Co (UAC)
  SAMUEL, Frank
United Alkali Co
  MUSPRATT, Sir Max
United Dairies
  BARHAM, Arthur Saxby
  BUTLER, Sir Robert Reginald Frederick
  MAGGS, Joseph Herbert
  PRICE, Sir William
United Kingdom Atomic Energy Authority
    (UKAEA)
  GROVE, Walter Patrick
  PLOWDEN, Edwin Noel August
  PORTAL, Charles Frederick Algernon
United Steel
  HILTON, Sir Robert Stuart
  JONES, Sir Walter Benton
  STEEL, Gerald

  STEEL, Henry
Urwick, Orr & Partners
  URWICK, Lyndall Fownes

V

Vauxhall Motors Ltd
  BARTLETT, Sir Charles John
  PEARSON, Sir James Reginald
Vickers
  BIRCH, Sir James Frederick Noel
  BIRD, Sir James
  BURNEY, Sir Charles Dennistoun
  CAILLARD, Sir Henry Vincent Penalver
  CASSEL, Sir Ernest Joseph
  DAWSON, Sir Arthur Trevor
  DOCKER, Frank Dudley
  EDWARDS, Sir George Robert
  JENKINSON, Sir Mark Webster
  KILNER, Sir Hew Ross
  KNOLLYS, Edward George William
    Tyrwhitt
  LAWRENCE, Sir Herbert Alexander
  MCLEAN, Sir Robert
  VICKERS, Albert
  VICKERS, Thomas Edward
  WEEKS, Ronald Morce
Victor Products
  MANN, Reginald William
Vivian, Younger & Bond
  BUDD, Sir Cecil Lindsay

W

Waddingtons
  WATSON, Victor Hugo
Wales Bank
  RAE, George
Walker, J & Sons
  STEVENSON, James
Wallpaper Manufacturers
  COCKSHUT, John
Wallsend Slipway Co
  BOYD, William
Walmsleys
  WALMSLEY, Benjamin
  WALMSLEY, William
Wardle, T & Co
  WARDLE, Sir Thomas
Warner & Sons
  WARNER, Sir Frank

Wates Group
  WATES, Norman Edward
Watney, Combe & Reid
  BONSOR, Sir Henry Cosmo Orme
  COMBE, Simon Harvey
Watson, Angus Ltd
  WATSON, Sir James Angus
Watson, J & Sons
  WATSON, Joseph
Watt, A P
  WATT, Alexander Pollock
Wedgwood
  WEDGWOOD, Josiah V
Weir, Andrew & Co
  WEIR, Andrew
Weir Group
  WEIR, William Douglas
Wellcome Foundation
  PERRIN, Sir Michael Willcox
  WELLCOME, Sir Henry Solomon
Wernher, Beit & Co
  BEIT, Alfred
  WERNHER, Sir Julius Carl
West's Gas Improvement Co
  WEST, John
Westminster Bank
  BECKETT, Rupert Evelyn
  LEAF, Walter
  LIDBURY, Sir Charles
Whatman Ltd
  BALSTON, Charles Henry
Wheeler, A & Co
  WHEELER, Sir Arthur
Whiffen Co
  WHIFFEN, Thomas
Whitbreads
  NEVILE, Sir Sydney Oswald
  WHITBREAD, Francis Pelham
Whiteleys
  WHITELEY, William
Whitworth, J Ltd
  WHITWORTH, Sir Joseph
Wigan Coal Corporation
  LINDSAY, David Alexander Edward
Wigan Coal & Iron Co
  HEWLETT, Alfred
  LINDSAY, David Alexander Edward
Wilkinsons
  WILKINSON, William Boutland
Willett, W Ltd
  WILLETT, William

Willey Group
  WILLEY, Francis Vernon
Williams, T & Sons
  WILLIAMS, Sir Evan
Williamson, Jas & Son
  WILLIAMSON, James
Wilson, Sons & Co
  WILSON, Arthur
  WILSON, Charles Henry
Wimpey
  MITCHELL, Sir Godfrey Way
Winn, R Ltd
  WINN, Rowland
Wogau Group
  LIPMAN, Michael Isaac
Wolseley Tool & Motor Co
  AUSTIN, Herbert
Woodall-Duckham Ltd
  DUCKHAM, Sir Arthur McDougall
Woodgers
  WOODGER, John
Woolwich Arsenal
  ANDERSON, Sir William
Woolworth, F W
  STEPHENSON, William Lawrence
Workman, Clark & Co
  CLARK, Sir George Smith
  WORKMAN, Francis
Wostenholm & Son
  WOSTENHOLM, George
Wyndham's Theatre
  WYNDHAM, Sir Charles

Y

Yates
  YATES, Edward
York Street Flax Spinning Co
  CRAWFORD, Sir William
  EWART, Sir William
  MULHOLLAND, John
Yorkshire Electricity Board
  BELLAMY, Dennis
Yorkshire Steel & Iron Works
  ADAMSON, Daniel

Z

Zeals
  ZEAL, Giles Henry

Index of business people, of subjects and of major figures in entries

Compiled by Francis Goodall
(Subject entries are indicated by ★)

Name	Vol	Page	Name	Vol	Page
ABERCONWAY, 1st Lord – see McLAREN, Charles Benjamin B			AITKEN, William Maxwell	II	604
			AITKEN, William Maxwell	III	55
			AITKEN, William Maxwell	III	60
ABERCONWAY, 2nd Lord – see McLAREN, Henry Duncan			AITKEN, William Maxwell	III	167
			AITKEN, William Maxwell	III	284
ABERNETHY, James	III	423	AITKEN, William Maxwell	III	386
ACKROYD, W H	II	141	AITKEN, William Maxwell	III	504
ADAM, William	★I	1	AITKEN, William Maxwell	III	513
ADAM, William	V	536	AITKEN, William Maxwell	III	857
ADAMS, William	★I	3	AITKEN, William Maxwell	III	907
ADAMS, William	V	395	AITKEN, William Maxwell	IV	172
ADAMSON, Daniel	★I	6	AITKEN, William Maxwell	IV	278
ADAMSON, Daniel	I	544	AITKEN, William Maxwell	IV	493
ADAMSON, Daniel	III	675	AITKEN, William Maxwell	IV	919
ADAMSON, Daniel	III	710	AITKEN, William Maxwell	V	274
ADAMSON, Daniel	V	313	AITKEN, William Maxwell	V	307
ADDIS, Charles Stewart	★I	13	AITKEN, William Maxwell	V	754
ADDIS, Charles Stewart	I	164	AITKEN, William Maxwell	VI	278
ADDIS, Charles Stewart	I	862	ALDENHAM, Lord – see GIBBS, Henry Hucks		
ADDISON, J G	V	362	ALEXANDER, George	★I	30
ADDISON, J S	III	723	ALEXANDER, George	I	147
AGNEW, Andrew	II	584	ALEXANDER, George	V	922
AINSWORTH, Thomas	III	326	ALEXANDER, L M	III	335
AIRD, John	★I	17	ALEXANDER, Robert	II	251
AIRD, John	I	108	ALLAN, Charles	V	892
AIRD, John	I	607	ALLAN, William	V	132
AIRD, John	I	753	ALLCROFT, John Derby	★I	32
AIRD, John	III	464	ALLCROFT, John Derby	V	831
AIRD, John	IV	583	ALLEN, J W	III	846
AIREDALE, Lord – see KITSON, James			ALLEN, Samuel	★I	35
AIREY, Edwin	★I	20	ALLEN, W D	I	311
AITKEN, William Maxwell	★I	23	ALLEN, William Edward	★I	37
AITKEN, William Maxwell	I	136	ALLERTON, Lord – see JACKSON, William Lawies		
AITKEN, William Maxwell	I	303	ALLHUSEN, Christian Augustus Henry	★I	39
AITKEN, William Maxwell	I	400			
AITKEN, William Maxwell	I	428	ALLHUSEN, Christian Augustus Henry	I	358
AITKEN, William Maxwell	I	539			
AITKEN, William Maxwell	I	867	ALLINSON, George White	V	432
AITKEN, William Maxwell	II	210	ALLPORT, James Joseph	★I	42
AITKEN, William Maxwell	II	263	AMBLER, Geoffrey Hill	★I	45
AITKEN, William Maxwell	II	268			

Name	Vol	Page	Name	Vol	Page
AMBLER, Geoffrey Hill	IV	847	ARMSTRONG, William		
ANDERSON, Alan Garrett	*I	47	George	V	231
ANDERSON, Alan Garrett	I	50	ARMSTRONG, William		
ANDERSON, Alan Garrett	II	502	George	V	625
ANDERSON, Alan Garrett	IV	245	ARMSTRONG, William		
ANDERSON, Donald Forsyth	*I	50	George	V	800
ANDERSON, James	I	47	ASHBURY, J	I	627
ANDERSON, James	*I	54	ASHFIELD, Lord – see		
ANDERSON, James	II	459	STANLEY, Albert Henry		
ANDERSON, John	*I	57	ASHTON, Lord – see		
ANDERSON, John	II	645	WILLIAMSON, James		
ANDERSON, John	III	405	ASHWORTH, George	IV	178
ANDERSON, John	V	799	ASPINALL, John Audley		
ANDERSON, William	*I	60	Frederick	*I	75
ANDERSON, William	II	570	ASPINALL, John Audley		
ANDREW, Nicholas	II	61	Frederick	II	657
ANGUS, Edmund Graham	*I	65	ASPINALL, John Audley		
ANGUS, George	*I	66	Frederick	IV	852
ANGUS, John Henry	I	67	ASPINALL, John Audley		
ANGUS, William Mathwin	I	67	Frederick	V	106
ARMSTRONG, William			ASSHETON SMITH,	II	147
George	I	58	ASTBURY, Thomas	III	570
ARMSTRONG, William			ASTLEY, Philip	V	52
George	*I	68	ASTOR, J J	III	55
ARMSTRONG, William			ATHERTON, Giles	*I	77
George	I	195	ATKINSON, William	III	703
ARMSTRONG, William			AUSTEN, J S	II	173
George	I	355	AUSTEN, J S	II	479
ARMSTRONG, William			AUSTEN, J S	III	376
George	I	481	AUSTEN, J S	IV	915
ARMSTRONG, William			AUSTEN, John	IV	665
George	I	860	AUSTIN, Herbert	*I	79
ARMSTRONG, William			AUSTIN, Herbert	II	48
George	II	218	AUSTIN, Herbert	II	290
ARMSTRONG, William			AUSTIN, Herbert	III	735
George	II	633	AUSTIN, Herbert	III	857
ARMSTRONG, William			AUSTIN, Herbert	V	61
George	III	123	AUSTIN, Herbert	V	137
ARMSTRONG, William			AUSTIN, Herbert	V	497
George	III	462	AUSTIN, S P	III	398
ARMSTRONG, William			AVEBURY, Lord – see		
George	IV	382	LUBBOCK, John		
ARMSTRONG, William			AVELING, Thomas Lake	*I	83
George	IV	444	AVELING, Thomas Lake	I	153
ARMSTRONG, William			AVELING, Thomas Lake	I	522
George	IV	519	AVELING, Thomas Lake	II	415
ARMSTRONG, William			AVERY, Thomas	*I	85
George	IV	540	BABCOCK, George H	III	579

Name	Vol	Page	Name	Vol	Page
BABINGTON, C H	II	491	BALL, John	III	35
BADER, Ernest	*I	87	BALLIN, Albert	I	611
BAER, A M	II	203	BALSTON, Charles Henry	*I	140
BAGNALL, John Nock	*I	91	BAMBERGER, Louis	*I	142
BAILEY, G E	IV	215	BANBURY, Frederick George	*I	144
BAILEY, James A	V	53	BANBURY, Frederick George	II	662
BAILLIEU, Clive Latham	*I	96	BANCROFT, Squire	*I	147
BAILLIEU, Clive Latham	II	317	BANCROFT, Squire	III	442
BAILLIEU, Clive Latham	III	906	BANTON, Alfred	V	13
BAIN, Albert Wellesley	*I	100	BARBER, Ami Lorenzo	I	569
BAIN, Albert Wellesley	III	140	BARBER, John	V	351
BAINBRIDGE, Emerson Muschamp (1817–1892)	*I	102	BARBER, Lionel	III	241
			BARBOUR, John Milne	*I	150
BAINBRIDGE, Emerson Muschamp (1845–1911)	*I	103	BARFORD, Edward James	I	83
			BARFORD, Edward James	*I	152
BAINBRIDGE, Emerson Muschamp (1845–1911)	IV	480	BARFORD, Edward James	IV	624
			BARFORD, Edward James	V	275
BAKER, Arthur	*I	105	BARHAM, Arthur Saxby	*I	156
BAKER, Arthur	I	400	BARHAM, George	*I	157
BAKER, Benjamin	*I	108	BARHAM, George Titus	*I	161
BAKER, Benjamin	II	412	BARING, John	*I	164
BAKER, Benjamin	II	632	BARING, John	I	608
BAKER, Benjamin	IV	356	BARING, John	II	682
BAKER, Benjamin	IV	583	BARING, John	III	295
BAKER, Joseph Allen	II	566	BARING, John	III	880
BALCHIN, Nigel	III	71	BARING, John	IV	560
BALCON, Michael Elias	*I	110	BARING, John	V	80
BALCON, Michael Elias	II	89	BARKER, Charles	V	391
BALCON, Michael Elias	IV	493	BARKER, Henry John	II	624
BALCON, Michael Elias	IV	834	BARKER, John	*I	167
BALCON, Michael Elias	V	885	BARKER, John	I	227
BALDWIN, Alfred	*I	116	BARKER, John	V	793
BALDWIN, Alfred	V	898	BARLOW, Frank Pratt	III	795
BALDWIN, Alfred	V	904	BARLOW, Henry	II	632
BALFOUR, Alexander	*I	119	BARLOW, Peter W	II	632
BALFOUR, Alexander	II	401	BARLOW, Robert	*I	169
BALFOUR, Alexander	V	834	BARLOW, Robert	III	494
BALFOUR, Arthur	*I	121	BARLOW, Thomas	IV	718
BALFOUR, Arthur	III	257	BARLOW, William Henry	*I	175
BALFOUR, Arthur	IV	618	BARLOW, William Henry	III	120
BALFOUR, Arthur	IV	1,008	BARNATO, Barney	V	738
BALFOUR, George	*I	125	BARNBY, Lord – see WILLEY, Francis Vernon		
BALFOUR, Jabez Spencer	*I	129			
BALFOUR, Jabez Spencer	V	860	BARNETT, Richard	III	46
BALFOUR, Jabez Spencer	V	903	BARNUM, P T	V	53
BALFOUR, Robert	V	835	BARON, Bernhard	*I	177
BALL, Charles James Prior	*I	135	BARRAN, John	*I	181
BALL, Charles James Prior	I	442	BARRAN, John	III	171
BALL, Charles James Prior	III	127	BARRAN, John	IV	136

Name	Vol	Page	Name	Vol	Page
BARRATT, Arthur William	*I	184	BEALE, George	*I	223
BARRATT, Bill	I	739	BEALE, George	III	802
BARRATT, Thomas James	*I	189	BEALE, George	IV	137
BARRATT, Thomas James	I	245	BEALE, George	IV	208
BARRATT, Thomas James	IV	573	BEALE, George	V	15
BARRETT-LENNARD, John	III	451	BEALE, George	V	606
BARRIE, Charles	II	652	BEALE, John	V	908
BARROW, Harrison	*I	192	BEALE, John Elmes	*I	226
BARROW, John Wylie	II	685	BEALE, Samuel Raymond	III	524
BARROW, Samuel	IV	474	BEALE, Samuel Raymond	V	908
BARRY, Arthur	V	902	BEAN, Jack	I	463
BARRY, Arthur John	I	196	BEARDMORE, William	V	516
BARRY, Charles & Edward	II	355	BEARDMORE, William	V	625
BARRY, John Wolfe	I	109	BEARSTED, 1st Viscount –		
BARRY, John Wolfe	*I	195	see SAMUEL, Marcus		
BARRY, John Wolfe	II	529	BEATTIE, William George	I	4
BARRY, John Wolfe	III	120	BEATTY, Alfred Chester	*I	230
BARRY, John Wolfe	III	530	BEATTY, Alfred Chester	IV	917
BARRY, John Wolfe	IV	196	BEATTY, Andrew	I	125
BARTLETT, Charles John	*I	198	BEAVER, Hugh Eyre		
BARTLETT, Charles John	IV	578	Campbell	*I	234
BARTLETT, Hardington			BEAVER, Hugh Eyre		
Arthur	I	205	Campbell	I	762
BARTLETT, Herbert Henry	I	195	BEAVER, Hugh Eyre		
BARTLETT, Herbert Henry	*I	203	Campbell	II	534
BARTON, Harold Montague	*I	208	BEAVERBROOK, Lord – see		
BARTON, Harold Montague	II	74	AITKEN, William Maxwell		
BARTON, Harold Montague	IV	207	BECK, Roger	V	898
BARTRAM, Robert Appleby	*I	210	BECKER	III	59
BARWICK, J S	II	444	BECKETT, Rupert Evelyn	*I	237
BASDEN, E D	V	38	BECKETT, Terry	III	168
BASS, Michael A	II	660	BEDDINGTON, Edmund	V	38
BATE, John	V	63	BEDFORD, John	*I	239
BATEMAN, Hezekiah	III	441	BEECHAM, Joseph	*I	243
BATEMAN, John Frederic La			BEECHAM, Joseph	II	294
Trobe	*I	212	BEECHAM, Joseph	III	236
BATEMAN, John Frederic La			BEECHAM, Joseph	IV	85
Trobe	III	123	BEECHAM, Joseph	IV	366
BATES, Percy	III	406	BEECHAM, Joseph	V	786
BATES, Percy	IV	455	BEECHAM, Thomas		
BATES, Percy	IV	618	(1820–1907)	*I	246
BATES, William	III	144	BEECHAM, Thomas		
BATEY, John Thomas	*I	215	(1820–1907)	II	581
BATEY, John Thomas	IV	958	BEECHAM, Thomas		
BATLEY, John	II	311	(1879–1961)	V	428
BATLEY, John	II	645	BEECHAM, Thomas		
BAXENDALE, Lloyd Henry	*I	218	(1879–1961)	V	760
BAYLIS, Lilian Mary	*I	219	BEECHAM, Thomas		
BAZLEY, Thomas	III	703	(1879–1961)	V	786

Name	Vol	Page	Name	Vol	Page
BEECHING, Richard	II	673	BERRY, Albert Eustace	II	492
BEGG, Ferdinand Faithfull	I	144	BERRY, Henry Seymour	I	25
BEGG, Ferdinand Faithfull	*I	249	BERRY, Henry Seymour	*I	299
BEHARRELL, George	II	72	BERRY, Henry Seymour	III	524
BEHARRELL, George	II	513	BERRY, Henry Seymour	III	823
BEHARRELL, George	V	431	BERRY, Henry Seymour	III	902
BEHRENS, Jacob	*I	251	BERRY, Henry Seymour	IV	272
BEHRENS, Jacob	IV	263	BERRY, Henry Seymour	V	62
BEIT, Alfred	*I	253	BERRY, Henry Seymour	V	479
BEIT, Alfred	I	609	BERRY, James Gomer	*I	301
BEIT, Alfred	V	74	BERRY, James Gomer	I	400
BEIT, Alfred	V	738	BERRY, James Gomer	III	55
BELL, David W	II	517	BERRY, James Gomer &		
BELL, Isaac Lowthian	*I	256	William Ewert	III	682
BELL, Isaac Lowthian	II	136	BERRY, James Gomer &		
BELL, Isaac Lowthian	III	392	William Ewert	III	830
BELL, John	*I	261	BERRY, William Ewert	*I	301
BELL, Thomas Hugh	I	258	BERRY, William Ewert	I	400
BELL, Thomas Hugh	*I	263	BERRY, William Ewert	III	55
BELL, Thomas Hugh	II	137	BERRY, William Ewert	III	60
BELL, Thomas Hugh	II	285	BERRY, William Ewert	III	385
BELLAMY, Dennis	*I	266	BERRY, William Ewert	III	412
BELLING, Charles Reginald	*I	269	BERRY, William Ewert	IV	23
BELLINGER, Robert Ian	*I	272	BERRY, William Ewert	IV	618
BELLINGHAM, Arthur	II	667	BERRY, William Ewert	IV	992
BELLMAN, Charles Harold	*I	273	BESSEMER, Henry	I	8
BELLMAN, Charles Harold	III	231	BESSEMER, Henry	*I	309
BELLMAN, Charles Harold	III	638	BESSEMER, Henry	I	475
BELLMAN, Charles Harold	V	270	BESSEMER, Henry	I	653
BELLMAN, Charles Harold	V	456	BESSEMER, Henry	I	689
BELLMAN, Charles Harold	V	918	BESSEMER, Henry	II	275
BENHAM, James	*I	279	BESSEMER, Henry	II	466
BENN, Ernest John Pickstone	*I	280	BESSEMER, Henry	II	633
BENN, Ernest John Pickstone	II	591	BESSEMER, Henry	IV	123
BENNETT, Peter	V	666	BESSEMER, Henry	IV	212
BENNION, Charles	*I	285	BESSEMER, Henry	IV	818
BENNION, Charles	V	778	BESSEMER, Henry	V	158
BENSON, Edward	II	617	BESSEMER, Henry	V	818
BENSON, Frank	V	543	BEST, Robert Hall	*I	314
BENSON, Henry Alexander	*I	287	BETTMANN, Siegfried	*I	317
BENSON, Henry Alexander	III	556	BETTMANN, Siegfried	V	56
BENSON, Rex & Con	V	579	BEVAN, Francis Augustus	*I	320
BENSON, Samuel Herbert	*I	289	BEVAN, Gerard Lee	*I	321
BENSON, Samuel Herbert	III	517	BEVAN, Gerard Lee	III	110
BENTALL, Leonard Hugh	*I	292	BEVINGTON, Timothy	I	33
BENTLEY, W O	IV	977	BIBBY, James	III	37
BERNSTEIN, Sidney	IV	859	BIBBY, Joseph	*I	325
BERRY, Albert Eustace	I	25	BICESTER, Lord – see		
BERRY, Albert Eustace	*I	295	SMITH, Vivian Hugh		

Name	Vol	Page	Name	Vol	Page
BIGELOW, Arthur Perkins	*I	328	BOOT, Jesse	II	211
BIGGART, Thomas	II	195	BOOT, Jesse	II	581
BIGGART, Thomas	V	198	BOOT, Jesse	III	237
BIGLAND, Reuben	I	395	BOOT, Jesse	V	210
BINNIE, Geoffrey Morse	*I	331	BOOTH, Alfred	*I	377
BIRCH, James Frederick Noel	*I	333	BOOTH, Alfred	I	380
BIRCH, James Frederick Noel	II	36	BOOTH, George Macaulay	I	125
BIRCH, Nigel	III	591	BOOTH, George Macaulay	*I	380
BIRD, Alfred Frederick	*I	336	BOOTH, George Macaulay	I	617
BIRD, James	*I	339	BOOTH, George Macaulay	II	31
BIRD, James	V	92	BOOTH, George Macaulay	II	572
BIRDSEYE, Clarence	II	567	BOOTH, George Macaulay	IV	489
BIRLEY family	III	432	BOOTH, George Macaulay	IV	686
BLACK, George	V	359	BOOTH, George Macaulay	V	742
BLACK, John	II	100	BOOTH, Robert Camm	*I	384
BLACK, John	III	247	BOOTH, Robert Camm	V	574
BLACK, John	IV	197	BORTHWICK, Thomas	*I	386
BLACKBURN, Robert	*I	342	BORTHWICK, Thomas	V	618
BLACKBURN, Robert	V	570	BOSTOCK, Henry John	*I	388
BLACKMORE, Hilary	V	336	BOSTOCK, Henry John	IV	764
BLACKWELL, Richard	*I	346	BOTTOMLEY, Horatio William	I	323
BLACKWOOD, Stevenson Arthur	*I	350	BOTTOMLEY, Horatio William	*I	391
BLAKE, Arthur	V	759	BOTTOMLEY, Horatio William	I	716
BLAKE, Ernest Edgar	*I	352	BOTTOMLEY, Horatio William	IV	181
BLAKE, Rustat	II	534	BOTTOMLEY, Horatio William	IV	480
BLOOM, John	I	288			
BLOOM, John	I	757	BOUCH, William	I	7
BLUNDELL, Henry Blundell-Hollinshead	*I	355	BOUCH, William	II	1
BOARD, Vyvyan & Tony	III	128	BOULT, Swinton	*I	396
BOGAARDT, Theodore	III	327	BOULT, Swinton	I	419
BOLCKOW, Henry William Ferdinand	I	40	BOULTON, Sidney	III	378
			BOWATER, Eric Vansittart	I	25
BOLCKOW, Henry William Ferdinand	*I	358	BOWATER, Eric Vansittart	I	105
			BOWATER, Eric Vansittart	I	209
BOLCKOW, Henry William Ferdinand	V	819	BOWATER, Eric Vansittart	*I	399
BOLITHO, Thomas Bedford	*I	360	BOWATER, Eric Vansittart	I	659
BOLTON, George Lewis French	*I	364	BOWATER, Eric Vansittart	III	61
			BOWATER, Eric Vansittart	IV	208
BOLTON, George Lewis French	I	709	BOWATER, Eric Vansittart	V	245
BOND, F M	IV	155	BOWDEN, Harold	*I	406
BOND, Stanley Shaw	*I	369	BOWES, John	*I	409
BONSOR, Henry Cosmo Orme	*I	372	BOWES, John	IV	515
BONSOR, Henry Cosmo Orme	II	491	BOWES, John	V	412
BOOT, Jesse	*I	374	BOWIE, James Alexander	*I	411
BOOT, Jesse	I	867	BOWLBY, Anthony	IV	724

Name	Vol	Page	Name	Vol	Page
BOWLES, F D	II	391	BROADHURST, Edward		
BOWMAN, James	★I	414	Tootal	III	708
BOWRING, Charles Tricks	★I	418	BROADHURST, Henry		
BOYD, William	★I	421	Tootal	III	703
BRABAZON, J T C	V	615	BROADWOOD, Henry Fowler	★I	458
BRABAZON, Moore	II	230	BROAKES, Nigel	I	756
BRABAZON, Moore	III	133	BROAKES, Nigel	III	552
BRACKLEY, Herbert George	★I	423	BROCKLEBANK, John	V	192
BRACKLEY, Herbert George	II	513	BROCKLEBANK, Ralph	★I	460
BRACKLEY, Herbert George	IV	297	BROCKLEBANK, Ralph	IV	301
BRACKLEY, Herbert George	V	92	BRODIE, John L P	III	13
BRACKLEY, Herbert George	V	882	BROMHEAD, A C & R C	IV	493
BRADLEY, John	II	409	BROOKE, Arthur	★I	461
BRAGGE, William	I	475	BROOKE, Arthur	II	176
BRAGGE, William	II	274	BROOKES, Raymond Percival	★I	463
BRAITHWAITE, John Bevan	★I	430	BROOKES, Raymond Percival	III	132
BRAITHWAITE, John Bevan	II	566	BROOKES, Raymond Percival	IV	570
BRAITHWAITE, Joseph			BROOM, Harry	III	805
Bevan	★I	433	BROUGH, Edward	★I	468
BRANCKER, Sefton	II	49	BROUGH, Joseph William	I	224
BRANCKER, Sefton	V	482	BROUGH, Joseph William	★I	469
BRAND, Henry Bouverie			BROWN, David	II	347
William	★I	436	BROWN, Frederick Herbert		
BRAND, Robert Henry	★I	437	Stanley	★I	472
BRAND, Robert Henry	III	199	BROWN, Frederick Herbert		
BRAND, Robert Henry	IV	784	Stanley	I	669
BRASSEY, Thomas	II	359	BROWN, Frederick Herbert		
BRASSEY, Thomas	IV	610	Stanley	II	539
BRASSEY, Thomas	IV	645	BROWN, George McLaren	II	653
BRETT, John Watkins	IV	610	BROWN, John	★I	475
BRETTLE, George	IV	322	BROWN, John	I	576
BRIDGEMAN, Maurice			BROWN, John	I	627
Richard	★I	440	BROWN, John	II	274
BRIDGEMAN, Maurice			BROWN, John	II	364
Richard	II	171	BROWN, John	III	5
BRIGGS, Arthur Harry	III	502	BROWN, John	IV	116
BRIGGS, Francis Henry	★I	443	BROWN, John	V	624
BRIGGS, Henry Currer	★I	445	BROWN, P B	III	7
BRINDLEY, Harry Samuel			BROWN, Sidney George	★I	478
Bickerton	I	60	BROWN, Stanley	II	225
BRINDLEY, Harry Samuel			BROWN, Sydney	IV	373
Bickerton	★I	448	BROWNE, Benjamin Chapman	★I	481
BRINDLEY, Harry Samuel			BROWNE, Benjamin Chapman	III	738
Bickerton	II	572	BROWNE, Benjamin Chapman	IV	158
BRINSMEAD, John	★I	450	BROWNE, Benjamin Chapman	IV	907
BROADHURST, Edward			BROWNE, Benjamin Chapman	IV	957
Tootal	★I	452	BRUCE-GARDNER, Charles		
BROADHURST, Edward			– see GARDNER, Charles Bruce		
Tootal	III	308	BRUCE-GARDNER, Douglas	II	483

Name	Vol	Page	Name	Vol	Page
BRUNEL, Isambard Kingdom	II	598	BURTON, Geoffrey	II	123
BRUNEL, Isambard Kingdom	V	436	BURTON, Lord	II	661
BRUNEL, Isambard Kingdom	V	736	BURTON, Montague Maurice	*I	526
BRUNEL, Marc	II	632	BURTON, William	II	282
BRUNLEES, James	III	120	BUTE, Lord	III	773
BRUNNER, C H	II	384	BUTLER, Alan	II	50
BRUNNER, Henry	IV	288	BUTLER, Alan	II	81
BRUNNER, John Tomlinson	*I	484	BUTLER, Isaac	V	898
BRUNNER, John Tomlinson	I	842	BUTLER, Robert Reginald		
BRUNNER, John Tomlinson	III	380	Frederick	*I	531
BRUNNER, John Tomlinson	IV	270	BUTLER, Robert Reginald		
BRUNNER, John Tomlinson	IV	289	Frederick	IV	79
BRUNNER, John Tomlinson	IV	296	BUTLER, William Waters	*I	533
BRUNNER, John Tomlinson	V	328	BUTLER, William Waters	II	491
BRYAN, Arthur	V	710	BUTLER, William Waters	II	661
BRYANT, Wilberforce	*I	488	BUTLER, William Waters	V	772
BUCKHAM, George	II	35	BUTLIN, William Heygate		
BUCKLAND, Lord – see			Edmund Colbourne	*I	535
BERRY, Henry Seymour			BUTLIN, William Heygate		
BUDD, Cecil Lindsay	*I	492	Edmund Colbourne	I	830
BUDD, Cecil Lindsay	II	666	BUTLIN, William Heygate		
BUDD, Cecil Lindsay	III	905	Edmund Colbourne	IV	238
BUDD, Henry	II	480	BUTTERWORTH, Alexander		
BULLOCK, William Edward	*I	496	Kaye	*I	542
BULLOUGH, George	*I	500	BUTTERWORTH, Alexander		
BULLOUGH, George	IV	414	Kaye	II	508
BULLOUGH, John	*I	502	BUTTERWORTH, Alexander		
BULMER, Edward Frederick	*I	504	Kaye	V	712
BUNTING, John	*I	506	BYERS, Frank	II	203
BUNTING, John	II	496	BYNG, Gustav	III	275
BUNTING, John	III	96	BYNG, Gustav	IV	812
BURBIDGE, Richard	I	241	BYTHELL, John Kenworthy	*I	544
BURBIDGE, Richard	*I	510	BYTHELL, John Kenworthy	V	314
BURBIDGE, Richard	V	793	BYTHELL, John Kenworthy	V	344
BURMAN, Stephen France	*I	513	CADBURY, George	*I	547
BURNAGE, F P	II	457	CADBURY, George	II	149
BURNAND, Percy G C	III	137	CADBURY, George	II	437
BURNEY, Charles Dennistoun	*I	516	CADBURY, George	III	333
BURNEY, Charles Dennistoun	II	36	CADBURY, George	IV	655
BURNHAM, Lord – see			CADBURY, Laurence John	*I	554
LAWSON, Edward Levy			CADBURY, Laurence John	IV	666
BURNS, Walter Hayes	II	655	CADBURY, Laurence John	IV	970
BURR, Arthur	*I	519	CADBURY, Richard Tapper	I	192
BURR, Arthur	II	98	CADMAN, John	I	427
BURR, Arthur	IV	591	CADMAN, John	I	440
BURRELL, Charles	*I	521	CADMAN, John	*I	558
BURROUGHS, Silas M	V	729	CADMAN, John	II	169
BURT, George Mowlem	*I	523	CADMAN, John	II	424
BURT, R A & F G	II	251	CADMAN, John	II	641

Name	Vol	Page	Name	Vol	Page
CADMAN, John	IV	16	CAPE, Charles F	II	71
CADMAN, John	IV	149	CARGILL, John Traill	★I	590
CAILLARD, Vincent Henry			CARGILL, John Traill	V	635
Penalver	★I	564	CARGILL, John Traill	V	693
CAILLARD, Vincent Henry			CARMICHAEL, James	★I	592
Penalver	II	34	CARNEGIE, Andrew	III	820
CAILLARD, Vincent Henry			CARNEGIE, Andrew	V	363
Penalver	II	351	CARNELLEY, William	IV	1,002
CAILLARD, Vincent Henry			CARPENTER, Guy	III	140
Penalver	II	557	CARR, Arthur	★I	594
CAILLARD, Vincent Henry			CARR, Arthur	IV	524
Penalver	III	200	CARR, Emsley	IV	911
CAILLARD, Vincent Henry			CARR, Jonathan Dodgson	★I	597
Penalver	III	449	CARR, Jonathan Dodgson	III	637
CAILLARD, Vincent Henry			CARR, Jonathan Dodgson	IV	905
Penalver	III	670	CARR, W M	III	531
CAILLARD, Vincent Henry			CARR, William	III	48
Penalver	IV	466	CARTER, W G	I	571
CAILLARD, Vincent Henry			CARTWRIGHT, W F	V	908
Penalver	V	137	CARVÈS, François	V	175
CAILLARD, Vincent Henry			CASH, John & Joseph	★I	601
Penalver	V	202	CASSEL, Ernest Joseph	I	18
CAILLARD, Vincent Henry			CASSEL, Ernest Joseph	I	164
Penalver	V	626	CASSEL, Ernest Joseph	★I	604
CALLAGHAN, T J	II	679	CASSEL, Ernest Joseph	III	154
CALLENDER, Thomas			CASSEL, Ernest Joseph	IV	947
Octavius	★I	568	CASSEL, Ernest Joseph	V	74
CALLINGHAM, Clement	II	124	CASSEL, Ernest Joseph	V	80
CAMERON, Ewan	II	612	CASSEL, Ernest Joseph	V	310
CAMERON, Robert	V	405	CASSEL, Ernest Joseph	V	543
CAMM, Sydney	★I	571	CASTNER, Hamilton Young	★I	614
CAMM, Sydney	II	161	CATTO, Thomas Sivewright	I	365
CAMM, Sydney	V	233	CATTO, Thomas Sivewright	★I	616
CAMMELL, Charles	I	311	CATTO, Thomas Sivewright	I	708
CAMMELL, Charles	★I	576	CATTO, Thomas Sivewright	IV	686
CAMMELL, Charles	I	627	CAVENDISH, William	★I	621
CAMMELL, Charles	II	364	CAVENDISH, William	IV	820
CAMMELL, Charles	IV	116	CAVENDISH, William	V	877
CAMMELL, Charles	V	624	CAWKWELL, William	II	360
CAMPBELL, Colin Frederick	★I	580	CAWKWELL, William	IV	302
CAMPBELL, Colin Minton	★I	582	CAYFORD, Ebenezer	III	355
CAMPBELL, John Middleton	★I	583	CAYZER family	V	913
CAMPION, Charles Aldworth			CAYZER, Nicholas	I	52
Gifford	V	102	CHADWICK, David	I	506
CAMROSE, 1st Viscount – see			CHADWICK, David	★I	625
BERRY, William Ewert			CHADWICK, David	IV	480
CANDLISH, John	★I	587	CHADWICK, David	IV	518
CANDLISH, John	V	363	CHADWICK, David	IV	727
CANTRELL, Thomas	I	720	CHAMBERLAIN, Arthur	★I	633

Name	Vol	Page	Name	Vol	Page
CHAMBERLAIN, Arthur	II	456	CHAPMAN, Charles	IV	625
CHAMBERLAIN, Arthur	III	251	CHAPMAN, William &		
CHAMBERLAIN, Arthur	III	632	Edward	III	36
CHAMBERLAIN, Arthur	III	753	CHAPMAN, William &		
CHAMBERLAIN, Joseph	I	86	Edward	III	83
CHAMBERLAIN, Joseph	*I	643	CHARLESWORTH, John		
CHAMBERLAIN, Joseph	I	777	Charlesworth Dodgson	*I	661
CHAMBERLAIN, Joseph	II	325	CHARLTON, George	III	217
CHAMBERLAIN, Joseph	II	463	CHEETHAM, Will	II	497
CHAMBERLAIN, Joseph	II	588	CHETWYND, Lord	II	514
CHAMBERLAIN, Joseph	II	662	CHILDE, Rowland	*I	664
CHAMBERLAIN, Joseph	III	29	CHILWORTH	II	35
CHAMBERLAIN, Joseph	III	35	CHIVERS, John	*I	665
CHAMBERLAIN, Joseph	III	186	CHIVERS, John	III	338
CHAMBERLAIN, Joseph	III	212	CHRISTIE, J A	III	291
CHAMBERLAIN, Joseph	III	465	CHURCHILL, Charles	II	455
CHAMBERLAIN, Joseph	III	528	CHURCHILL, Victor Spencer	III	352
CHAMBERLAIN, Joseph	III	571	CHURCHWARD, George		
CHAMBERLAIN, Joseph	III	677	Jackson	III	425
CHAMBERLAIN, Joseph	III	756	CHURCHWARD, George		
CHAMBERLAIN, Joseph	III	833	Jackson	IV	241
CHAMBERLAIN, Joseph	IV	181	CITRINE, Walter McLennan	*I	667
CHAMBERLAIN, Joseph	IV	314	CITRINE, Walter McLennan	II	272
CHAMBERLAIN, Joseph	IV	428	CITRINE, Walter McLennan	III	1
CHAMBERLAIN, Joseph	IV	489	CLARE, George	III	388
CHAMBERLAIN, Joseph	IV	821	CLAREMONT, A E	III	501
CHAMBERLAIN, Joseph	IV	830	CLARK, Alfred Corning	*I	671
CHAMBERLAIN, Joseph	IV	923	CLARK, Alfred Corning	III	758
CHAMBERLAIN, Joseph	V	24	CLARK, Alfred Corning	III	834
CHAMBERLAIN, Joseph	V	79	CLARK, Alfred Corning	IV	509
CHAMBERLAIN, Joseph	V	246	CLARK, Alfred Corning	V	507
CHAMBERLAIN, Joseph	V	663	CLARK, Allen George	*I	676
CHAMBERLAIN, Joseph	V	848	CLARK, Allen George	V	507
CHAMBERLAIN, Joseph	V	861	CLARK, Francis Joseph	II	76
CHAMBERLAIN, Joseph	V	877	CLARK, George	*I	680
CHAMBERLAIN, Neville &			CLARK, George	IV	683
Arthur	III	251	CLARK, George	V	857
CHAMBERS, Stanley Paul	*I	649	CLARK, George	V	892
CHAMBERS, Stanley Paul	III	25	CLARK, George Smith	*I	683
CHANCE, James Timmins	*I	653	CLARK, George Smith	IV	854
CHANCE, James Timmins	III	341	CLARK, George Thomas	*I	686
CHANCE, Robert Lucas	I	653	CLARK, George Thomas	III	480
CHANCE, William	III	94	CLARK, George Thomas	III	571
CHANCELLOR, Christopher			CLARK, George Thomas	IV	212
John Howard	*I	656	CLARK, William Stephens	*I	691
CHANDOS, 1st Viscount – see			CLARK, William Stephens	II	76
LYTTELTON, Oliver			CLARK, William Stephens	IV	521
CHAPLIN, Eric	II	649	CLARKE, A B H	III	7
CHAPLIN, Ernest	II	649	CLARKE, Stephenson	III	256

Name	Vol	Page	Name	Vol	Page
CLAUGHTON, Gilbert	II	620	COKAYNE, Brien	IV	449
CLAYTON, Nathaniel	*I	693	COLE, Eric Kirkham	*I	733
CLAYTON, Nathaniel	V	134	COLE, Eric Kirkham	III	798
CLIFF family	II	563	COLE, George	V	40
CLIFFORD-TURNER, Harry	*I	695	COLEMAN, J E	IV	792
CLIFFORD-TURNER, Harry	III	388	COLEMAN, James Edward	V	582
CLORE, Charles	*I	697	COLES, Henry James	*I	736
CLORE, Charles	I	760	COLGRAIN, Lord — see		
CLORE, Charles	I	798	CAMPBELL, Colin Frederick		
CLORE, Charles	III	242	COLLARD, Alfred	III	371
CLORE, Charles	V	100	COLLINS, Douglas Raymond	*I	737
CLUTTON, John	*I	701	COLLINS, Willliam	II	124
COATALEN, Louis	V	498	COLLS, John Howard	*I	743
COATES, John Bernard			COLMAN family	IV	209
Maurice	I	88	COLMAN, Cecil	*I	747
COATES, John Bernard			COLMAN, Cecil	V	777
Maurice	*I	704	COLMAN, Frederick Edward	II	5
COATES, William Henry	*I	705	COLMAN, Jeremiah James	*I	750
COATES, William Henry	IV	685	COLSON, Alfred	*I	753
COATS family	II	255	COLSTON, Charles Blampied	*I	755
COBBOLD, Cameron			COLSTON, Charles Blampied	IV	776
Fromanteel	I	365	COMBE, Richard	II	491
COBBOLD, Cameron			COMBE, Simon Harvey	*I	759
Fromanteel	I	619	COOK, John Mason	*I	763
COBBOLD, Cameron			COOK, John Mason	V	828
Fromanteel	*I	707	COOK, Thomas	*I	766
COBHAM, Alan John	I	343	COOKSON family	V	412
COBHAM, Alan John	*I	710	COOKSON, Clive	*I	770
COBHAM, Alan John	I	829	COOKSON, Norman Charles	*I	772
COBHAM, Alan John	V	127	COOKSON, Norman Charles	III	644
COBHAM, Alan John	V	882	COOKSON, Norman Charles	IV	434
COCHRAN, Charles Blake	*I	715	COOKSON, Roland Antony	*I	774
COCHRAN, Charles Blake	V	356	COOPER, Arthur	*I	776
COCHRANE, Henry	*I	720	COOPER, Arthur	III	35
COCKCROFT, John	III	270	COOPER, Arthur	IV	794
COCKSHUT, John	*I	721	COOPER, Arthur	V	767
CODY, William	V	53	COOPER, Ernest	*I	778
COHEN, John Edward	*I	724	COOPER, Ernest	V	767
COHEN, John Edward	III	476	COOPER, Francis D'Arcy	I	287
COHEN, John Edward	V	5	COOPER, Francis D'Arcy	*I	781
COHEN, John Edward	V	755	COOPER, Francis D'Arcy	II	489
COHEN, Lewis Coleman	*I	730	COOPER, Francis D'Arcy	III	750
COHEN, Louis Samuel	III	754	COOPER, Francis D'Arcy	IV	43
COHEN, Louis Samuel & Rex	III	333	COOPER, George Beverley	III	246
COHEN, Rex D	IV	147	COOPER, William	IV	794
COHEN, Robert Waley	V	38	COOTE, Arthur	III	738
COHEN, Robert Waley	V	693	COPELAND, Richard Ronald		
COKAYNE, Brien	I	863	John	*I	786
COKAYNE, Brien	II	556	COPEMAN, Henry John	*I	788

Name	Vol	Page	Name	Vol	Page
CORLEY, Kenneth	V	667	CRITCHLEY, Alfred Cecil	I	539
CORY, William	IV	441	CRITCHLEY, Alfred Cecil	*I	827
COSSOR, Alfred Charles	*I	790	CRITCHLEY, Alfred Cecil	III	240
COSTAIN, Richard Rylandes	*I	792	CRITCHLEY, Alfred Cecil	III	618
COSTAIN, Richard Rylandes	III	544	CRITCHLEY, Alfred Cecil	V	334
COTTON, Jack	I	699	CRITCHLEY, Alfred Cecil	V	912
COTTON, Jack	*I	796	CRITTALL, Francis Henry	I	381
COUNTWAY, Francis	III	193	CRITTALL, Francis Henry	*I	831
COURTAULD, Samuel	III	24	CROFTON, Harold B	IV	104
COURTAULD, Samuel	IV	350	CROMER, Lord	III	198
COURTAULD, Samuel	IV	430	CROMPTON, Rookes Evelyn		
COURTAULD, Samuel III	*I	800	Bell	I	478
COURTAULD, Samuel III	III	616	CROMPTON, Rookes Evelyn		
COURTAULD, Samuel III	V	470	Bell	*I	835
COURTAULD, Samuel IV	*I	803	CROMPTON, Rookes Evelyn		
COURTAULD, Samuel IV	III	509	Bell	III	558
COURTAULD, Samuel IV	V	796	CROMPTON, Thomas	I	17
COUSSMAKER, Arthur			CRONSHAW, Cecil John		
Blakeney	*I	807	Turrell	*I	838
COWDRAY family	V	912	CROS – see DU CROS		
COWDRAY, 1st Viscount – see			CROSFIELD, John	I	486
PEARSON, Weetman			CROSFIELD, John	*I	841
Dickinson			CROSFIELD, John	II	471
COWLIN, Francis Nicholas	*I	809	CROSS, Herbert Shepherd	*I	845
CRAIG, John	IV	73	CROSS, Herbert Shepherd	V	420
CRAMMOND, Edgar	II	352	CROSS, J K & Edward	III	314
CRAMPTON, Thomas Russell	IV	648	CROSSLEY, Francis	*I	847
CRAVEN, Charles	II	36	CROSSLEY, Francis William	*I	850
CRAVEN, Charles	III	592	CROSSLEY, Francis William	III	744
CRAVEN, Charles	IV	66	CROSSLEY, Francis William	III	891
CRAWFORD and			CROSSLEY, Francis William	IV	654
BALCARRES, 27th Earl of – see			CROSSLEY, Francis William	V	616
LINDSAY, David A E			CROSSLEY, Kenneth	III	744
CRAWFORD, William	*I	812	CROSSLEY, William John	*I	852
CRAWFORD, William	IV	376	CROTHERS, Isaac Holden	III	300
CRAWFORD, William Smith	*I	814	CROWTHER, Geoffrey	*I	854
CRAWSHAY family	IV	213	CROWTHER, Geoffrey	III	546
CRAWSHAY, George	*I	816	CRUDDAS, William		
CREED, Frederick George	*I	819	Donaldson	*I	860
CREWDSON, A	III	314	CRUM, Walter	III	366
CRIBBETT, George	II	78	CRUTTWELL, G E W	I	196
CRIBBETT, George	V	191	CUBITT, Thomas	II	428
CRISP, Charles Birch	*I	822	CULLEN, Lord – see		
CRISP, Charles Birch	II	6	COKAYNE, Brien		
CRISP, Charles Birch	II	351	CUNDY, James	I	33
CRISP, Charles Birch	III	44	CUNLIFFE, Walter	I	165
CRISP, Charles Birch	III	450	CUNLIFFE, Walter	*I	861
CRISP, Charles Birch	IV	529	CUNLIFFE, Walter	II	656
CRISP, Charles Birch	IV	783	CUNLIFFE, Walter	IV	449

Name	Vol	Page	Name	Vol	Page
CUNLIFFE, Walter	V	80	DARLINGTON, James	III	190
CUNLIFFE, Walter	V	901	DARTMOUTH, 6th Earl of – see		
CUNLIFFE-OWEN, Hugo			LEGGE, William Heneage		
von Reitzenstein	*I	865	DARWIN, Ernest Emil	V	177
CUNLIFFE-OWEN, Hugo			DARWIN, Horace	*II	14
von Reitzenstein	II	211	DARWIN, Horace	IV	789
CUNLIFFE-OWEN, Hugo			DAVENPORT, F R	V	431
von Reitzenstein	II	531	DAVIDSON, Samuel Clement	*II	18
CUNLIFFE-OWEN, Hugo			DAVIES, David	*II	21
von Reitzenstein	V	814	DAVIES, David	II	58
CURRIE, Donald	*I	869	DAVIES, David	V	473
CURRIE, Laurence	III	670	DAVIES, David Jr.	II	22
CURRIE, William	I	51	DAVIES, Hector Leighton	V	909
CURRY, Henry	*I	874	DAVIES, Herbert	V	41
CURZON, Frank	IV	86	DAVIS, Edmund Gabriel	IV	481
CZARNIKOW, Julius Caesar	*I	876	DAVIS, Edmund Gabriel	*II	24
CZARNIKOW, Julius Caesar	V	72	DAVIS, Edmund Gabriel	IV	109
D'ARCY, William Knox	I	591	DAVIS, Edmund Gabriel	V	901
D'ARCY, William Knox	*II	12	DAVIS, John	IV	834
D'ARCY, William Knox	IV	863	DAW, William Adams	*II	28
D'ARCY, William Knox	V	635	DAW, William Adams	II	429
d'ERLANGER, Gerard John			DAWES, Thomas	II	430
Regis Leo	*II	77	DAWNAY, Guy Payan	*II	30
d'ERLANGER, Gerard John			DAWNAY, Guy Payan	III	673
Regis Leo	II	144	DAWNAY, Guy Payan	IV	22
d'ERLANGER, Gerard John			DAWNAY, Guy Payan	V	814
Regis Leo	V	191	DAWSON, Arthur Trevor	I	517
d'ERLANGER, Gerard John			DAWSON, Arthur Trevor	I	566
Regis Leo	V	499	DAWSON, Arthur Trevor	*II	33
d'ERLANGER, Leo Frederic			DAWSON, Arthur Trevor	IV	466
Alfred	*II	80	DAWSON, Arthur Trevor	V	626
d'ERLANGER, Leo Frederic			DAY, Julian C	II	31
Alfred	III	244	DEELEY – see		
d'ERLANGER, Leo Frederic			MALLABY-DEELEY, Harry C		
Alfred	IV	15	DE FERRANTI, Gerard		
DADE, C H	III	376	Vincent Sebastian	*II	38
DALE, David	*II	1	DE FERRANTI, Sebastian		
DALE, David	III	481	Ziani	*II	43
DALE, David Sr.	II	1	DE FERRANTI, Sebastian		
DALZIEL, Davison Alexander	*II	5	Ziani	II	394
DALZIEL, Davison Alexander	II	132	DE FERRANTI, Sebastian		
DALZIEL, Davison Alexander	II	652	Ziani	IV	223
DALZIEL, Davison Alexander	III	46	DE FERRANTI, Sebastian		
DALZIEL, Davison Alexander	III	154	Ziani	IV	894
DALZIEL, Davison Alexander	III	385	DE FERRANTI, Sebastian		
DALZIEL, Davison Alexander	III	447	Ziani	V	430
DALZIEL, Davison Alexander	V	901	DE HAVILLAND, Geoffrey	I	711
DALZIEL, Henry	III	830	DE HAVILLAND, Geoffrey	*II	48
DARBY, John	III	900	DE HAVILLAND, Geoffrey	III	12

Name	Vol	Page	Name	Vol	Page
DE HAVILLAND, Geoffrey	III	133	DEUCHAR, James	*II	83
DE HAVILLAND, Geoffrey	V	126	DEUCHAR, John James		
DE HAVILLAND, Geoffrey	V	481	Walker	*II	85
DE LA RUE, Warren	*II	52	DEUCHAR, Robert	II	84
DE PAULA, Frederic Rudolf			DEUTSCH, Oscar	I	111
Mackley	*II	71	DEUTSCH, Oscar	*II	89
DE PAULA, Frederic Rudolf			DEUTSCH, Oscar	III	237
Mackley	II	512	DEUTSCH, Oscar	IV	366
DE REUTER – see REUTER			DEUTSCH, Oscar	IV	833
DE ROTHSCHILD – see			DEUTSCH, Oscar	V	359
ROTHSCHILD			DEUTSCH, Oscar	V	885
DE STEIN, Edward	II	31	DEVEREAUX, Col.	II	81
DE STEIN, Edward	II	462	DEVONPORT, 1st Viscount – see		
DE STEIN, Edward	III	834	KEARLEY, Hudson Ewbanke		
DE STERN – see STERN,			DEVONSHIRE, 7th Duke of – see		
Edward			CAVENDISH, William		
DE STERN, Hermann	V	25	DEW-SMITH, A G	II	15
DE STERN, Hermann	V	309	DEWAR, John Arthur	II	94
DE WALDEN, Howard	II	667	DEWAR, Thomas Robert	I	190
DEACON, Henry	II	499	DEWAR, Thomas Robert	*II	94
DEASY, Henry P P	V	137	DEWAR, Thomas Robert	III	371
DEBENHAM, A M G	III	101	DEWRANCE, John	*II	96
DEBENHAM, Archibald	II	584	DEWRANCE, John	III	580
DEBENHAM, Ernest	III	590	DICK, Alick Sydney	*II	100
DEBENHAM, Ernest	IV	488	DICK, Alick Sydney	II	348
DEELEY – see MALLABY-			DICK, Alick Sydney	V	257
DEELEY, Harry C			DICKINSON, Arthur Lowes	*II	103
DELANE, John Thadeus	III	682	DICKINSON, Arthur Lowes	V	676
DELOITTE, William Welch	*II	57	DICKINSON, John	II	301
DELOITTE, William Welch	III	153	DICKSEE, Lawrence	II	71
DELOITTE, William Welch	IV	737	DIXON, Alfred Herbert	I	455
DELOITTE, William Welch	IV	792	DIXON, Alfred Herbert	*II	107
DEMPSTER, John	III	527	DIXON, Alfred Herbert	III	306
DENNIS, Herbert Raymond &			DIXON, Alfred Herbert	III	363
John Cawsey	*II	60	DIXON, Alfred Herbert	III	723
DENNIS, Herbert Raymond &			DIXON, Raylton	*II	112
John Cawsey	III	582	DIXON, Raylton	IV	773
DENNISON, Aaron Lufkin	*II	64	DOBSON, Benjamin Alfred	*II	115
DENNY, Maurice	I	344	DOBSON, Roy Hardy	*II	118
DENT, Arthur	IV	199	DOBSON, Roy Hardy	V	235
DENT, Francis Henry	*II	66	DOBSON, Roy Hardy	V	252
DENT, Joseph Malaby	*II	68	DOCKER, Bernard Dudley		
DENTON, John Dunshon	II	630	Frank	*II	121
DETERDING, Henri	III	652	DOCKER, Bernard Dudley		
DETERDING, Henri	IV	590	Frank	IV	919
DETERDING, Henri	IV	723	DOCKER, Bernard Dudley		
DETERDING, Henri	V	44	Frank	V	57
DETERDING, Henri	V	695	DOCKER, Bernard Dudley		
DEUCHAR, David	II	85	Frank	V	566

Name	Vol	Page	Name	Vol	Page
DOCKER, Bernard Dudley Frank	V	571	DOUGLAS, William Sholto	IV	251
DOCKER, Frank Dudley	I	24	DOUGLAS, William Sholto	V	499
DOCKER, Frank Dudley	I	565	DOUGLAS-PENNANT, George Sholto Gordon	★II	146
DOCKER, Frank Dudley	I	824	DOUGLAS-PENNANT, George Sholto Gordon	IV	629
DOCKER, Frank Dudley	II	8	DOULTON, Henry	★II	152
DOCKER, Frank Dudley	II	35	DOVE, Frederick John	★II	154
DOCKER, Frank Dudley	II	121	DOVERCOURT, Lord – see HOLMES, Stanley		
DOCKER, Frank Dudley	★II	128	DOWN, Alastair Frederick	★II	158
DOCKER, Frank Dudley	II	351	DOWTY, George Herbert	II	81
DOCKER, Frank Dudley	II	667	DOWTY, George Herbert	★II	161
DOCKER, Frank Dudley	III	154	DOWTY, George Herbert	II	334
DOCKER, Frank Dudley	III	200	DOWTY, George Herbert	IV	463
DOCKER, Frank Dudley	III	251	DOXFORD, William Theodore	★II	165
DOCKER, Frank Dudley	III	448	DOXFORD, William Theodore	IV	773
DOCKER, Frank Dudley	III	484	DOXFORD, William Theodore	IV	943
DOCKER, Frank Dudley	III	572	DOXFORD, William Theodore	V	503
DOCKER, Frank Dudley	III	670	DRAKE, Arthur Eric Courtney	★II	169
DOCKER, Frank Dudley	III	735	DRAKE, W R	I	628
DOCKER, Frank Dudley	IV	34	DRAYTON, Harold Charles Gilbert	I	154
DOCKER, Frank Dudley	IV	111	DRAYTON, Harold Charles Gilbert	I	618
DOCKER, Frank Dudley	IV	168	DRAYTON, Harold Charles Gilbert	I	829
DOCKER, Frank Dudley	IV	466	DRAYTON, Harold Charles Gilbert	★II	173
DOCKER, Frank Dudley	IV	755	DRAYTON, Harold Charles Gilbert	III	376
DOCKER, Frank Dudley	IV	784	DRAYTON, Harold Charles Gilbert	IV	667
DOCKER, Frank Dudley	IV	918	DRAYTON, Harold Charles Gilbert	IV	916
DOCKER, Frank Dudley	IV	925	DREW, Julius Charles	★II	176
DOCKER, Frank Dudley	IV	1,007	DREW, Julius Charles	III	880
DOCKER, Frank Dudley	V	431	DREW, Julius Charles	V	187
DOCKER, Frank Dudley	V	626	DREYFUS, Henry	★II	178
DOCKER, Frank Dudley	V	633	DREYFUS, Henry	IV	69
DOCKER, Frank Dudley	V	656	DREYFUS, Henry	V	431
DODD, John	IV	730	DRUMMOND, Dugald	I	5
DOMVILLE, William Cecil	V	516	DRUMMOND, Dugald	★II	181
DONALDSON, John	V	515	DRUMMOND, Dugald	II	658
DONISTHORPE, George Edmund	III	806	DRUMMOND, Dugald	V	888
DONKIN, John	III	586	DRUMMOND, Hugh	V	629
DORMAN, Arthur John	I	257	DREW, Julius Charles	V	187
DORMAN, Arthur John	I	264	DREYFUS, Henry	IV	69
DORMAN, Arthur John	II	98	DRYSDALE, Daniel	IV	92
DORMAN, Arthur John	★II	136	DU CROS, Arthur Philip	I	97
DORMAN, Arthur John	II	563	DU CROS, Arthur Philip	I	111
DORMAN, Arthur John	III	391			
DORMAN, Arthur John	V	48			
DOUGLAS, George	★II	140			
DOUGLAS, William Sholto	II	79			
DOUGLAS, William Sholto	★II	142			
DOUGLAS, William Sholto	IV	172			

Name	Vol	Page	Name	Vol	Page
DU CROS, Arthur Philip	II	26	DUNLEATH, Lord – see		
DU CROS, Arthur Philip	*II	191	MULHOLLAND, John		
DU CROS, Arthur Philip	II	511	DUNLOP, John Boyd	II	194
DU CROS, Arthur Philip	IV	22	DUNLOP, John Boyd	*II	206
DU CROS, Arthur Philip	IV	85	DUNN, James Hamet	I	28
DU CROS, Arthur Philip	IV	833	DUNN, James Hamet	*II	210
DU CROS, Arthur Philip	V	427	DUNN, James Hamet	II	651
DU CROS, Arthur Philip	V	431	DUNN, James Hamet	IV	531
DU CROS, Arthur Philip	V	785	DUNN, James Hamet	IV	917
DU CROS, William Harvey	*II	194	DUNN, James Hamet	V	455
DU CROS, William Harvey	II	207	DUNNE, J W	II	315
DU CROS, William Harvey	II	227	DUNPHIE, Charles	III	593
DU CROS, William Harvey	IV	406	DUVEEN, Joseph	*II	213
DUCKHAM, Alexander	II	185	DYER, Henry Clement		
DUCKHAM, Arthur			Swinnerton	I	70
McDougall	I	753	DYER, Henry Clement		
DUCKHAM, Arthur			Swinnerton	*II	217
McDougall	*II	185	DYER, Henry Clement		
DUCKHAM, Arthur			Swinnerton	IV	731
McDougall	III	281	DYER, Henry Clement		
DUCKHAM, Arthur			Swinnerton	V	198
McDougall	III	436	EADIE, Albert	*II	222
DUCKHAM, Arthur			EADIE, Albert	IV	925
McDougall	IV	618	EASTMAN, George	IV	194
DUCKHAM, Arthur			EASTMAN, George	IV	481
McDougall	V	874	EASTMAN, George	V	406
DUCKWORTH, James	I	375	ECCLES, Josiah	I	472
DUCKWORTH, Nicholas	IV	849	ECCLES, Josiah	I	669
DUDLEY, 1st Earl of – see			ECCLES, Josiah	*II	225
WARD, William			ECCLES, Josiah	II	539
DUDLEY, 3rd Earl of – see			ECCLES, Josiah	III	2
WARD, William Humble Eric			EDGAR, Edward Mackay	V	788
DUKE, James Buchanan	I	865	EDGE, Selwyn Francis	*II	227
DUKE, James Buchanan	V	844	EDGE, Selwyn Francis	IV	406
DUNCAN, Andrew Rae	I	126	EDGE, Selwyn Francis	IV	930
DUNCAN, Andrew Rae	*II	196	EDGE, Selwyn Francis	IV	974
DUNCAN, Andrew Rae	II	211	EDGE, Selwyn Francis	V	140
DUNCAN, Andrew Rae	III	392	EDGECUMBE, Robert	II	25
DUNCAN, Andrew Rae	III	540	EDISON, Thomas	III	341
DUNCAN, Andrew Rae	IV	456	EDISON, Thomas	V	407
DUNCAN, Andrew Rae	V	122	EDWARDES, Michael	II	242
DUNCAN, Andrew Rae	V	202	EDWARDS, Ebby	III	259
DUNCAN, Andrew Rae	V	909	EDWARDS, George Robert	*II	230
DUNCAN, James Blair	III	162	EDWARDS, George Robert	III	593
DUNCAN, John Norman			EDWARDS, George Robert	III	620
Valette	*II	200	EDWARDS, George Robert	IV	425
DUNCAN, John Norman			EDWARDS, George Robert	IV	747
Valette	V	580	EDWARDS, George Robert	IV	761

Name	Vol	Page	Name	Vol	Page
EDWARDS, George Robert	V	716	ELLIS, John Devonshire	I	578
EDWARDS, J Passmore	II	626	ELLIS, John Devonshire	★II	274
EDWARDS, J Passmore	V	364	ELLIS, John Devonshire	II	283
EDWARDS, J R	V	351	ELLIS, John Devonshire	IV	58
EDWARDS, James Coster	★II	234	ELLIS, Richard Adam	★II	281
EDWARDS, Ronald	I	474	ELLIS, William Henry	★II	283
EDWARDS, Ronald	I	669	ENGELBACH, Charles		
EDWARDS, Ronald	★II	237	Richard Fox	★II	288
EDWARDS, Ronald	V	915	ENGLISH, John	★II	291
EGERTON, Hubert Wingfield	IV	101	ENO, James Crossley	★II	293
ELBOURNE, E T	I	448	ENTHOVEN, Henry John	V	217
ELDER, Alexander	III	527	ERCOLANI, Lucian Randolph	★II	295
ELDERTON, William Palin	★II	245	ERDMAN, Edward	III	544
ELEY, Geoffrey	II	421	ERIKS, Sierd Sint	II	40
ELIAS, J S	I	392	ERIKS, Sierd Sint	★II	297
ELKINGTON, George			ERIKS, Sierd Sint	IV	379
Richards	V	158	ERLANGER – see		
ELKINGTON, George			D'ERLANGER		
Richards & Henry	IV	180	ESSENDON, Lord – see		
ELLERMAN, John Reeves			LEWIS, Frederick William		
(1862–1933)	II	243	EVANS, D H	IV	505
ELLERMAN, John Reeves			EVANS, John	★II	301
(1862–1933)	★II	248	EVANS, John	III	847
ELLERMAN, John Reeves			EVANS, John	IV	955
(1862–1933)	II	444	EVANS, Laming Worthington	II	667
ELLERMAN, John Reeves			EVANS, Louis	III	795
(1862–1933)	IV	480	EVANS, Samuel	IV	866
ELLERMAN, John Reeves			EVANS, William	★II	304
(1862–1933)	IV	794	EVANS, William	III	338
ELLERMAN, John Reeves			EVETTS, George	III	531
(1862–1933)	V	849	EWART, William	★II	307
ELLERMAN, John Reeves			FAIRBAIRN, Andrew	★II	311
(1909–1973)	II	255	FAIRBAIRN, Peter	II	645
ELLERMAN, John Reeves			FAIRBAIRN, William	III	849
(1909–1973)	★II	262	FAIREY, Charles Richard	I	97
ELLERTON, Frederick Cecil	★II	265	FAIREY, Charles Richard	★II	314
ELLIOT, A G	III	284	FAIREY, Charles Richard	II	333
ELLIOT, George	II	59	FAIRRIE family	V	415
ELLIOT, John	★II	268	FALK, Herman Eugen	★II	318
ELLIOT, John	III	150	FALK, Oswald Toynbee	III	589
ELLIOT, John	IV	254	FALK, Robert Julius	II	318
ELLIOT, John	IV	678	FALKNER, John Meade	II	573
ELLIOT, John	V	631	FARINGDON, Lord – see		
ELLIOTT, D H	III	345	HENDERSON, Alexander		
ELLIOTT, J W	III	395	FARLEY, Reuben	★II	323
ELLIOTT, Norman Randall	★II	272	FARLEY, Reuben	III	266
ELLIS, Charles	II	283	FARMER, John Stinson	V	68
ELLIS, Charles	IV	783	FARNDON, Jonathan	II	616
ELLIS, John Devonshire	I	475	FARRAR, E	III	371

Name	Vol	Page	Name	Vol	Page
FARRER, Gaspard	I	164	FIRTH, William	II	560
FARRER, Henry	III	880	FIRTH, William	V	906
FAY, Samuel	*II	328	FISCHER, Charles Louis	II	210
FAY, Samuel	V	66	FISHER, Edwin	II	607
FEDDEN, Alfred Hubert Roy	II	81	FISON, Frank Guy Clavering	*II	367
FEDDEN, Alfred Hubert Roy	II	164	FITZWILLIAM, William		
FEDDEN, Alfred Hubert Roy	*II	332	Thomas Spencer Wentworth	*II	370
FEDDEN, Alfred Hubert Roy	III	14	FLACK, Walter	I	798
FEDDEN, Alfred Hubert Roy	III	284	FLADGATE, W Francis	V	430
FEDDEN, Alfred Hubert Roy	V	141	FLAVEL, Percival William	II	372
FEDDEN, Alfred Hubert Roy	V	484	FLAVEL, Sidney Smith	*II	372
FEDDEN, Alfred Hubert Roy	V	791	FLECK, Alexander	*II	374
FEDDEN, Alfred Hubert Roy	V	931	FLECK, Alexander	III	358
FELLOWS, Joshua	II	324	FLEMING, Arthur Percy		
FELLS, John Manger	*II	335	Morris	*II	380
FELLS, John Manger	II	475	FLEMING, Arthur Percy		
FELLS, John Manger	V	220	Morris	III	471
FENTON, Myles	*II	338	FLEMING, Arthur Percy		
FENWICK, John James	*II	340	Morris	IV	215
FEREDAY, Samuel	V	205	FLEMING, Robert	V	459
FERENS, Thomas Robinson	*II	342	FLEMING, Sandford	III	820
FERENS, Thomas Robinson	IV	857	FLETCHER, George		
FERGUSON, Henry George	*II	346	Hamilton	III	456
FERGUSON, Henry George	IV	643	FLETT, George	IV	109
FERGUSON, John	III	801	FLOYD, C M	II	442
FERRANTI – see DE			FODEN, William & Edwin		
FERRANTI			Richard	*II	383
FFRENCH, Charles Austin			FOLEY, Patrick James	*II	388
Thomas Robert John Joseph	II	133	FORBES, Archibald	III	393
FFRENCH, Charles Austin			FORBES, James Staats	I	44
Thomas Robert John Joseph	*II	350	FORBES, James Staats	I	262
FFRENCH, Charles Austin			FORBES, James Staats	*II	392
Thomas Robert John Joseph	III	155	FORBES, James Staats	II	396
FIELD, Andrew	I	646	FORBES, James Staats	II	600
FIELD, Cyrus W	II	59	FORBES, James Staats	V	683
FIELD, Cyrus W	IV	610	FORBES, William	V	631
FIELD, H C	II	610	FORBES, William de Guise	*II	395
FIELD, Marshall	V	109	FORBES-ROBERTSON,		
FIELD, William	*II	354	Johnston	IV	230
FIELDING, Charles William			FORD, Henry	II	346
Ewing	*II	356	FORD, Henry	III	165
FINDLAY, George	*II	358	FORRES of Glenogil, Lord –		
FINDLAY, George	IV	304	see WILLIAMSON, Archibald		
FINNISTON, H M	IV	286	FORRESTER, George	II	86
FIRTH, Bernard	IV	783	FORTE, Charles	I	857
FIRTH, Mark	*II	363	FORWOOD, Arthur	II	398
FIRTH, Mark	V	623	FORWOOD, William Bower	*II	398
FIRTH, Thomas	II	278	FORWOOD, William Bower	II	431

Name	Vol	Page	Name	Vol	Page
FOSTER, Alfred James	*II	404	FULLER, Henry	II	441
FOSTER, James	II	409	FULLER, Robert	II	441
FOSTER, Nevile	III	46	FULTON, Hamilton	I	8
FOSTER, Richard A	III	10	FURNESS, Christopher	I	545
FOSTER, William	*II	406	FURNESS, Christopher	II	249
FOSTER, William	III	536	FURNESS, Christopher	*II	443
FOSTER, William Henry	II	411	FURNESS, Christopher	II	631
FOSTER, William Orme	*II	409	FURNESS, Christopher	II	652
FOTHERGILL, Benjamin	III	849	FURNESS, Christopher	II	668
FOTHERGILL, Rowland	IV	211	FURNESS, Christopher	III	761
FOWLER, Alfred	IV	995	FURNESS, Christopher	IV	481
FOWLER, John	I	17	FURNESS, Christopher	IV	598
FOWLER, John	I	108	FURNESS, Christopher	IV	944
FOWLER, John	*II	412	FURNESS, Christopher	V	344
FOWLER, John	II	633	FURNESS, Christopher	V	434
FOWLER, John	IV	583	FURNESS, Marmaduke	*II	449
FOWLER, Robert Henry	I	83	FURNESS, Marmaduke	III	761
FOWLER, Robert Henry	I	522	FURNESS, Stephen William	II	447
FOWLER, Robert Henry	*II	414	FURNESS, Stephen William	II	449
FOWLER, Robert Henry	IV	842	FYFFE, Edward Wathen	*II	452
FOX, Charles	I	17	FYFFE, Edward Wathen	III	528
FOX, Douglas	II	633	GABRIEL, John Beresford		
FRANKLIN, Ellis Abraham	IV	298	Stuart	*II	455
FRASER, Hugh	I	241	GABRIEL, John Beresford		
FRASER, Hugh	I	698	Stuart	IV	746
FRASER, William Lionel	I	760	GABRIEL, Ralph	II	458
FRASER, William Lionel	*II	417	GAINFORD, Lord – see		
FRASER, William Lionel	III	150	PEASE, Joseph Albert		
FRASER, William Lionel	III	162	GALLAHER, Thomas	*II	461
FRASER, William Milligan	*II	423	GALLOWAY, George & W W	III	313
FRASER, William Milligan	IV	70	GALLOWAY, John	*II	465
FRASER, William Milligan	V	693	GALLOWAY, William	I	310
FRASER-NASH, Archie	V	497	GAMAGE, Albert Walter	*II	468
FREAKE, Charles James	*II	427	GAMAGE, Eric	II	470
FREEBOROUGH, John H	I	185	GAMAGE, Leslie	III	281
FREEMAN, Gerry	V	913	GAMAGE, Leslie	IV	813
FREEMAN, Ralph	II	534	GAMBLE, David	*II	471
FREMANTLE, Charles	II	474	GANONG, J E	III	192
FRENCH, Walter Flexman	II	478	GARCKE, Emile Oscar	II	336
FRESHFIELD, Edwin	*II	430	GARCKE, Emile Oscar	*II	474
FRESHFIELD, Edwin	III	732	GARCKE, Emile Oscar	III	160
FRESHFIELD, James William	II	430	GARCKE, Emile Oscar	III	376
FRISWELL, Charles Ernest			GARCKE, Emile Oscar	IV	663
Hain	*II	433	GARCKE, Sidney Emile	I	433
FRISWELL, Charles Ernest			GARCKE, Sidney Emile	II	475
Hain	IV	197	GARCKE, Sidney Emile	*II	478
FRY, Joseph Storrs	*II	436	GARCKE, Sidney Emile	III	148
FRY, Joseph Storrs	IV	970	GARCKE, Sidney Emile	III	376
FULLER, George Pargiter	*II	440	GARDNER, Charles Bruce	*II	480

Name	Vol	Page	Name	Vol	Page
GARDNER, Charles Bruce	III	257	GEDDES, Eric Campbell	IV	223
GARDNER, Charles Bruce	III	487	GEDDES, Eric Campbell	IV	241
GARDNER, Charles Bruce	III	673	GEDDES, Eric Campbell	IV	467
GARDNER, Charles Bruce	III	840	GEDDES, Eric Campbell	IV	562
GARDNER, Charles Bruce	III	906	GEDDES, Eric Campbell	IV	666
GARDNER, Charles Bruce	IV	452	GEDDES, Eric Campbell	IV	925
GARDNER, Charles Bruce	IV	531	GEDDES, Eric Campbell	V	92
GARDNER, Charles Bruce	IV	1,008	GEDDES, Eric Campbell	V	275
GARDNER, James	V	46	GEDDES, Eric Campbell	V	427
GARDNER, Robert	III	703	GEDDES, Eric Campbell	V	431
GARFORTH, William Edward	*II	484	GEDDES, Eric Campbell	V	712
GARNSEY, Gilbert Francis	I	784	GEDDES, Eric Campbell	V	742
GARNSEY, Gilbert Francis	II	71	GEDDES, Eric Campbell	V	785
GARNSEY, Gilbert Francis	II	286	GEDDES, Eric Campbell	V	811
GARNSEY, Gilbert Francis	*II	487	GEDDES, Eric Campbell	V	881
GARNSEY, Gilbert Francis	III	111	GEDDES, Irvine Campbell	II	502
GARNSEY, Gilbert Francis	III	839	GEE, Harry Percy	II	518
GARNSEY, Gilbert Francis	IV	208	GEE, Henry Simpson	*II	516
GARNSEY, Gilbert Francis	V	460	GEOGHEGAN	II	681
GARTON, Richard Charles	I	297	GESTETNER, David	*II	519
GARTON, Richard Charles	I	534	GESTETNER, David	III	602
GARTON, Richard Charles	*II	491	GESTETNER, Sigmund	II	523
GARTON, Richard Charles	II	661	GHALIB, Selchouk Ahmed	*II	525
GARTON, Richard Charles	IV	432	GIBB, Alexander	I	234
GARTON, Richard Charles	V	772	GIBB, Alexander	*II	529
GARTSIDE, James Brewer	II	498	GIBB, Alexander	IV	196
GARTSIDE, John Henry	III	726	GIBB, Alexander	V	88
GARTSIDE, Thomas Edmund	*II	494	GIBB, Alexander Easton	II	529
GARTSIDE, Thomas Edmund	V	447	GIBB, Claude Dixon	*II	537
GASKELL, Holbrook	*II	499	GIBB, Claude Dixon	IV	545
GATES, Ernest Henry	*II	500	GIBB, George Stegmann	I	542
GAUDIN, H de G	III	310	GIBB, George Stegmann	II	508
GEDDES, Auckland Campbell	*II	502	GIBB, George Stegmann	II	529
GEDDES, Eric Campbell	I	48	GIBB, George Stegmann	*II	543
GEDDES, Eric Campbell	I	126	GIBB, George Stegmann	IV	222
GEDDES, Eric Campbell	II	72	GIBB, George Stegmann	IV	678
GEDDES, Eric Campbell	II	192	GIBB, George Stegmann	V	274
GEDDES, Eric Campbell	II	502	GIBB, George Stegmann	V	712
GEDDES, Eric Campbell	*II	507	GIBBONS, Edward Stanley	*II	546
GEDDES, Eric Campbell	II	534	GIBBONS, James Boatwright	III	33
GEDDES, Eric Campbell	II	543	GIBBS, Henry Hucks	*II	548
GEDDES, Eric Campbell	II	621	GIBBS, Henry Hucks	II	608
GEDDES, Eric Campbell	III	156	GIBBS, Henry Hucks	II	626
GEDDES, Eric Campbell	III	350	GIBBS, Henry Hucks	III	17
GEDDES, Eric Campbell	III	435	GIBBS, Herbert Cokayne	I	862
GEDDES, Eric Campbell	III	821	GIBBS, Herbert Cokayne	*II	555
GEDDES, Eric Campbell	IV	22	GIBBS, Walter Durant	II	557
GEDDES, Eric Campbell	IV	31	GIBBS, William	II	549
GEDDES, Eric Campbell	IV	216	GIFFARD, Edward	IV	432

Name	Vol	Page	Name	Vol	Page
GIFFARD, Edward	V	772	GOLLANCZ, Victor	*II	591
GILBERTSON, Cecil Frederic	II	559	GOMME, Ebenezer	II	295
GILBERTSON, Charles Geoffrey	II	559	GOMME, Ebenezer	*II	595
GILBERTSON, Francis William	*II	558	GOOCH, Daniel	II	59
			GOOCH, Daniel	*II	597
GILCHRIST, Percy Carlisle	I	605	GOOCH, Daniel	IV	610
GILCHRIST, Percy Carlisle	II	136	GOODAY, J F S	II	396
GILCHRIST, Percy Carlisle	*II	562	GOODENOUGH, Frederick Crauford	I	320
GILCHRIST, Percy Carlisle	III	211	GOODENOUGH, Frederick Crauford	*II	603
GILCHRIST, Percy Carlisle	IV	898	GOODENOUGH, Frederick Crauford	V	78
GILCHRIST, Percy Carlisle	V	491	GOODENOUGH, Frederick Crauford	V	78
GILCHRIST, Percy Carlisle	V	653	GOODENOUGH, William Macnamara	*II	607
GILLESPIE, Thomas	II	84	GOODENOUGH, William Macnamara	IV	761
GILLETT, Ronald Brodie	*II	564	GOODENOUGH, William Macnamara	V	559
GILPIN, Edmund Henry	*II	565	GOODMAN, Frederick Buck	*II	609
GIROUARD, Edouard Percy Cranwill	I	380	GOODMAN, John Dent	II	609
GIROUARD, Edouard Percy Cranwill	*II	570	GOODMAN, John Dent	III	291
GIROUARD, Edouard Percy Cranwill	III	199	GORDON, Harry Panmure	*II	611
GIROUARD, Edouard Percy Cranwill	V	742	GORDON, Harry Panmure	IV	949
GLASS, Richard	II	59	GORDON-SMITH, Allan	*II	614
GLENDYNE, Lord – see NIVISON, Robert			GORRINGE, Frederick	III	765
			GOSCHEN, Lord	III	673
GLIKSTEN, Albert Arnold	*II	574	GOSCHEN, Lord	III	695
GLIKSTEN, Reuben	II	574	GOSCHEN, Lord	III	788
GLIKSTEN, Stanley	II	576	GOSCHEN, W H N	I	863
GLOVER,	V	748	GOSSAGE, William	I	842
GLUCKSTEIN, Montague	I	717	GOSSAGE, William	*II	616
GLUCKSTEIN, Montague	*II	578	GRAHAM-WHITE, Claude	IV	461
GLUCKSTEIN, Montague	III	888	GRANET, William Guy	*II	620
GLUCKSTEIN, Montauge	V	20	GRANET, William Guy	III	156
GLYN, Maurice	III	670	GRANET, William Guy	IV	456
GLYN-JONES, William Samuel	I	376	GRANET, William Guy	IV	531
GLYN-JONES, William Samuel	*II	581	GRANET, William Guy	IV	784
			GRANET, William Guy	V	264
GLYNN, Walter	II	444	GRANET, William Guy	V	431
GODBER, Frederick	*II	583	GRANT, Albert Zachariah	*II	623
GODFREY, A H	III	796	GRANT, Albert Zachariah	IV	480
GOLDIE, George Dashwood Taubman-	*II	586	GRANT, Maurice	II	626
GOLDSMID-STERN-SALOMONS – see SALOMONS, David L			GRANTLEY, Lord – see FURNESS, Christopher		
			GRANVILLE, Keith	V	884
			GRAY, William	II	443
			GRAY, William	*II	629
GOLLANCZ, Victor	I	282	GRAY, William	IV	941

Name	Vol	Page	Name	Vol	Page
GREATHEAD, James Henry	I	108	GRINNELL-MILNE,		
GREATHEAD, James Henry	*II	632	Douglas	II	649
GREATHEAD, James Henry	IV	183	GRINNELL-MILNE,		
GREATHEAD, James Henry	IV	355	George	II	649
GREATHEAD, James Henry	IV	587	GRINSTEAD, Stanley	III	550
GREENE, Benjamin Buck	II	637	GRISSELL, Thomas	II	355
GREENE, Edward	*II	634	GRISSELL, Thomas	IV	644
GREENE, Walter	II	637	GROVE, Walter Patrick	*II	675
GREENLY, John	II	419	GROVE, Walter Patrick	IV	637
GREENWAY, Charles	I	561	GUÉRET, Louis Jean		
GREENWAY, Charles	I	591	Baptiste	*II	678
GREENWAY, Charles	I	823	GUÉRET, Louis Jean		
GREENWAY, Charles	*II	639	Baptiste	III	824
GREENWAY, Charles	V	635	GUÉRET, Louis Jean		
GREENWELL, Thomas	I	588	Baptiste	V	478
GREENWOOD, Arthur	*II	642	GUEST, Ivor	III	571
GREENWOOD, Thomas	II	311	GUEST, Josiah John	I	686
GREENWOOD, Thomas	*II	645	GUEST, Josiah John	III	480
GREENWOOD, Thomas	III	153	GUEST, Josiah John	IV	212
GREG, Henry Philips	*II	647	GUINNESS family	V	912
GREG, Henry Philips	III	308	GUINNESS, Edward Cecil	I	234
GREG, Robert Hyde	IV	849	GUINNESS, Edward Cecil	I	613
GRENFELL, Arthur Morton	II	10	GUINNESS, Edward Cecil	II	252
GRENFELL, Arthur Morton	II	30	GUINNESS, Edward Cecil	II	635
GRENFELL, Arthur Morton	II	211	GUINNESS, Edward Cecil	*II	680
GRENFELL, Arthur Morton	*II	649	GUTHRIE, Edwin	*II	684
GRENFELL, Arthur Morton	II	667	GUTHRIE, Giles	II	232
GRENFELL, Arthur Morton	III	904	GUTHRIE, Giles	*II	687
GRENFELL, Arthur Morton	IV	529	GUTHRIE, Giles	V	192
GRENFELL, Arthur Morton	V	218	GUTHRIE, Giles	V	915
GRENFELL, Edward Charles	II	649	GUY, J H	II	487
GRENFELL, Edward Charles	*II	655	HACKING, John	I	669
GRENFELL, Edward Charles	V	223	HACKING, John	II	225
GRENFELL, Henry			HACKING, John	*III	1
Riversdale	II	655	HACKING, John	IV	225
GRENFELL, Riversdale			HACKWORTH, Timothy	I	6
Nonus	II	651	HADDOCK, Thomas	II	471
GRESLEY, Herbert Nigel	*II	657	HADFIELD, John	*III	3
GRESLEY, Herbert Nigel	IV	851	HADFIELD, Robert Abbott	*III	5
GRESLEY, Herbert Nigel	V	713	HADFIELD, Robert Abbott	V	814
GRETTON, John	*II	660	HAGUE, Kenneth	II	419
GREY, Lord	II	650	HAIN, Edward	*III	9
GRIFFIN, John Ross	*II	664	HALDANE, James S	I	559
GRIFFITHS, John Norton	II	651	HALDIN or		
GRIFFITHS, John Norton	*II	666	HALDINSTEIN, Philip	IV	668
GRIFFITHS, John Norton	IV	529	HALFORD, Alfred	II	24
GRIFFITHS, John Norton	IV	927	HALFORD, Arthur	II	24
GRIFFITHS, William Thomas	*II	672	HALFORD, Ernest Samuel	IV	109

Name	Vol	Page	Name	Vol	Page
HALFORD, Frank Bernard	II	51	HARLEY, Harry	III	176
HALFORD, Frank Bernard	*III	12	HARMAN, Alfred Hugh	*III	41
HALFORD, Frank Bernard	IV	408	HARMAN, Alfred Hugh	III	616
HAMBRO, Charles	IV	687	HARMAN, Alfred Hugh	IV	195
HAMBRO, Eric	II	652	HARMER, Oscar	III	174
HAMBRO, Eric	III	18	HARMOOD-BANNER, John		
HAMBRO, Everard Alexander	*III	16	Sutherland	II	662
HAMBRO, H C	V	814	HARMOOD-BANNER, John		
HAMILTON, Claud John	*III	18	Sutherland	*III	43
HAMILTON, Claud John	III	153	HARMOOD-BANNER, John		
HAMILTON, Claud John	V	510	Sutherland	IV	793
HAMMOND, John Hays	I	230	HARMOOD-BANNER, John		
HAMMOND, Robert	II	44	Sutherland	IV	917
HAMMOND, Robert	*III	21	HARMOOD-BANNER, John		
HAMPDEN, 1st Viscount – see			Sutherland	IV	1,006
BRAND, Henry Bouverie			HARMSWORTH, Alfred		
William			Charles William	I	24
HANBURY-WILLIAMS,			HARMSWORTH, Alfred		
John Coldbrook	I	651	Charles William	I	190
HANBURY-WILLIAMS,			HARMSWORTH, Alfred		
John Coldbrook	I	708	Charles William	I	303
HANBURY-WILLIAMS,			HARMSWORTH, Alfred		
John Coldbrook	*III	23	Charles William	I	394
HANBURY-WILLIAMS,			HARMSWORTH, Alfred		
John Coldbrook	III	565	Charles William	II	6
HANDASYDE, George H	I	571	HARMSWORTH, Alfred		
HANDLEY-PAGE – see			Charles William	II	255
PAGE, Frederick Handley			HARMSWORTH, Alfred		
HANDYSIDE, Andrew	*III	26	Charles William	*III	47
HANN, Edmund	III	256	HARMSWORTH, Alfred		
HANN, Edmund	III	824	Charles William	III	57
HANSON, John F	II	431	HARMSWORTH, Alfred		
HARBEN, Henry	*III	29	Charles William	III	384
HARCOURT, Lewis	I	560	HARMSWORTH, Alfred		
HARDAY, Henry	IV	94	Charles William	III	411
HARDIE, Stephen	III	392	HARMSWORTH, Alfred		
HARDING, Robert Palmer	*III	32	Charles William	III	502
HARDING, Robert Palmer	V	583	HARMSWORTH, Alfred		
HARDING, Robert Palmer	V	766	Charles William	III	682
HARGREAVES, C R	III	722	HARMSWORTH, Alfred		
HARGREAVES, John	III	206	Charles William	III	746
HARGREAVES, William	III	206	HARMSWORTH, Alfred		
HARLAND, Edward James	I	684	Charles William	III	828
HARLAND, Edward James	*III	36	HARMSWORTH, Alfred		
HARLAND, Edward James	III	456	Charles William	IV	52
HARLAND, Edward James	IV	703	HARMSWORTH, Alfred		
HARLAND, Edward James	V	195	Charles William	IV	437
HARLAND, Edward James	V	854	HARMSWORTH, Alfred		
HARLAND, Edward James	V	892	Charles William	IV	575

Name	Vol	Page	Name	Vol	Page
HARMSWORTH, Alfred Charles William	IV	591	HARRISON, William Edward	*III	87
HARMSWORTH, Alfred Charles William	IV	738	HARTLEY, Harold Brewer	*III	89
HARMSWORTH, Alfred Charles William	IV	867	HARTLEY, Harold Brewer	IV	456
HARMSWORTH, Alfred Charles William	V	244	HARTLEY, Harold Brewer	V	265
HARMSWORTH, Alfred Charles William	V	365	HARTLEY, Harold Brewer	V	376
HARMSWORTH, Esmond Cecil	II	80	HARTLEY, James	I	589
HARMSWORTH, Harold Sidney	I	24	HARTLEY, James	*III	93
HARMSWORTH, Harold Sidney	I	303	HARTLEY, Jesse	III	120
HARMSWORTH, Harold Sidney	I	400	HARTLEY, John	III	94
HARMSWORTH, Harold Sidney	III	49	HARTLEY, William Pickles	I	507
HARMSWORTH, Harold Sidney	*III	57	HARTLEY, William Pickles	*III	96
HARMSWORTH, Harold Sidney	III	385	HARTLEY, William Pickles	III	338
HARMSWORTH, Harold Sidney	III	413	HARVEY, Ernest	IV	453
HARMSWORTH, Harold Sidney	IV	870	HARVEY, Wilfred	I	856
HARMSWORTH, Harold Sidney	V	483	HARWOOD, Harold Marsh	*III	99
HARMSWORTH, Harold Sidney	V	724	HASLAM, Alfred Seale	*III	105
HARMSWORTH, Hildebrand	III	54	HASLAM, Alfred Seale	III	370
HARMSWORTH, Leicester	III	54	HASWELL, George	I	210
HARMSWORTH, St John	III	55	HATFIELD, Edgar Richard	III	159
HARRIMAN, George William	*III	65	HATRY, Clarence Charles	I	430
HARRIMAN, George William	III	858	HATRY, Clarence Charles	II	193
HARRIMAN, George William	III	893	HATRY, Clarence Charles	II	488
HARRIMAN, George William	V	351	HATRY, Clarence Charles	*III	110
HARRIS, George James	*III	70	HATRY, Clarence Charles	IV	210
HARRISON, Cyril Ernest	*III	74	HATRY, Clarence Charles	IV	490
HARRISON, Robert	*III	78	HATTERSLEY, Richard Longden	*III	115
HARRISON, Stanley	III	138	HAWKER, Harry G	V	232
HARRISON, Thomas & James	II	399	HAWKER, Harry G	V	497
HARRISON, Thomas & James	*III	81	HAWKSHAW, John	I	175
HARRISON, Thomas & James	III	380	HAWKSHAW, John	I	195
HARRISON, Thomas & James	IV	840	HAWKSHAW, John	II	412
HARRISON, Thomas Elliot	*III	83	HAWKSHAW, John	*III	119
			HAWKSLEY, Thomas	*III	122
			HAWTHORN, Robert	IV	905
			HAYMAN, Cecil George Graham	I	442
			HAYMAN, Cecil George Graham	*III	127
			HAYWARD, Charles William	I	465
			HAYWARD, Charles William	*III	130
			HEAD, John	IV	844
			HEARLE, Francis Trounson	II	48
			HEARLE, Francis Trounson	*III	133
			HEATH, Cuthbert Eden	I	100
			HEATH, Cuthbert Eden	I	459
			HEATH, Cuthbert Eden	*III	136
			HEATH, Cuthbert Eden	IV	364

Name	Vol	Page	Name	Vol	Page
HEATH, Robert II	*III	142	HEYWORTH, Geoffrey	*III	192
HEATH, Robert III, James & Arthur H	*III	145	HEYWORTH, Geoffrey	V	602
			HICHENS, William Lionel	I	824
HEATON, John Frederick	II	420	HICHENS, William Lionel	II	653
HEATON, John Frederick	II	479	HICHENS, William Lionel	*III	198
HEATON, John Frederick	*III	148	HICHENS, William Lionel	III	486
HEATON, John Frederick	III	376	HICHENS, William Lionel	III	671
HEDLEY, Thomas	*III	151	HICHENS, William Lionel	III	904
HEDLEY, Thomas	III	699	HICHENS, William Lionel	IV	216
HENDERSON, Alexander	I	708	HICHENS, William Lionel	IV	783
HENDERSON, Alexander	II	131	HICHENS, William Lionel	IV	1,007
HENDERSON, Alexander	II	351	HICK, Benjamin	III	205
HENDERSON, Alexander	*III	153	HICK, John	*III	205
HENDERSON, Alexander	III	385	HICKMAN, Alfred	II	326
HENDERSON, Alexander	III	450	HICKMAN, Alfred	*III	209
HENDERSON, Alexander	III	672	HICKMAN, Alfred	III	264
HENDERSON, Alexander	III	820	HICKMAN, T E, E & V H	III	211
HENDERSON, Alexander	III	838	HICKSON, Robert	III	37
HENDERSON, Alexander	IV	344	HIGGS, William	*III	217
HENDERSON, Alexander	IV	465	HIGHAM, C S S	III	847
HENDERSON, Alexander	IV	926	HIGHAM, Charles Frederick	*III	220
HENDERSON, Brodie	III	153	HIGHAM, J S	I	507
HENDERSON, Brodie	III	821	HIGHAM, James	*III	222
HENMAN, Frank Espinett	III	162	HILEY, Ernest	III	251
HENMAN, Philip Sydney	*III	158	HILGER, Adam	V	588
HENMAN, Philip Sydney	III	641	HILL, Arthur	III	536
HENNESSY, Patrick	*III	165	HILL, Enoch	*III	226
HENNESSY, Patrick	IV	642	HILL, Enoch	IV	44
HENNESSY, Patrick	IV	761	HILL, Enoch	V	862
HEPWORTH, Joseph	*III	170	HILL, G H	I	213
HEPWORTH, Norris	III	171	HILL, John Cathles	*III	232
HERBERT, Alfred Edward	*III	174	HILL, John Edgar	III	234
HERBERT, Alfred Edward	III	246	HILL, Philip Ernest	I	245
HERBERT, Alfred Edward	V	750	HILL, Philip Ernest	II	82
HERBERT, Alfred Edward	V	931	HILL, Philip Ernest	II	92
HERBERT, Edwin	II	239	HILL, Philip Ernest	*III	235
HERBERT, William Henry	III	246	HILL, Philip Ernest	III	690
HERMON, Edward	*III	178	HILL, Philip Ernest	IV	366
HERMON, Edward	III	313	HILL, Philip Ernest	V	760
HETHERINGTON, Arthur Ford	*III	181	HILL, Philip Ernest	V	787
			HILL, Rowland	V	531
HETHERINGTON, Arthur Ford	III	534	HILL, Rowland & Joseph	III	218
HEWITT, Joseph	*III	184	HILL, Walter	I	201
HEWITT, Thomas Peter	*III	186	HILL, William	*III	239
HEWLETT, Alfred	*III	188	HILLINGDON, Lord – see MILLS, Charles Henry		
HEWLETT, Alfred	III	251	HILLMAN, Edward Henry	II	80
HEWLETT, William Henry	III	189	HILLMAN, Edward Henry	*III	242
HEYWORTH, Geoffrey	I	784	HILLMAN, Edward Henry	IV	15

Name	Vol	Page	Name	Vol	Page
HILLMAN, William	II	100	HOLDEN, Edward Hopkinson	II	518
HILLMAN, William	*III	245	HOLDEN, Edward Hopkinson	II	604
HILLMAN, William	V	805	HOLDEN, Edward Hopkinson	III	277
HILLS, Arnold Frank	III	596	HOLDEN, Edward Hopkinson	*III	290
HILTON, Ralph	*III	248	HOLDEN, Edward Hopkinson	III	572
HILTON, Ralph John	III	250	HOLDEN, Edward Hopkinson	III	695
HILTON, Robert Stuart	*III	251	HOLDEN, Edward Hopkinson	IV	34
HILTON, Robert Stuart	III	539	HOLDEN, Edward Hopkinson	IV	109
HILTON, Robert Stuart	IV	784	HOLDEN, Edward Hopkinson	IV	589
HILTON, Robert Stuart	V	291	HOLDEN, Edward Hopkinson	V	78
HINDLEY, John Scott	I	415	HOLDEN, Isaac	*III	299
HINDLEY, John Scott	I	668	HOLDEN, Isaac	III	419
HINDLEY, John Scott	*III	255	HOLDEN, Isaac	III	806
HINGLEY, Benjamin	III	212	HOLDEN, Jonathan	I	627
HINGLEY, Benjamin	*III	261	HOLDEN, Jonathan	III	300
HINGLEY, Noah	III	261	HOLLAND, William Henry	*III	303
HINTON, Christopher	I	473	HOLLINGS, J S	V	908
HINTON, Christopher	II	226	HOLLINS, Denis Machell	II	648
HINTON, Christopher	II	540	HOLLINS, Denis Machell	*III	308
HINTON, Christopher	*III	268	HOLLINS, Denis Machell	III	316
HINTON, Christopher	IV	634	HOLLINS, Frank	III	180
HINTON, Christopher	IV	745	HOLLINS, Frank	*III	313
HINTON, Christopher	IV	760	HOLLINS, Frank	III	320
HIRST, Hugo	I	668	HOLLINS, Frank	V	418
HIRST, Hugo	II	557	HOLLINS, Henry Ernest	III	308
HIRST, Hugo	II	573	HOLLINS, Henry Ernest	III	315
HIRST, Hugo	III	252	HOLLINS, Henry Ernest	*III	318
HIRST, Hugo	*III	275	HOLLINS, I F E	III	310
HIRST, Hugo	IV	111	HOLLINS, William	III	318
HIRST, Hugo	IV	417	HOLLOWAY, Thomas	I	244
HIRST, Hugo	IV	467	HOLLOWAY, Thomas	I	247
HIRST, Hugo	IV	784	HOLLOWAY, Thomas	II	294
HIRST, Hugo	IV	812	HOLLOWAY, Thomas	*III	323
HIRST, Hugo	V	812	HOLMES, Stanley	III	691
HITCHCOCK, George	V	826	HOLT, Alfred	II	398
HIVES, Ernest Walter	II	81	HOLT, Alfred	*III	326
HIVES, Ernest Walter	II	164	HOLT, Alfred & Philip	V	414
HIVES, Ernest Walter	*III	283	HOLT, Follett	II	352
HIVES, Ernest Walter	IV	977	HOLT, George	III	326
HOBBS, J W	I	130	HOLT, John	III	527
HOBHOUSE, Charles	III	449	HOLT, Lawrence	III	328
HODDER, Martin	V	828	HOLT, Philip	III	326
HODDER-WILLIAMS, J E	V	828	HOLT, Vesey	III	670
HODGE, Julian Stephen			HOOKER, Stanley	I	574
Alfred	*III	286	HOOKHAM, George	I	634
HODGSON, Richard	III	85	HOOLEY, Ernest Terah	I	393
HOLDEN, E T	V	363	HOOLEY, Ernest Terah	II	194
HOLDEN, Edward Hopkinson	I	237	HOOLEY, Ernest Terah	*III	329
HOLDEN, Edward Hopkinson	II	130	HOOLEY, Ernest Terah	III	510

Name	Vol	Page	Name	Vol	Page
HOOLEY, Ernest Terah	III	517	HOULDSWORTH, William Henry	III	849
HOOLEY, Ernest Terah	III	603	HOUSTON, Robert Paterson	★III	369
HOOLEY, Ernest Terah	III	685	HOWARD, Frederick	III	373
HOOLEY, Ernest Terah	IV	134	HOWARD, James	★III	373
HOOLEY, Ernest Terah	IV	162	HOWARD, James	IV	842
HOOLEY, Ernest Terah	IV	480	HOWARD, James	V	136
HOOLEY, Ernest Terah	IV	661	HOWLETT, John Godfrey	V	776
HOOLEY, Ernest Terah	V	315	HOWLEY, Richard Joseph	II	174
HOOLEY, Ernest Terah	V	903	HOWLEY, Richard Joseph	II	479
HOOPER, Frederic Collins	★III	333	HOWLEY, Richard Joseph	★III	375
HOOPER, Frederic Collins	IV	148	HOZIER, Henry Montague	★III	377
HOOVER, Herbert Clark	I	231	HOZIER, William Wallace	III	377
HOOVER, Herbert Clark	IV	312	HUBBARD, William S	III	174
HOOVER, Herbert Clark	IV	685	HUCKS, Bentfield C	I	342
HOOVER, Herbert Clark	V	217	HUDSON, Edward	III	879
HOPE, Samuel	III	326	HUDSON, George	I	43
HOPKINSON, John	I	634	HUDSON, George	III	84
HOPKINSON, John	I	836	HUDSON, George	III	401
HOPKINSON, John	★III	340	HUDSON, George	IV	792
HOPKINSON, John	III	558	HUGHES, John William	III	81
HOPKINSON, John	IV	373	HUGHES, John William	★III	380
HOPWOOD, Frank	IV	723	HUGHES, T Harrison	III	383
HOPWOOD, Herbert	V	565	HUISH, Mark	IV	302
HOPWOOD, Herbert	V	572	HUISH, Mark	V	66
HORLICK, James	★III	343	HUISH, Mark	V	682
HORLICK, William	III	343	HULTON, Edward	I	25
HORNBY, Frank	★III	345	HULTON, Edward	III	59
HORNE, Robert Stevenson	★III	349	HULTON, Edward	★III	384
HORNIMAN, John	V	586	HULTON, Edward	III	413
HORROCKS, James	IV	1,002	HULTON, Edward	V	244
HOULDER, Alfred & Augustus	III	354	HULTON, Edward Sr.	III	384
HOULDER, Edwin Savory	★III	354	HUME, Hubert Nutcombe	★III	388
HOULDSWORTH, Hubert Stanley	I	415	HUNSDON, Lord – see GIBBS, Herbert Cokayne		
HOULDSWORTH, Hubert Stanley	III	259	HUNT, Henry	II	428
HOULDSWORTH, Hubert Stanley	★III	356	HUNTER, Ellis	II	199
HOULDSWORTH, Thomas	III	359	HUNTER, Ellis	★III	390
HOULDSWORTH, William Henry	II	107	HUNTER, Ellis	V	122
HOULDSWORTH, William Henry	III	304	HUNTER, Ernest John	★III	394
HOULDSWORTH, William Henry	★III	359	HUNTER, George Burton	III	394
HOULDSWORTH, William Henry	III	711	HUNTER, George Burton	★III	398
			HUNTER, George Burton	IV	906
			HUNTER, Summers	IV	959
			HUNTING, Charles Samuel	III	402
			HUNTING, Gerald Lindsay	III	402
			HUNTING, Percy Llewellyn	II	232
			HUNTING, Percy Llewellyn	★III	402

Name	Vol	Page	Name	Vol	Page
HUNTING, Percy Llewellyn	V	913	ISAACS, Godfrey Charles	III	281
HUNTLEY, Thomas	IV	522	ISAACS, Godfrey Charles	*III	446
HURCOMB, Cyril William	*III	405	ISAACS, Godfrey Charles	IV	466
HURCOMB, Cyril William	IV	254	ISAACS, Godfrey Charles	IV	512
HUTCHINSON, John	IV	288	ISAACS, Godfrey Charles	V	246
HUTCHINSON, William	III	211	ISAACS, Rufus	I	612
HUTCHISON, William			ISHERWOOD, Joseph		
Kenneth	III	182	William	*III	453
HUTCHISON, William			ISMAY, Joseph Bruce	III	456
Kenneth	III	534	ISMAY, Joseph Bruce	V	856
HYAM, Benjamin	III	754	ISMAY, Thomas Henry	*III	455
HYAMS, Harry	III	544	ISMAY, Thomas Henry	IV	704
HYDE, Charles	III	413	ISMAY, Thomas Henry	V	856
HYDE, Clarendon	III	484	IVEAGH, 1st Earl of, – see		
HYDE, Robert Robertson	*III	408	GUINNESS, Edward Cecil		
HYDE, Robert Robertson	IV	960	JACKSON, John	I	18
HYDE, Robert Robertson	IV	962	JACKSON, John	I	195
HYNDLEY, 1st Viscount – see			JACKSON, John	*III	462
HINDLEY, John Scott			JACKSON, John	IV	583
ILIFFE, Edward Langton	III	414	JACKSON, Ralph Ward	I	257
ILIFFE, Edward Mauger	I	25	JACKSON, William Lawies	III	153
ILIFFE, Edward Mauger	I	302	JACKSON, William Lawies	*III	468
ILIFFE, Edward Mauger	*III	411	JACKSON, Willis	*III	470
ILIFFE, Edward Mauger	V	244	JACQUES, John Henry	*III	475
ILLINGWORTH family	III	301	JAFFE, Otto	IV	39
ILLINGWORTH, Alfred	*III	417	JAMIESON, Archibald	III	592
ILLINGWORTH, Alfred	V	33	JAPHET, Saemy	I	611
ILLINGWORTH, Henry	III	418	JARROTT, Charles	III	744
IMRIE, William	III	455	JARVIE, Gibson	IV	366
INCHCAPE, 1st Earl of – see			JEFFERIES, John Robert	IV	842
MACKAY, James Lyle			JENKINS, Robert	V	59
INGLIS, James Charles	*III	423	JENKINS, William	I	687
INGLIS, James Charles	IV	241	JENKINS, William	*III	480
INGLIS, James Charles	IV	748	JENKINSON, Mark Webster	I	62
INMAN, William	*III	427	JENKINSON, Mark Webster	I	565
INSTONE, Samuel	*III	434	JENKINSON, Mark Webster	*III	483
INSTONE, Samuel	III	825	JENKINSON, Mark Webster	III	670
INVERFORTH, Lord – see			JENKINSON, Mark Webster	III	839
WEIR, Andrew			JENKINSON, Mark Webster	IV	204
IRVIN, John	III	439	JENKINSON, Mark Webster	IV	755
IRVIN, Richard	*III	437	JENKINSON, Mark Webster	V	658
IRVING, Henry	I	148	JEPHCOTT, Harry	*III	491
IRVING, Henry	*III	441	JOBLING, James A	III	498
IRVING, Henry	III	683	JOBLING-PURSER, Ernest		
IRVING, Henry	IV	864	Joseph	*III	498
IRVING, Henry	V	357	JOEL, S B	III	315
IRVING, Henry	V	543	JOHNSON, C O	III	439
IRVING, Henry	V	877	JOHNSON, Claude Goodman	*III	499
IRVING, Henry	V	920	JOHNSON, Claude Goodman	IV	930

Name	Vol	Page	Name	Vol	Page
JOHNSON, Claude Goodman	IV	974	KEARTON, Christopher Frank	*III	564
JOHNSON, Eldridge R	I	671			
JOHNSON, Ernest James	*III	505	KEARTON, Christopher Frank	III	612
JOHNSON, Henry	*III	508			
JOHNSON, Henry	III	663	KEARTON, Christopher Frank	V	351
JOHNSON, Herbert	III	880			
JOHNSON, Percival Norton	IV	192	KEAY, John	*III	567
JOHNSON, Robert	III	505	KEAY, John	V	343
JOHNSON, S W	I	4	KEBLE, Arthur	V	333
JOHNSON, S W	V	393	KEELING, Jack	I	741
JOHNSTON, George Lawson	*III	510	KEELING, John	I	739
JOHNSTON, George Lawson	IV	833	KEEN, Arthur	III	251
JOHNSTON, George Lawson	V	620	KEEN, Arthur	III	526
JOHNSTON, George Lawson	V	886	KEEN, Arthur	*III	570
JOHNSTON, John Lawson	I	290	KEEN, Arthur	IV	430
JOHNSTON, John Lawson	III	510	KEEN, Arthur	IV	900
JOHNSTON, John Lawson	*III	516	KEEN, Arthur	V	583
JOICEY, James	*III	521	KEEVIL, Ambrose	*III	575
JOICEY, James	IV	618	KEEVIL, C Percy	III	575
JOLLY, James Hornby	*III	523	KEITH, Kenneth	I	798
JOLLY, James Hornby	IV	570	KEITH, Kenneth	III	691
JONES, Alfred Lewis	*III	527	KEITH, Kenneth	IV	284
JONES, Alfred Lewis	IV	706	KELLAWAY, Frederick	III	451
JONES, Alfred Lewis	V	594	KEMNAL, James	*III	578
JONES, Frank Harding	III	530	KEMNAL, James	III	838
JONES, Frederick John	III	539	KEMP-Welch, John	IV	661
JONES, Henry Frank Harding	III	182	KEMSLEY, 1st Viscount – see BERRY, James Gomer		
JONES, Henry Frank Harding	*III	530			
JONES, Peter	III	769	KENILWORTH, Lord – see SIDDELEY, John Davenport		
JONES, Roderick	I	656			
JONES, Theodore Brooke	*III	536	KENNING, David	III	585
JONES, Walter Benton	III	252	KENNING, George	*III	582
JONES, Walter Benton	*III	539	KENRICK, Martin	III	587
JONES, Walter Benton	V	291	KENRICK, Timothy	I	644
JOSEPH, Maxwell	I	793	KENRICK, William Edmund	*III	586
JOSEPH, Maxwell	*III	543	KENT, Stephenson	III	256
JOWITT, F McCullock	III	554	KEVILLE, Errington	I	52
JOWITT, John	*III	553	KEYNES, John Maynard	I	13
JOYCE, James W	III	334	KEYNES, John Maynard	I	25
JUDGE, Edward Thomas	*III	555	KEYNES, John Maynard	I	438
JURGENS, Anton	V	604	KEYNES, John Maynard	I	805
JURGENS, Anton	V	692	KEYNES, John Maynard	I	863
KAPP, Gisbert	*III	558	KEYNES, John Maynard	*III	588
KAPP, Gisbert	IV	767	KEYNES, John Maynard	IV	35
KAPP, Jack	III	758	KEYNES, John Maynard	IV	73
KEARLEY, Hudson Ewbanke	I	166	KEYNES, John Maynard	IV	131
KEARLEY, Hudson Ewbanke	*III	561	KEYNES, John Maynard	IV	205
KEARLEY, Hudson Ewbanke	IV	481	KEYNES, John Maynard	IV	452

Name	Vol	Page	Name	Vol	Page
KEYSER, Assur	IV	299	KOCH, Willie	II	613
KILNER, Hew Ross	*III	591	KORDA, Alexander	*III	624
KILNER, Hew Ross	V	716	KORDA, Alexander	IV	201
KIMBER, Cecil	*III	594	KORDA, Alexander	V	886
KINDERSLEY, Robert			KREITMAN, Hyman	I	728
Molesworth	*III	596	KREUGER, Ivar	II	622
KINDERSLEY, Robert			KULLBERG, Victor	*III	628
Molesworth	IV	47	KULLBERG, Victor	IV	220
KINDERSLEY, Robert			KYLSANT, Lord – see		
Molesworth	IV	453	PHILIPPS, Owen Cosby		
KINDERSLEY, Robert			KYNOCH, George	I	635
Molesworth	IV	761	KYNOCH, George	*III	630
KING, Cecil	I	658	LACEY, Stephen	III	183
KITSON, James	II	312	LACY, Pierce	II	128
KITSON, James	*III	598	LACY, Pierce	II	352
KITSON, James	IV	540	LAING, Hugh	III	635
KITSON, James	IV	589	LAING, James	*III	633
KLABER, Augustus David	II	522	LAING, James	IV	682
KLABER, Augustus David	*III	602	LAING, John Maurice	III	640
KLEINWORT family	II	281	LAING, John William	I	600
KLEINWORT, Alexander			LAING, John William	III	162
Drake	*III	605	LAING, John William	*III	637
KLEINWORT, Cyril	III	606	LAING, John William	IV	257
KLEINWORT, Ernest			LAING, John William	IV	502
Greverus	*III	607	LAING, John William	V	456
KLEINWORT, Ernest			LAING, Samuel	V	65
Greverus	V	579	LAING, William Kirby	III	640
KNIGHT, Alfred Edward	*III	609	LAKER, Freddie	V	913
KNIGHT, Arthur William	III	565	LAMBURY, Lord – see		
KNIGHT, Arthur William	*III	612	LORD, Leonard Percy		
KNIGHT, Charles A	III	578	LANCASTER, Arthur Henry	*III	643
KNIGHT, Jasper	V	38	LANCASTER, John	III	189
KNOBEL, Edward Ball	III	42	LANCHESTER, Frederick W	IV	167
KNOBEL, Edward Ball	*III	616	LANCHESTER, Frederick W	IV	781
KNOLLYS, Edward George			LANCHESTER, Frederick W	IV	930
William Tyrwhitt	I	428	LANE, Allen	*III	645
KNOLLYS, Edward George			LANE, Frederick	*III	652
William Tyrwhitt	*III	618	LANE, Frederick	IV	947
KNOLLYS, Edward George			LANE, Frederick	V	43
William Tyrwhitt	IV	761	LANE, John	III	645
KNOLLYS, Edward George			LANE, Richard	III	646
William Tyrwhitt	V	717	LARKE, William	V	812
KNOTT, James	*III	621	LASCELLES, William Henry	*III	655
KNOTT, James	IV	979	LATHAM, Edward Bryan	*III	659
KNOTT, James	V	131	LATHAM, Thomas Paul	*III	662
KNOTT, James	V	365	LATHAM, Thomas Paul	V	470
KNOWLES, Thomas	III	43	LAVERTON, Abraham	*III	665
KOBLER, Fred	III	546	LAWRENCE, Charles Napier	III	668

Name	Vol	Page	Name	Vol	Page
LAWRENCE, Herbert Alexander	I	333	LEE, Joseph Cocksey	I	452
			LEE, Joseph Cocksey	I	544
LAWRENCE, Herbert Alexander	II	31	LEE, Joseph Cocksey	*III	703
			LEE, Joseph Cocksey	III	715
LAWRENCE, Herbert Alexander	III	201	LEE, Joseph Cocksey	V	314
			LEE, Lennox Bertram	III	703
LAWRENCE, Herbert Alexander	III	486	LEE, Lennox Bertram	*III	715
			LEE, R M	III	722
LAWRENCE, Herbert Alexander	*III	667	LEECH,	II	399
			LEEK, James	II	123
LAWRENCE, Herbert Alexander	IV	66	LEEK, James	V	57
LAWRENCE, Joseph	*III	674	LEES, William Clare	*III	726
LAWRENCE, Jospeh	IV	753	LEES, William Clare	V	380
LAWSON, Edward Levy	II	652	LEES, William Clare	V	422
LAWSON, Edward Levy	*III	679	LEESE, William Hargreaves	*III	732
LAWSON, Edward Levy	IV	910	LEESE, William Hargreaves	IV	615
LAWSON, Edward Levy	V	645	LEGGE, William Heneage	*III	734
LAWSON, Henry John	II	227	LEMON, E J	V	265
LAWSON, Henry John	II	433	LEO, H	I	627
LAWSON, Henry John	III	683	LEPPER family	III	433
LAWSON, Henry John	*III	685	LEPPOC, H J	I	627
LAWSON, Henry John	IV	109	LESLIE, Andrew	I	481
LAWSON, Henry John	IV	639	LESLIE, Andrew	*III	737
LAWSON, Henry John	IV	929	LETTS, Charles John	*III	740
LAWSON, Henry John	V	165	LETTS, Charles John	IV	101
LAWSON, Samuel	II	312	LETTS, William Malesbury	*III	744
LAYBORN, Thomas Alec Edwin	*III	687	LEVER, Hardman	II	513
			LEVER, William Hesketh	I	100
LAYTON, Walter	II	568	LEVER, William Hesketh	I	778
LAZELL, Henry George Leslie	II	241	LEVER, William Hesketh	I	781
			LEVER, William Hesketh	II	252
LAZELL, Henry George Leslie	III	236	LEVER, William Hesketh	II	588
			LEVER, William Hesketh	III	52
LAZELL, Henry George Leslie	*III	690	LEVER, William Hesketh	III	192
			LEVER, William Hesketh	*III	745
LEACH, C H	III	182	LEVER, William Hesketh	V	595
LEAF, Walter	*III	694	LEVER, William Hesketh	V	606
LEAF, Walter	V	78	LEVER, William Hesketh	V	686
LEATHART, James	*III	698	LEVER, William Hesketh	V	691
LEATHART, James	IV	805	LEVERHULME, 1st Viscount – see LEVER, William Hesketh		
LEBUS, Harris	*III	700	LEVINSTEIN, Herbert	I	839
LEBUS, Hermann Andrew	*III	701	LEVENSTEIN, Ivan	*III	752
LEBUS, Solomon	III	700	LEVY, Joseph	III	679
LEE, H W	III	703	LEWIS, Alfred Edward	III	757
LEE, Harold	III	703	LEWIS, David	*III	754
LEE, Henry	I	452	LEWIS, David	IV	147
LEE, Henry	*III	703	LEWIS, David	V	792
LEE, Joseph Cocksey	I	9	LEWIS, Edward Roberts	*III	757

Name	Vol	Page	Name	Vol	Page
LEWIS, Frederick William	I	618	LIVESEY, Fernando Harry		
LEWIS, Frederick William	II	447	Whitehead	III	821
LEWIS, Frederick William	II	652	LIVESEY, George Thomas	II	185
LEWIS, Frederick William	*III	761	LIVESEY, George Thomas	III	531
LEWIS, Frederick William	IV	394	LIVESEY, George Thomas	*III	813
LEWIS, H	II	624	LIVESEY, George Thomas	IV	906
LEWIS, John	*III	764	LIVESEY, George Thomas	V	872
LEWIS, John Spedan	III	765	LIVESEY, James	*III	819
LEWIS, John Spedan	*III	766	LIVESEY, William	III	308
LEWIS, William Thomas	III	480	LLEWELLYN, David Richard	*III	822
LEWIS, William Thomas	*III	773	LLEWELLYN, David Richard	IV	272
LEWIS, William Thomas	IV	443	LLEWELLYN, Rees	III	822
LEWIS, William Thomas	V	476	LLOYD, Edward	*III	827
LEWIS, William Thomas	V	487	LLOYD, Edward	III	829
LEYLAND, Frederick	II	249	LLOYD, Frank	I	303
LIBERTY, Arthur Lasenby	*III	778	LLOYD, Frank	*III	829
LIBERTY, Arthur Lasenby	V	336	LLOYD, Frank	IV	666
LIBERTY, Arthur Lasenby	V	661	LLOYD, Harry	I	315
LIDBURY, Charles	*III	783	LLOYD, Howard	*III	831
LIDBURY, Charles	V	560	LLOYD, Howard	IV	676
LIDDERDALE, William	*III	786	LLOYD, Robert Donald	III	830
LIGGETT, Lewis K	I	376	LLOYD, Samuel	III	831
LINDSAY, Coutts	II	44	LOBNITZ, Frederick	IV	587
LINDSAY, Coutts	II	394	LOCH, James	V	205
LINDSAY, David Alexander			LOCKWOOD, Joseph Flawith	*III	834
Edward	*III	790	LOCOCK, Guy Harold	*III	837
LING, Reuben Herbert	*III	795	LOCOCK, Guy Harold	IV	466
LINGS, Scott	II	107	LOCOCK, Guy Harold	IV	919
LINGS, Scott	III	363	LOEBL, Henry	I	738
LIPMAN, Michael Isaac	*III	797	LOEWENSTEIN, Alfred	II	211
LIPTON, Thomas Johnstone	I	224	LONDONDERRY, Lord	III	403
LIPTON, Thomas Johnstone	II	95	LONG, Albert de Lande	II	136
LIPTON, Thomas Johnstone	*III	799	LONG, Albert de Lande	II	563
LIPTON, Thomas Johnstone	IV	137	LONG, Albert de Lande	V	48
LIPTON, Thomas Johnstone	IV	557	LONGLEY, Basil	III	842
LIPTON, Thomas Johnstone	V	15	LONGLEY, Norman	*III	841
LIPTON, Thomas Johnstone	V	606	LONGMAN, Charles James	*III	845
LISTER, Charles Percy	*III	803	LONGRIDGE, Michael	II	597
LISTER, Robert Ashton	III	803	LONGRIDGE, Robert Bewick	*III	848
LISTER, Samuel Cunliffe	III	300	LONGSDON, Robert	I	311
LISTER, Samuel Cunliffe	III	418	LORD, Cyril	*III	852
LISTER, Samuel Cunliffe	*III	806	LORD, Leonard Percy	II	290
LISTER, Samuel Cunliffe	V	213	LORD, Leonard Percy	III	66
LITHGOW, James	II	196	LORD, Leonard Percy	*III	856
LITHGOW, James	IV	216	LORD, Leonard Percy	IV	336
LITHGOW, James	IV	705	LORD, Leonard Percy	V	498
LITTLER brothers	V	359	LOVELL, John Carey	III	576
LITTLETON, Henry	*III	809	LOWNDES, Noble Frank	*III	860

Name	Vol	Page	Name	Vol	Page
LOWOOD, John Grayson	*III	865	MACKAY, James Lyle	III	11
LOWSON, Denys	II	31	MACKAY, James Lyle	III	240
LOYD, Edward	III	869	MACKAY, James Lyle	*IV	27
LOYD, Samuel Jones	*III	868	MACKAY, James Lyle	IV	242
LUBBOCK, Cecil	IV	432	MACKAY, James Lyle	IV	673
LUBBOCK, Edgar	II	491	MACKAY, James Lyle	IV	755
LUBBOCK, Edgar	II	661	MACKAY, James Lyle	IV	958
LUBBOCK, John	III	696	MACKAY, James Lyle	V	80
LUBBOCK, John	*III	873	MACKENNA, F	II	625
LUBBOCK, John	IV	170	MACKIE, James	*IV	38
LUBBOCK, John	V	24	MACKIE, Thomas	IV	38
LUBBOCK, John	V	558	MACKINNON, William	II	286
LUCAS, Harry	III	877	MACKINNON, William	IV	28
LUCAS, Joseph	III	583	MACKINTOSH, Harold Vincent	*IV	41
LUCAS, Joseph	*III	877			
LUCAS, Joseph	V	666	MACKINTOSH, Harold Vincent	IV	54
LUGARD, Frederick	II	588			
LUKE, Lord – see JOHNSTON, George Lawson			MACKINTOSH, Harold Vincent	IV	741
LUM, John	V	367	MACKINTOSH, John	IV	41
LUTYENS, Edwin Landseer	*III	879	MACKINTOSH, John	*IV	49
LUTYENS, Edwin Landseer	IV	36	MACLEAN, Alexander	III	690
LUTYENS, Edwin Landseer	IV	415	MACMILLAN, Frederick Orridge	II	70
LUTYENS, Edwin Landseer	IV	460			
LUTYENS, Edwin Landseer	V	87	MACMILLAN, Frederick Orridge	III	846
LYLE, Charles Ernest Leonard	*III	884			
LYLE, Charles Ernest Leonard	V	442	MACMILLAN, Frederick Orridge	*IV	76
LYONS, Joseph Nathaniel	II	579			
LYONS, Joseph Nathaniel	*III	888	MACMILLAN, Frederick Orridge	V	246
LYONS, Joseph Nathaniel	V	619	MACPHERSON, A S	II	311
LYONS, William	*III	890	MADDERS, J M	III	293
LYSAGHT, Daniel Conner	III	900	MADGEN, W L	II	474
LYSAGHT, John	*III	895	MAGGS, Joseph Herbert	I	532
LYSAGHT, John	III	899	MAGGS, Joseph Herbert	*IV	79
LYSAGHT, William Royse	*III	899	MAGGS, Leonard	IV	79
LYSTER, A G	I	196	MAGGS, Leonard	*IV	81
LYTTELTON, Oliver	*III	904	MALCOLM, George William	*IV	82
LYTTELTON, Oliver	IV	751	MALLABY-DEELEY, Harry C	*IV	84
MACARA, Charles Wright	II	108	MALLABY-DEELEY, Harry C	IV	915
MACARA, Charles Wright	III	364	MALLINSON, Stuart Sidney	*IV	88
MACARA, Charles Wright	*IV	7	MALLINSON, William James	II	576
MACARA, Charles Wright	IV	1,006	MALLINSON, William James	IV	88
MACARA, Charles Wright	V	449	MALLINSON, William James	*IV	90
MACHONOCHIE, Archibald W	I	84	MANBRÉ Alexandre	I	296
MACILWAINE, John H	V	857	MANBY, Charles	II	413
MACINTOSH, Charles	IV	359	MANDER, Charles	I	448
MACIVER, Charles	I	870	MANFIELD, James	IV	97
MACKAY, James Lyle	I	48	MANFIELD, Moses Philip	*IV	94
MACKAY, James Lyle	I	863			

Name	Vol	Page	Name	Vol	Page
MANN, Gerard Noel Cornwallis	*IV	101	MARKS, Simon	IV	279
			MARKS, Simon	V	16
MANN, Gerard Noel Cornwallis	V	809	MARKS, Simon	V	142
MANN, Reginald William	*IV	104	MARQUIS, Frederick James	III	333
MANN, Reginald William	V	868	MARQUIS, Frederick James	III	756
MANNABERG, Maximilian	II	563	MARQUIS, Frederick James	III	909
MANNABERG, Maximilian	III	252	MARQUIS, Frederick James	*IV	146
MANNABERG, Maximilian	III	539	MARQUIS, Frederick James	IV	473
MANNERS family	II	661	MARQUIS, Frederick James	IV	826
MANSFIELD, Walter & George	III	327	MARR, James	III	635
			MARR, James	*IV	151
MANTON, Lord – see WATSON, Joseph			MARR, James	V	504
			MARRIOTT, Thomas Geoffrey	*IV	154
MANVILLE, Edward	II	24	MARS, Forrest	III	71
MANVILLE, Edward	II	133	MARSHALL, Arthur	III	388
MANVILLE, Edward	III	759	MARSHALL, Francis Carr	I	481
MANVILLE, Edward	*IV	108	MARSHALL, Francis Carr	*IV	158
MANVILLE, Edward	IV	466	MARSHALL, Stewart Ray	V	102
MANVILLE, Edward	IV	755	MARSLAND, Henry	III	313
MANVILLE, Edward	IV	918	MARTI, Otto	I	88
MANVILLE, Edward	IV	925	MARTIN, Cecil	*IV	162
MANVILLE, Edward	V	812	MARTIN, Edward Pritchard	V	487
MANZI-FÉ, George	III	450	MARTIN, Edward Pritchard	V	491
MANZI-FÉ, George	III	672	MARTIN, James	*IV	164
MANZI-FÉ, George	IV	466	MARTIN, Kingsley	II	569
MAPPIN, Frederick Thorpe	*IV	115	MARTIN, Lionel	V	498
MAPPIN, Frederick Thorpe	V	896	MARTIN, Percy	II	50
MAPPIN, John Newton	IV	115	MARTIN, Percy	IV	112
MARCONI, Guglielmo	II	272	MARTIN, Percy	*IV	167
MARCONI, Guglielmo	III	447	MARTIN, Percy	IV	756
MARCONI, Guglielmo	IV	612	MARTIN, Percy	IV	916
MARCONI, Guglielmo	IV	767	MARTIN, Percy	IV	926
MARCROFT, William	*IV	120	MARTIN, Percy	V	431
MARGARY, Peter	III	424	MARTIN, Richard Biddulph	*IV	169
MARKHAM, Charles Paxton	IV	60	MARTIN, Richard Biddulph	V	558
MARKHAM, Charles Paxton	*IV	123	MARTINEAU, David	V	441
MARKHAM, Charles Paxton	IV	215	MARTYN, A W	II	162
MARKLAND, Stanley	*IV	128	MARWICK, James	IV	603
MARKLAND, Stanley	V	257	MASEFIELD, Peter Gordon	II	78
MARKLAND, Stanley	V	350	MASEFIELD, Peter Gordon	II	145
MARKS, Geoffrey	III	589	MASEFIELD, Peter Gordon	*IV	171
MARKS, Geoffrey	*IV	130	MASEFIELD, Peter Gordon	IV	233
MARKS, Harry Hananel	*IV	133	MASHAM, Lord – see LISTER, Samuel Cunliffe		
MARKS, Michael	*IV	135			
MARKS, Michael	V	147	MASON, Hugh	*IV	176
MARKS, Simon	III	71	MASON, Josiah	I	646
MARKS, Simon	IV	136	MASON, Josiah	*IV	179
MARKS, Simon	*IV	138	MASTERMAN, J	II	624

Name	Vol	Page	Name	Vol	Page
MATHER, William	I	614	McGOWAN, Harry Duncan	IV	68
MATHER, William	III	716	McGOWAN, Harry Duncan	IV	73
MATHER, William	*IV	182	McGOWAN, Harry Duncan	IV	273
MATHER, William	V	550	McGOWAN, Harry Duncan	IV	281
MATHESON, Hugh Mackay	*IV	187	McGOWAN, Harry Duncan	IV	404
MATHESON, Hugh Mackay	IV	891	McGOWAN, Harry Duncan	V	261
MATHESON, James	IV	187	McGOWAN, Harry Duncan	V	785
MATHIESON, John	II	620	McINSTREY, Archibald	I	172
MATTHEY, George	*IV	192	McIVER, Thomas	III	396
MATTINSON, Miles	II	250	McKENNA, Reginald	I	863
MATTISON, Francis Charles	*IV	194	McKENNA, Reginald	I	867
MAUDSLAY, Reginald Walter	II	433	McKENNA, Reginald	II	130
MAUDSLAY, Reginald Walter	II	531	McKENNA, Reginald	III	201
MAUDSLAY, Reginald Walter	*IV	196	McKENNA, Reginald	III	296
MAUDSLAY, Reginald Walter	V	797	McKENNA, Reginald	III	485
MAXIM, Hiram	I	62	McKENNA, Reginald	III	670
MAXIM, Hiram	I	80	McKENNA, Reginald	III	880
MAXIM, Hiram	V	624	McKENNA, Reginald	*IV	33
MAXWELL, Arthur	III	670	McKENNA, Reginald	IV	452
MAXWELL, James Clerk	II	15	McKENNA, Reginald	IV	854
MAXWELL, John	*IV	199	McKENNA, Reginald	V	73
MAXWELL, John	IV	494	McKENNA, Reginald	V	138
MAY, Francis	I	488	McKENNA, Reginald	V	261
MAY, George Ernest	II	198	McKENNA, Reginald	V	528
MAY, George Ernest	III	487	McLAREN, Charles Benjamin Bright	I	627
MAY, George Ernest	IV	34	McLAREN, Charles Benjamin Bright	II	277
MAY, George Ernest	*IV	203	McLAREN, Charles Benjamin Bright	II	284
MAY, George Oliver	V	677	McLAREN, Charles Benjamin Bright	*IV	57
MAYER, Carl	V	543	McLAREN, Charles Benjamin Bright	IV	126
MAYHEW, Basil Edgar	I	208	McLAREN, Charles Benjamin Bright	IV	488
MAYHEW, Basil Edgar	I	400	McLAREN, Charles Benjamin Bright	IV	785
MAYHEW, Basil Edgar	*IV	207	McLAREN, Charles Benjamin Bright	V	106
McALPINE, Alfred David	*IV	1	McLAREN, Charles Melville	IV	64
McALPINE, Robert	IV	1	McLAREN, Henry Duncan	*IV	62
McALPINE, Thomas Malcolm	IV	1	McLAREN, Henry Duncan	IV	216
McALPINE, Thomas Malcolm	*IV	3	McLEAN, Robert	I	675
McCALL, A K	II	457	McLEAN, Robert	III	592
McCRINDLE, John Ronald	*IV	15	McLEAN, Robert	*IV	65
McCRINDLE, John Ronald	V	882	McLELLAN, William	II	534
McCULLOCH, N G	III	722	McLELLAN, William	III	1
McDOUGALL, Arthur	V	175	McLELLAN, William	IV	222
McFADZEAN, William Hunter	*IV	19			
McFADZEAN, William Hunter	IV	921			
McGOWAN, Harry Duncan	I	706			
McGOWAN, Harry Duncan	II	376			
McGOWAN, Harry Duncan	III	24			
McGOWAN, Harry Duncan	*IV	21			

Name	Vol	Page	Name	Vol	Page
McLELLAN, William	IV	907	MICKLEM, Robert	V	716
McLINTOCK, Thomas	II	426	MILES, Frederick George	IV	165
McLINTOCK, William	II	488	MILES, Frederick George	IV	173
McLINTOCK, William	*IV	68	MILES, Frederick George	*IV	230
McLINTOCK, William	IV	281	MILES, Frederick George	IV	513
McLINTOCK, William	IV	456	MILES, Frederick George	V	375
McLINTOCK, William	IV	674	MILFORD, Humphrey		
McLINTOCK, William	IV	740	Sumner	*IV	235
McLINTOCK, William	IV	854	MILFORD, Lord – see		
McLINTOCK, William	V	261	PHILIPPS, Laurence Richard		
McMILLAN, William	III	852	MILLBANK, Lord – see		
McTAGGART, Andrew	I	126	DUVEEN, Joseph		
MELCHETT, 1st Lord – see			MILLER, H Eric	IV	687
MOND, Alfred Moritz			MILLER, O B	III	770
MELCHETT, 2nd Lord – see			MILLER, Thomas	III	178
MOND, Henry Ludwig			MILLS, Algernon	III	670
MELCHETT, 3rd Lord – see			MILLS, Bertram Wagstaff	I	536
MOND, Julian Edward Alfred			MILLS, Bertram Wagstaff	*IV	237
MENDL, Sigismund	III	759	MILLS, Charles Henry	III	668
MENDL, Sigismund	IV	109	MILLS, Percy	II	226
MENELAUS, William	I	687	MILLS, Percy	II	239
MENELAUS, William	III	480	MILNE, James	*IV	240
MENELAUS, William	*IV	211	MILNE, James	IV	254
MENELAUS, William	IV	898	MILNE-WATSON, David	III	814
MENELAUS, William	V	818	MILNE-WATSON, David	IV	208
MENSFORTH, Holberry	III	201	MILNE-WATSON, David	*IV	247
MENSFORTH, Holberry	*IV	214	MILNE-WATSON, David	V	873
MENSFORTH, Holberry	IV	417	MILNE-WATSON, Michael	IV	250
MENSFORTH, Holberry	IV	784	MILNER, Lord	II	359
MERCER, Thomas	III	628	MILNER, Lord	II	504
MERCER, Thomas	*IV	219	MILNER, Lord	III	198
MERRETT, Herbert Henry	III	823	MILWARD, Anthony Horace	*IV	250
MERTHYR, Lord, – see			MISSENDEN, Eustace James	II	268
LEWIS, William Thomas			MISSENDEN, Eustace James	*IV	253
MERTON family	II	650	MITCHELL, Charles	II	112
MERTON, Wilhelm	II	480	MITCHELL, Charles	III	737
MERZ, Charles Hesterman	II	534	MITCHELL, Godfrey Way	III	639
MERZ, Charles Hesterman	III	1	MITCHELL, Godfrey Way	*IV	256
MERZ, Charles Hesterman	*IV	221	MITCHELL, Godfrey Way	V	456
MERZ, Charles Hesterman	IV	894	MITCHELL, H J	IV	281
MERZ, Charles Hesterman	IV	907	MITCHELL, Henry	*IV	262
METHUEN, Algernon			MITCHELL, J H	III	230
Methuen Marshall	*IV	227	MITCHELL, John Thomas		
MEYER, Carl	IV	947	Whitehead	*IV	265
MICHAELS, John Gallaher	II	462	MOND, Alfred Moritz	I	618
MICHELHAM, Lord – see			MOND, Alfred Moritz	I	804
STERN, Herbert			MOND, Alfred Moritz	II	376
MICKLEM, Robert	II	36	MOND, Alfred Moritz	II	481
MICKLEM, Robert	III	592	MOND, Alfred Moritz	III	281

Name	Vol	Page	Name	Vol	Page
MOND, Alfred Moritz	III	557	MORRELL, J B	IV	966
MOND, Alfred Moritz	III	823	MORRIS, Herbert	I	199
MOND, Alfred Moritz	IV	23	MORRIS, Herbert	*IV	325
MOND, Alfred Moritz	*IV	270	MORRIS, John	*IV	328
MOND, Alfred Moritz	IV	404	MORRIS, John	IV	344
MOND, Alfred Moritz	IV	599	MORRIS, Mowbray	V	645
MOND, Alfred Moritz	IV	1,007	MORRIS, William	III	780
MOND, Alfred Moritz	V	428	MORRIS, William	*IV	331
MOND, Alfred Moritz	V	812	MORRIS, William	IV	349
MOND, Henry Ludwig	IV	23	MORRIS, William	V	84
MOND, Henry Ludwig	IV	73	MORRIS, William	V	661
MOND, Henry Ludwig	IV	271	MORRIS, William Richard	I	868
MOND, Henry Ludwig	*IV	280	MORRIS, William Richard	II	255
MOND, Julian Edward Alfred	*IV	283	MORRIS, William Richard	II	289
MOND, Ludwig	I	485	MORRIS, William Richard	II	608
MOND, Ludwig	I	668	MORRIS, William Richard	III	65
MOND, Ludwig	I	842	MORRIS, William Richard	III	582
MOND, Ludwig	II	672	MORRIS, William Richard	III	594
MOND, Ludwig	IV	270	MORRIS, William Richard	III	856
MOND, Ludwig	*IV	287	MORRIS, William Richard	*IV	334
MOND, Ludwig	V	328	MORRIS, William Richard	IV	407
MOND, Robert Ludwig	I	424	MORRIS, William Richard	IV	532
MOND, Robert Ludwig	IV	271	MORRIS, William Richard	V	498
MOND, Robert Ludwig	*IV	296	MORRIS, William Richard	V	889
MONTAGU, Charles	V	427	MORRISON, Charles	II	252
MONTAGU, Samuel	*IV	298	MORRISON, Charles	IV	328
MOON, Richard	II	360	MORRISON, Charles	*IV	341
MOON, Richard	*IV	301	MORSON, Thomas	*IV	346
MOORE, Mary	V	921	MORSON, Thomas	V	764
MOORE-BRABAZON, J T C	V	126	MORTIMER, William Egerton	*IV	348
MOORES, John	*IV	306	MORTON, Charles	I	446
MORDEN, Grant	II	34	MORTON, James	*IV	349
MOREING, Charles Algernon	II	25	MOSS, Harry Neville	*IV	352
MOREING, Charles Algernon	*IV	311	MOSS, Horace Edward	V	356
MOREING, Charles Algernon	IV	481	MOSS, William Miles	II	402
MORETON, Stanley	V	919	MOTT, Basil	II	535
MORGAN family	III	36	MOTT, Basil	*IV	355
MORGAN, David	*IV	315	MOUILLOT, Fred	I	37
MORGAN, J Pierpont	II	444	MOULTON, Stephen	*IV	359
MORGAN, J Pierpont	II	649	MOULTON, Stephen	V	240
MORGAN, J Pierpoint	II	655	MOUNTAIN, Edward Mortimer	I	810
MORGAN, Octavious V	III	33	MOUNTAIN, Edward Mortimer	II	92
MORLEY, Eric	III	551	MOUNTAIN, Edward Mortimer	III	139
MORLEY, Francis	II	471	MOUNTAIN, Edward Mortimer	*IV	361
MORLEY, Samuel	III	711			
MORLEY, Samuel	*IV	319			
MORLEY, Samuel	IV	382			
MORLEY, Samuel	V	829			
MORPHY, Donal William	*IV	324			

Name	Vol	Page	Name	Vol	Page
MOYSES, H J S	II	122	NELSON, Amos	*IV	413
MUDIE, Charles Edward	*IV	368	NELSON, George Horatio	IV	217
MUIR, Rowland	V	38	NELSON, George Horatio	*IV	417
MUIRHEAD, Alexander	*IV	371	NELSON, George Horatio	IV	747
MULHOLLAND, John	*IV	374	NELSON, George Horatio	IV	784
MULHOLLAND, John	IV	396	NELSON, George Horatio	V	507
MULLARD, Stanley Robert	II	298	NELSON, Henry George	IV	421
MULLARD, Stanley Robert	*IV	378	NELSON, Henry George	*IV	423
MÜLLER, Hugo	II	55	NETTLEFOLD, John S	I	634
MUNDELLA, Anthony John	II	2	NETTLEFOLD, John S	I	643
MUNDELLA, Anthony John	IV	118	NETTLEFOLD, Joseph		
MUNDELLA, Anthony John	*IV	380	Henry	*IV	428
MUNTZ, Alan	V	911	NEVILE, Sydney Oswald	*IV	431
MUNTZ, Gerard	III	251	NEWALL, Robert Stirling	*IV	433
MURPHY, Frank	*IV	385	NEWALL, Robert Stirling	V	159
MURPHY, Frank	IV	987	NEWMAN, F D O'Brien	II	122
MURPHY, William Martin	*IV	389	NEWMARCH, William	I	628
MURRANT, Ernest Henry	*IV	393	NEWMARK, Augustus S	III	603
MURRANT, Ernest Henry	V	914	NEWNES, George	III	48
MURRAY, George Evelyn			NEWNES, George	*IV	436
Pemberton	II	572	NEWNES, George	IV	575
MURRAY, George Evelyn			NEWNES, George	IV	592
Pemberton	*IV	396	NEWNES, George	IV	911
MURRAY, John	III	846	NEWNES, George	V	244
MURRAY, SB	III	277	NICHOLSON, J G	III	723
MURRAY, Samuel	III	293	NICHOLSON, John	I	52
MUSGRAVE, John	*IV	400	NICKALLS, Thomas	*IV	439
MUSKER, John	II	176	NICKOLS, Harold	V	691
MUSKER, John	V	110	NIEMEYER, Otto	IV	70
MUSKER, John	V	187	NIMMO, Adam	V	823
MUSPRATT, James	II	471	NIVEN, John B	V	540
MUSPRATT, Max	IV	23	NIVISON, Robert	II	653
MUSPRATT, Max	*IV	403	NIXON, John	*IV	441
MUSPRATT, Max	IV	918	NIXON, W E	III	134
MYLCHREEST, T G	II	312	NOBEL	II	35
NAGELMACKERS, Georges	II	7	NOBLE, Andrew	I	71
NAPIER, Montague Stanley	II	227	NOBLE, Andrew	II	221
NAPIER, Montague Stanley	*IV	406	NOBLE, Andrew	II	573
NAPIER, Montague Stanley	IV	930	NOBLE, Andrew	*IV	444
NAPIER, Montague Stanley	IV	974	NOBLE, Herbert	III	74
NAPIER, Montague Stanley	V	140	NORMAN, Duncan	IV	506
NAPIER, Montague Stanley	V	722	NORMAN, Montagu Collet	I	14
NAPIER, Robert	III	398	NORMAN, Montagu Collet	I	164
NASH, Philip	III	252	NORMAN, Montagu Collet	I	382
NASMYTH, James	II	499	NORMAN, Montagu Collet	I	618
NATHAN, Alex	III	491	NORMAN, Montagu Collet	I	863
NAYLOR, J W	II	311	NORMAN, Montagu Collet	II	196
NEALE, Edward Vansittart	*IV	409	NORMAN, Montagu Collet	II	418
NEELE, G P	II	66	NORMAN, Montagu Collet	II	481

Name	Vol	Page	Name	Vol	Page
NORMAN, Montagu Collet	II	605	OPPENHEIMER, Ernest	II	504
NORMAN, Montagu Collet	II	621	OSTRER, Isidore	IV	199
NORMAN, Montagu Collet	III	112	OSTRER, Isidore	*IV	492
NORMAN, Montagu Collet	III	670	OSTRER, Isidore	IV	833
NORMAN, Montagu Collet	III	732	OSTRER, Mark	V	886
NORMAN, Montagu Collet	IV	35	OTTLEY, Charles	II	572
NORMAN, Montagu Collet	*IV	447	OURY, Libert	III	154
NORMAN, Montagu Collet	IV	531	OVERSTONE, Lord – see		
NORMAN, Montagu Collet	IV	560	LOYD, Samuel Jones		
NORMAN, Montagu Collet	IV	719	OWEN, Alfred George Beech	*IV	497
NORMAN, Montagu Collet	V	104	OWEN, Leonard	III	272
NORMAN, Montagu Collet	V	461	OWEN, Owen	III	765
NORMAN, Montagu Collet	V	528	OWEN, Owen	*IV	504
NORMAN, Montagu Collet	V	813	OWEN, Robert	II	1
NORMAN, Montagu Collet	V	908	OWEN, Robert	IV	866
NORMAN, Nigel	V	911	OWEN, William Barry	I	672
NORTH, Jonathan	*IV	458	OWEN, William Barry	III	820
NORTH, John Dudley	*IV	461	OWEN, William Barry	*IV	507
NORTHCLIFFE, 1st Viscount – see			PAGE, Frederick Handley	III	13
HARMSWORTH, Alfred			PAGE, Frederick Handley	III	451
Charles W			PAGE, Frederick Handley	IV	417
NORTHUMBERLAND, 1st Duke			PAGE, Frederick Handley	*IV	510
of – see PERCY, Alan Ian			PAGE, Frederick Handley	V	880
NORTON-GRIFFITHS – see			PAGET, W B	III	318
GRIFFITHS, John Norton			PALMER, Charles Mark	I	409
NOVELLO, Alfred	III	809	PALMER, Charles Mark	IV	158
NUFFIELD, Viscount – see			PALMER, Charles Mark	*IV	515
MORRIS, William Richard			PALMER, Charles Mark	IV	797
NUGENT, Roland Thomas	III	838	PALMER, Charles Mark	V	412
NUGENT, Roland Thomas	*IV	465	PALMER, George	*IV	521
NUNBURNHOLME, Lord –			PAM, Albert Samuel	II	667
see WILSON, Charles Henry			PAM, Albert Samuel	*IV	526
O'GORMAN, Mervyn	II	49	PAM, Albert Samuel	V	527
O'HAGAN, Henry Osborne	I	392	PANMURE-GORDON – see		
O'HAGAN, Henry Osborne	II	249	GORDON, Harry Panmure		
O'HAGAN, Henry Osborne	II	612	PARKER, Peter	IV	724
O'HAGAN, Henry Osborne	III	562	PARKES, Charles Henry	III	19
O'HAGAN, Henry Osborne	IV	109	PARKINSON, Albert Lindsay	*IV	535
O'HAGAN, Henry Osborne	*IV	479	PARNELL, Val	III	855
O'HAGAN, Henry Osborne	IV	587	PARNELL, Val	V	359
O'HAGAN, Henry Osborne	IV	663	PARSONS, Charles Algernon	I	482
OAKLEY, Henry	II	620	PARSONS, Charles Algernon	I	683
OAKLEY, Henry	*IV	470	PARSONS, Charles Algernon	II	537
OATES, Francis	I	361	PARSONS, Charles Algernon	III	279
ODEY, George William	*IV	473	PARSONS, Charles Algernon	III	459
OKEY, W H	I	228	PARSONS, Charles Algernon	IV	221
OLDROYD, Mark	*IV	484	PARSONS, Charles Algernon	*IV	539
OLIVER, Frederick Scott	*IV	488	PARSONS, Charles Algernon	IV	894
OPPENHEIMER family	II	281	PARSONS, Charles Algernon	V	126

Name	Vol	Page	Name	Vol	Page
PARSONS, Charles Algernon	V	431	PEARSON, Weetman		
PARSONS, Jim	IV	724	Dickinson	III	305
PASOLD, Eric Walter	*IV	549	PEARSON, Weetman		
PATERSON, John Craig	*IV	554	Dickinson	III	448
PATHÉ, Charles	IV	195	PEARSON, Weetman		
PATON, Alexander Allan	*IV	556	Dickinson	III	463
PATON, Angus	II	534	PEARSON, Weetman		
PATTINSON, Hugh Lee	IV	434	Dickinson	III	484
PAULING, George	II	351	PEARSON, Weetman		
PAULING, George	II	669	Dickinson	IV	438
PAYTON, Ernest L	II	289	PEARSON, Weetman		
PEACE, William	III	189	Dickinson	IV	481
PEACOCK, Edward Robert	I	164	PEARSON, Weetman		
PEACOCK, Edward Robert	III	672	Dickinson	*IV	582
PEACOCK, Edward Robert	IV	451	PEARSON, Weetman		
PEACOCK, Edward Robert	IV	489	Dickinson	IV	723
PEACOCK, Edward Robert	*IV	559	PEARSON, Weetman		
PEACOCK, Edward Robert	V	459	Dickinson	IV	863
PEACOCK, John Atkins	*IV	567	PEARSON, Weetman		
PEACOCK, Kenneth Swift	I	466	Dickinson	V	45
PEACOCK, Kenneth Swift	III	524	PEASE, John William		
PEACOCK, Kenneth Swift	*IV	570	Beaumont	*IV	594
PEAKE, H	V	910	PEASE, Joseph Albert	I	257
PEARS, Andrew	*IV	573	PEASE, Joseph Albert	II	3
PEARS, Francis	I	189	PEASE, Joseph Albert	*IV	597
PEARSON, Clive	II	688	PEASE, Joseph Albert	IV	603
PEARSON, Cyril Arthur	III	50	PEAT, William Barclay	*IV	602
PEARSON, Cyril Arthur	III	513	PEAT, William Barclay	V	813
PEARSON, Cyril Arthur	IV	52	PEDDIE, James Mortimer	*IV	605
PEARSON, Cyril Arthur	IV	437	PEEBLES, Bruce	III	557
PEARSON, Cyril Arthur	*IV	575	PEECH, Alan J	III	541
PEARSON, Cyril Arthur	IV	911	PEECH, Alan J	III	557
PEARSON, Cyril Arthur	V	244	PEECH, Alan J	V	291
PEARSON, Edward	III	484	PEECH, Albert	III	539
PEARSON, James Reginald	I	199	PEECH, William	V	294
PEARSON, James Reginald	*IV	578	PEEK, Henry W	II	176
PEARSON, M H	I	285	PEEK, James	I	595
PEARSON, Weetman			PEMBERTON-BILLING,		
Dickinson	I	18	Noel	V	91
PEARSON, Weetman			PENDER, John	II	59
Dickinson	I	524	PENDER, John	*IV	609
PEARSON, Weetman			PENNANT, Richard	II	146
Dickinson	I	827	PENNEY, William	III	270
PEARSON, Weetman			PENRHYN, Lord – see		
Dickinson	II	652	DOUGLAS-PENNANT,		
PEARSON, Weetman			George Sholto G.		
Dickinson	II	667	PEPPIATT, Leslie Ernest	*IV	614
PEARSON, Weetman			PERCY, Alan Ian	*IV	616
Dickinson	III	294	PERKIN, William Henry	*IV	621

Name	Vol	Page	Name	Vol	Page
PERKINS, Francis Arthur	IV	346	PHILIPPS, Owen Cosby	V	857
PERKINS, Francis Arthur	*IV	623	PHILLIPS, Charles J	II	547
PERKS, Robert William	IV	486	PHILLIPS, John Spencer	III	832
PERKS, Robert William	*IV	628	PHILLIPS, John Spencer	*IV	676
PERKS, Robert William	V	778	PHORSON, Peter	V	504
PERRIN, Michael Willcox	*IV	633	PICK, Frank	II	273
PERRY, John	I	203	PICK, Frank	II	544
PERRY, Percival Lee			PICK, Frank	*IV	678
Dewhurst	I	283	PICK, Frank	V	274
PERRY, Percival Lee			PICKERING, W B	III	7
Dewhurst	III	167	PICKERSGILL, William	*IV	682
PERRY, Percival Lee			PICKERSGILL, William	IV	773
Dewhurst	*IV	639	PIERCY, William Stuckey	I	708
PETERSEN, William	II	652	PIERCY, William Stuckey	*IV	684
PETO family	III	36	PIGGOT	III	189
PETO, Samuel Morton	II	355	PILE, William	I	210
PETO, Samuel Morton	II	625	PILE, William	III	398
PETO, Samuel Morton	*IV	644	PILKINGTON, Lionel		
PETO, Samuel Morton	V	82	Alexander Bethune (Alastair)	*IV	689
PETO, Samuel Morton	V	239	PILKINGTON, William		
PETTER brothers	IV	715	Henry	III	94
PETTER, Ernest Willoughby	IV	625	PILKINGTON, William		
PETTER, Ernest Willoughby	*IV	653	Henry	IV	690
PETTER, Percival Waddams	*IV	653	PILKINGTON, William		
PETTIGREW, W F	I	5	Henry	*IV	693
PHELPS, Douglas	IV	694	PILKINGTON, William		
PHILIPPS brothers	IV	71	Henry	V	716
PHILIPPS, Ivor	*IV	659	PINKER, J B	V	701
PHILIPPS, John Wynford	II	173	PIPKIN, Samuel James	*IV	700
PHILIPPS, John Wynford	IV	482	PIRRIE, William James	II	285
PHILIPPS, John Wynford	IV	528	PIRRIE, William James	II	463
PHILIPPS, John Wynford	*IV	662	PIRRIE, William James	III	39
PHILIPPS, John Wynford	IV	671	PIRRIE, William James	III	294
PHILIPPS, John Wynford	IV	915	PIRRIE, William James	III	529
PHILIPPS, Laurence Richard	*IV	668	PIRRIE, William James	IV	665
PHILIPPS, Owen Cosby	I	48	PIRRIE, William James	IV	672
PHILIPPS, Owen Cosby	I	618	PIRRIE, William James	*IV	702
PHILIPPS, Owen Cosby	II	73	PIRRIE, William James	IV	739
PHILIPPS, Owen Cosby	II	488	PIRRIE, William James	IV	853
PHILIPPS, Owen Cosby	III	152	PIRRIE, William James	V	857
PHILIPPS, Owen Cosby	III	156	PITMAN, Isaac	III	665
PHILIPPS, Owen Cosby	III	529	PITMAN, Isaac	*IV	710
PHILIPPS, Owen Cosby	III	762	PITT, Robert	V	367
PHILIPPS, Owen Cosby	IV	663	PITTARD, Wreford John Charles	*IV	713
PHILIPPS, Owen Cosby	*IV	670	PLATT, Frank	IV	562
PHILIPPS, Owen Cosby	IV	704	PLATT, Frank	*IV	716
PHILIPPS, Owen Cosby	IV	739	PLATT, Frank	V	382
PHILIPPS, Owen Cosby	IV	853	PLATT, James Westlake	*IV	722
PHILIPPS, Owen Cosby	V	595	PLATT, John	I	8

Name	Vol	Page	Name	Vol	Page
PLATT, John	*IV	725	PORTAL, Charles Frederick		
PLATT, John	IV	729	Algernon	IV	425
PLATT, John	V	418	PORTAL, Charles Frederick		
PLATT, Samuel Radcliffe	*IV	729	Algernon	IV	634
PLATT, William	IV	183	PORTAL, Charles Frederick		
PLAYER, John	*IV	733	Algernon	IV	745
PLAYER, John Dane	*IV	733	PORTAL, Charles Frederick		
PLAYER, William Goodacre	III	880	Algernon	*IV	759
PLAYER, William Goodacre	*IV	733	PORTER, Leslie	I	728
PLENDER, William	III	485	PORTER, Richard Thomas	I	83
PLENDER, William	IV	69	POSNETT, Robert Harold	*IV	763
PLENDER, William	IV	204	POSNETT, William A	IV	473
PLENDER, William	*IV	736	POTTER, Henry Thomas	I	519
PLOWDEN, Edwin Noel			POTTER, Kenneth	III	846
August	II	226	POTTER, Richard	II	599
PLOWDEN, Edwin Noel			POTTER, Rupert	V	172
August	IV	426	POWELL, Thomas	IV	441
PLOWDEN, Edwin Noel			PRATT brothers	II	292
August	*IV	744	PREECE, William Henry	*IV	766
POCHIN, Henry Davis	I	476	PREECE, William Henry	V	238
POCHIN, Henry Davis	I	627	PRESCOTT, W G	III	870
POCHIN, Henry Davis	II	276	PRESTWICK, J A	V	615
POCHIN, Henry Davis	IV	58	PRICE, Robert	II	650
POCHIN, Henry Davis	IV	123	PRICE, Samuel Lowell	III	35
PODE, E Julian	V	908	PRICE, Samuel Lowell	V	675
POLE, Felix John Clewett	II	622	PRICE, William	*IV	769
POLE, Felix John Clewett	III	287	PRIESTMAN, Francis	*IV	771
POLE, Felix John Clewett	IV	241	PRIESTMAN, John	*IV	773
POLE, Felix John Clewett	*IV	748	PRINSEP, Throby	II	250
POLLARD, William	III	178	PUCKEY, Walter Charles	*IV	776
POLLEN, Arthur Joseph			PUGH, Charles Vernon	*IV	780
Hungerford	II	133	PULLEIN, Edmund	III	33
POLLEN, Arthur Joseph			PULLINGER, C T	III	12
Hungerford	IV	112	PURSER, J T	II	681
POLLEN, Arthur Joseph			PYBUS, Percy John	III	201
Hungerford	*IV	753	PYBUS, Percy John	III	252
POLLEN, Arthur Joseph			PYBUS, Percy John	IV	217
Hungerford	IV	918	PYBUS, Percy John	*IV	783
POLLEN, Arthur Joseph			PYE, Harold John	*IV	787
Hungerford	IV	926	PYE, William George	II	16
POLLEN, Arthur Joseph			PYE, William George	IV	787
Hungerford	V	432	PYE, William George	*IV	789
POLLEN, Stephen	V	432	QUILTER, Cuthbert	II	249
POLLOCK, D G H	III	293	QUILTER, William	*IV	791
PORGES, Jules	V	737	QUILTER, William	V	584
PORTAL of Laverstoke, Lord	V	886	QUILTER, William	V	767
PORTAL, Charles Frederick			RACE, George	I	1
Algernon	III	639	RADCLIFFE, Henry	*IV	796

Name	Vol	Page	Name	Vol	Page
RADCLIFFE, Henry	IV	941	REDWOOD, Thomas Boverton	I	559
RADFORD, Francis	*IV	800			
RAE, Edward	*IV	803	REDWOOD, Thomas Boverton	I	590
RAE, George	IV	803			
RAE, George	*IV	806	REDWOOD, Thomas Boverton	*IV	862
RAE, George	V	27			
RAILING, Harry	*IV	812	REED, Albert	V	246
RAILING, Max John	*IV	812	REED, Albert Edwin	III	59
RALLI family	II	431	REED, Albert Edwin	*IV	866
RAMSBOTTOM, John	*IV	816	REED, Albert Edwin	V	114
RAMSBOTTOM, John	V	69	REED, Albert Ralph	IV	868
RAMSBOTTOM, John	V	340	REED, Albert Ralph	*IV	870
RAMSDEN, James	I	622	REED, Albert Ralph	V	114
RAMSDEN, James	*IV	820	REED, Austin Leonard	*IV	873
RANK, James Voase	*IV	823	REED, Carol	V	545
RANK, James Voase	V	755	REID, Charles	III	259
RANK, Joseph	I	100	REISS, Emil	III	23
RANK, Joseph	IV	823	REITH, John Charles Walsham	I	427
RANK, Joseph	*IV	828			
RANK, Joseph	V	175	REITH, John Charles Walsham	II	513
RANK, Joseph Arthur	II	92			
RANK, Joseph Arthur	III	237	REITH, John Charles Walsham	IV	17
RANK, Joseph Arthur	IV	46			
RANK, Joseph Arthur	IV	200	REITH, John Charles Walsham	IV	680
RANK, Joseph Arthur	IV	494			
RANK, Joseph Arthur	IV	825	REITH, John Charles Walsham	*IV	877
RANK, Joseph Arthur	*IV	832			
RANK, Joseph Arthur	V	886	REITH, John Charles Walsham	V	882
RANKIN, John	*IV	837			
RANSOME, James Edward	*IV	841	RENDEL, George	I	70
RANSOME, Robert Charles	IV	841	RENDEL, James Meadows	I	69
RANSOME, Robert Charles	*IV	844	RENDEL, James Meadows	III	120
RAPER, George Frederick	I	46	RENOLD, Charles Garonne	IV	215
RAPER, George Frederick	*IV	846	RENOLD, Charles Garonne	*IV	882
RASTRICK, J U	II	412	REUTER, Paul Julius	IV	189
RATCLIFF, Richard	II	660	REUTER, Paul Julius	*IV	887
RATHBONE, William Benson	*IV	848	REUTER, Paul Julius	V	645
RAVEN, Vincent Litchfield	II	657	REVELSTOKE, Lord – see BARING, John		
RAVEN, Vincent Litchfield	*IV	850			
RAWORTH, J S	II	474	REYROLLE, Alphonse Constant	*IV	893
RAYNER, Derek	V	601			
READ, Robert Sawle	III	10	RHODES, Cecil	II	25
READHEAD, John	III	10	RHODES, Cecil	IV	311
REBBECK, Frederick Ernest	*IV	853	RHODES, Cecil	IV	950
RECKITT, James	II	343	RHODES, Cecil	V	738
RECKITT, James	*IV	856	RHONDDA, 1st Viscount – see THOMAS, David Alfred		
REDDISH, Halford Walter Lupton	*IV	858			
			RICARDO, Harry R	III	13

Name	Vol	Page	Name	Vol	Page
RICHARDS, Charles Frederick	IV	324	ROGER, Alexander Forbes Proctor	IV	926
RICHARDS, Edward Windsor	I	359	ROGERS, Hallewell	III	251
RICHARDS, Edward Windsor	*IV	897	ROGERS, Hallewell	IV	755
RICHARDS, Edward Windsor	V	492	ROGERS, Hallewell	IV	918
RICHARDS, Edward Windsor	V	821	ROGERS, Hallewell	*IV	923
RICHARDS, Westley	II	645	ROLLS, Charles Stewart	I	24
RICHARDSON brothers	III	427	ROLLS, Charles Stewart	II	228
RICHARDSON, James Nicholson	*IV	901	ROLLS, Charles Stewart	III	283
			ROLLS, Charles Stewart	III	500
RICHARDSON, John Wigham	I	483	ROLLS, Charles Stewart	IV	101
			ROLLS, Charles Stewart	IV	406
RICHARDSON, John Wigham	IV	221	ROLLS, Charles Stewart	*IV	929
			ROLLS, Charles Stewart	IV	974
RICHARDSON, John Wigham	*IV	904	ROLLS, Charles Stewart	V	126
			ROLLS, Charles Stewart	V	231
RICHARDSON, John Wigham	IV	957	ROLLS, Charles Stewart	V	614
RICHES, J O & O H	V	473	ROLLS, Charles Stewart	V	722
RIDDELL, George Allardice	III	880	ROOKE, Denis E	III	533
RIDDELL, George Allardice	*IV	910	ROOTES brothers	V	805
RILEY, Ed	I	201	ROOTES, Reginald Claud	*IV	933
RIPLEY, Henry	III	418	ROOTES, William Edward	I	867
RITCHIE, Charles Thomson	V	78	ROOTES, William Edward	IV	933
RITCHIE, John	II	18	ROOTES, William Edward	*IV	935
RITSON, Utrick Alexander	*IV	913	ROPNER, Robert	*IV	940
RIVERDALE, Lord – see BALFOUR, Arthur			ROSENTHAL, James Hermann – see KEMNAL, James H R		
ROBERTS, James	II	501	ROTHERHAM, Lord – see HOLLAND, William Henry		
ROBERTSON, Brian	II	270			
ROBINSON, J G	II	657	ROTHERMERE, 1st Viscount – see HARMSWORTH, Harold Sidney		
ROBINSON, Peter	III	764			
ROBINSON, W S	I	96			
ROBINSON, W S	III	906	ROTHSCHILD family	II	255
ROE, A V – see VERDUN-ROE, Edwin Alliott Verdon			ROTHSCHILD, Nathan Meyer	II	356
			ROTHSCHILD, Nathan Meyer	II	682
			ROTHSCHILD, Nathan Meyer	III	153
ROGER, Alexander Forbes Proctor	II	173	ROTHSCHILD, Nathan Meyer	III	295
			ROTHSCHILD, Nathan Meyer	III	788
ROGER, Alexander Forbes Proctor	III	46	ROTHSCHILD, Nathan Meyer	*IV	946
			ROTHSCHILD, Nathan Meyer	V	80
ROGER, Alexander Forbes Proctor	III	840	ROTHSCHILD, Nathan Meyer	V	309
			ROTHSCHILD, Nathan Meyer	V	543
ROGER, Alexander Forbes Proctor	IV	17	ROUSE, H L	V	560
			ROUTLEDGE, Thomas	II	302
ROGER, Alexander Forbes Proctor	IV	756	ROUTLEDGE, Thomas	*IV	954
			ROUTLEDGE, Thomas	V	243
ROGER, Alexander Forbes Proctor	*IV	915	ROWELL, Herbert Babington	I	215
			ROWELL, Herbert Babington	I	482

Name	Vol	Page	Name	Vol	Page
ROWELL, Herbert Babington	*IV	957	RYDER, Donald	III	893
ROWLAND, Gwilym E	I	84	RYDER, Donald	V	352
ROWLAND, Roland 'Tiny'	I	366	RYKENS, Paul	III	194
ROWLAND, Roland 'Tiny'	V	193	RYLANDS, John	III	180
ROWLANDSON, Hervy S	III	576	RYLANDS, John	III	711
ROWNTREE, Benjamin Seebohm	II	568	RYLANDS, John	*IV	999
			RYLANDS, John	V	705
ROWNTREE, Benjamin Seebohm	III	70	RYLANDS, William Peter	III	45
			RYLANDS, William Peter	IV	466
ROWNTREE, Benjamin Seebohm	III	409	RYLANDS, William Peter	IV	531
			RYLANDS, William Peter	*IV	1,004
ROWNTREE, Benjamin Seebohm	*IV	961	RYLANDS, William Peter	V	431
			SADLER, S A	II	114
ROWNTREE, Benjamin Seebohm	V	117	SAINSBURY family	III	71
			SAINSBURY, Alan John	I	728
ROWNTREE, Benjamin Seebohm	V	600	SAINSBURY, Alan John	*V	1
			SAINSBURY, Alan John	V	14
ROWNTREE, Benjamin Seebohm	V	648	SAINSBURY, David	V	6
			SAINSBURY, John	V	6
ROWNTREE, Joseph	II	437	SAINSBURY, John Benjamin	V	1
ROWNTREE, Joseph	III	70	SAINSBURY, John Benjamin	*V	11
ROWNTREE, Joseph	III	333	SAINSBURY, John Benjamin	V	18
ROWNTREE, Joseph	IV	961	SAINSBURY, John James	V	11
ROWNTREE, Joseph	*IV	965	SAINSBURY, John James	*V	15
ROYCE, Frederick Henry	II	228	SAINSBURY, Robert	*V	1
ROYCE, Frederick Henry	III	283	SAINSBURY, Robert	V	14
ROYCE, Frederick Henry	III	501	SAINSBURY, Simon	V	6
ROYCE, Frederick Henry	IV	109	SAINSBURY, Timothy	V	6
ROYCE, Frederick Henry	IV	327	SALISBURY, Frederick	V	2
ROYCE, Frederick Henry	IV	406	SALISBURY, Frederick	V	12
ROYCE, Frederick Henry	IV	930	SALMON family	III	888
ROYCE, Frederick Henry	*IV	973	SALMON, Barnett	II	579
ROYCE, Frederick Henry	V	140	SALMON, Henry	*V	20
ROYCE, Frederick Henry	V	722	SALMON, Julius	V	20
RUBERY, John T	IV	497	SALMON, Maurice	V	20
RUCKER, Martin	III	330	SALOMONS, David Lionel Goldsmid-Stern-	IV	929
RUNCIMAN, Walter	IV	854			
RUNCIMAN, Walter	*IV	978	SALOMONS, David Lionel Goldsmid-Stern-	*V	22
RUSHBROOKE, Frederick William	*IV	982			
			SALOMONS, David Lionel Goldsmid-Stern-	V	167
RUSSELL, Ernest Frank	V	525			
RUSSELL, Sydney Gordon	IV	388	SALOMONS, David Lionel Goldsmid-Stern-	V	310
RUSSELL, Sydney Gordon	*IV	985			
RUSSELL, Thomas Baron	*IV	991	SALT, Daniel	V	29
RUSSELL, W J	V	640	SALT, Thomas	*V	26
RUSTON, Joseph	*IV	994	SALT, Titus	II	408
RUTTER, Frederick William Pascoe	*IV	996	SALT, Titus	II	501
			SALT, Titus	IV	588
RYDER, Donald	II	241	SALT, Titus	*V	29

Name	Vol	Page	Name	Vol	Page
SALTER, Arthur	III	405	SCHUSTER, Felix Otto	*V	77
SAMUEL, Frank	*V	37	SCHWABE, Gustavus		
SAMUEL, Frank	V	456	Christian	III	37
SAMUEL, Marcus	II	584	SCHWABE, Gustavus		
SAMUEL, Marcus	II	630	Christian	III	456
SAMUEL, Marcus	III	652	SCHWABE, Gustavus		
SAMUEL, Marcus	IV	283	Christian	V	854
SAMUEL, Marcus	IV	947	SCOTT, George Gilbert	I	44
SAMUEL, Marcus	*V	43	SCOTT, George Gilbert	III	643
SAMUEL, Marcus	V	579	SCOTT, George Gilbert	*V	82
SAMUEL, Wilfred, Conrad &			SCOTT, George Gilbert	V	86
Max	V	37	SCOTT, Giles Gilbert	*V	86
SAMUELSON, Bernhard	IV	383	SCOTT, Hudson	I	598
SAMUELSON, Bernhard	*V	46	SCOTT, Percy	II	35
SANDEMAN, Albert G	III	732	SCOTT, Terence	II	576
SANDEMAN, N Stewart	II	31	SCOTT-PAINE, Charles		
SANDILANDS, Francis	I	857	Hubert	I	339
SANGER, George	*V	51	SCOTT-PAINE, Charles		
SANGSTER, John Young	II	123	Hubert	*V	91
SANGSTER, John Young	*V	55	SCOTT-PAINE, Charles		
SANGSTER, John Young	V	565	Hubert	V	884
SANGSTER, John Young	V	571	SCUDAMORE, Frank Ives	I	350
SANKEY, John William	*V	59	SCUDAMORE, Frank Ives	IV	399
SANKEY, John William	V	64	SCUDAMORE, Frank Ives	*V	93
SANKEY, Joseph	V	59	SCUDAMORE, Frank Ives	V	532
SANKEY, Joseph	V	63	SEAGRAVE, H O D	V	497
SARLE, Allen Lanyon	*V	65	SEARS, John George	IV	459
SARNOFF, David	I	673	SEARS, John George	*V	97
SAVILE, Leopold	II	534	SEARS, William Thomas	V	98
SAVILLE, Alfred	II	282	SECCOMBE, Lawrence Henry	*V	102
SAVILLE, Victor	II	89	SEDDON-BROWN, N	III	315
SAVIN, Thomas	II	359	SELBIE, Robert Hope	IV	59
SAXBY, John	*V	67	SELBIE, Robert Hope	*V	106
SCHIFF, Jacob	I	605	SELF, Henry	III	1
SCHLUSSER, Alexander	V	71	SELFRIDGE, Harry Gordon	I	228
SCHNEIDER, H W	I	622	SELFRIDGE, Harry Gordon	I	511
SCHNEIDER, H W	IV	820	SELFRIDGE, Harry Gordon	II	417
SCHRÖDER, Helmut	V	75	SELFRIDGE, Harry Gordon	III	294
SCHRÖDER, John Henry	V	71	SELFRIDGE, Harry Gordon	*V	109
SCHRÖDER, John Henry			SELFRIDGE, Harry Gordon	V	303
William	IV	530	SELFRIDGE, Harry Gordon	V	787
SCHRÖDER, John Henry			SEROCOLD, Oswald P	II	491
William	V	71	SHARP, Milton	II	141
SCHRÖDER, John Henry			SHELDON, Alfred	V	114
William	V	526	SHELDON, Clifford Dommett	IV	871
SCHRÖDER, Rudolph Bruno	*V	70	SHELDON, Clifford Dommett	*V	114
SCHRÖDER, Rudolph Bruno	V	526	SHELDON, Oliver	IV	963
SCHUSTER, Felix Otto	II	604	SHELDON, Oliver	*V	116
SCHUSTER, Felix Otto	III	295	SHELDON, Oliver	V	600

Name	Vol	Page	Name	Vol	Page
SHIPPAM, Alfred Ernest Cooper	*V	119	SIMMS, Frederick Richard	*V	165
			SIMMS, Frederick Richard	V	930
SHONE, Robert Minshull	*V	121	SIMON, Ernest Emil Darwin	*V	169
SHORT, Horace & Eustace	V	126	SIMON, Ernest Emil Darwin	V	386
SHORT, Hugh Oswald	IV	655	SIMON, Henry	III	834
SHORT, Hugh Oswald	*V	126	SIMON, Henry	IV	829
SHORT, Hugh Oswald	V	231	SIMON, Henry	V	169
SHORT, Hugh Oswald	V	616	SIMON, Henry	*V	174
SHORT, Hugh Oswald, Horace & Eustace	II	315	SIMONDS, Frederick Adolphus	*V	178
SHORT, John Young	*V	130	SIMPSON, Edward	II	516
SHUTTLEWORTH, Joseph	I	693	SIMPSON, John Bell	*V	182
SHUTTLEWORTH, Joseph	*V	134	SIMPSON, Samuel Leonard	*V	183
SIDDELEY, John Davenport	II	48	SIMPSON, Samuel Leonard	V	814
SIDDELEY, John Davenport	II	118	SIMPSON, Simeon	V	183
SIDDELEY, John Davenport	IV	168	SINGER, John Y	I	318
SIDDELEY, John Davenport	*V	136	SINGER, Paris	III	500
SIDDELEY, John Davenport	V	234	SKINNER, John	III	739
SIDDELEY, John Davenport	V	251	SKINNER, W T	II	272
SIDDELEY, John Davenport	V	616	SKIPWORTH, R W	II	649
SIDDELEY, John Davenport	V	743	SLADE, Edmund	I	559
SIDGREAVES, Arthur Frederick	IV	66	SLATTERY, Matthew	II	79
			SLATTERY, Matthew	II	688
SIDGREAVES, Arthur Frederick	*V	139	SLATTERY, Matthew	V	191
SIEFF, Israel Moses	IV	137	SLAUGHTER, Edward	V	367
SIEFF, Israel Moses	IV	139	SLAUGHTER, William Capel	II	177
SIEFF, Israel Moses	V	16	SLAUGHTER, William Capel	IV	348
SIEFF, Israel Moses	*V	142	SLAUGHTER, William Capel	*V	187
SIEFF, J Edward	V	152	SLAUGHTER, William Capel	V	606
SIEFF, Marcus	V	151	SLINGO, William	III	450
SIEMENS, Alexander	*V	155	SLOAN, Alfred P Jr	I	199
SIEMENS, Alexander	V	160	SMALLEY, Joseph	I	502
SIEMENS, Charles William	I	117	SMALLPEICE, Basil	I	366
SIEMENS, Charles William	I	654	SMALLPEICE, Basil	II	79
SIEMENS, Charles William	II	45	SMALLPEICE, Basil	II	688
SIEMENS, Charles William	V	155	SMALLPEICE, Basil	IV	861
SIEMENS, Charles William	*V	157	SMALLPEICE, Basil	*V	190
SIEMENS, Charles William	V	624	SMEDLEY, William T	III	603
SIEMENS, Charles William	V	820	SMILES, Samuel	V	194
SIEMENS, Charles William	V	897	SMILES, William Holmes	*V	194
SIEMENS, Werner, Karl & Frederick	V	157	SMILES, William Holmes	V	858
			SMITH, A Rowland	IV	642
SIGRIST, Fred	V	232	SMITH, Alfred	III	118
SIKES, Charles William	*V	162	SMITH, Allan MacGregor	III	449
SIMMS, Frederick Richard	III	500	SMITH, Allan MacGregor	IV	466
SIMMS, Frederick Richard	III	685	SMITH, Allan MacGregor	IV	618
SIMMS, Frederick Richard	III	744	SMITH, Allan MacGregor	IV	1,007
SIMMS, Frederick Richard	IV	929	SMITH, Allan MacGregor	*V	197
			SMITH, Allan MacGregor	V	811

Name	Vol	Page	Name	Vol	Page
SMITH, Arthur	V	40	SPICER family	II	419
SMITH, David W	III	229	SPICER, Albert	III	448
SMITH, Donald, Lord			SPICER, Albert	★V	242
Strathcona	V	635	SPICER, Albert	V	596
SMITH, George Samuel			SPRAGUE, Thomas Bond	★V	248
Fereday	★V	205	SPRIGGS, Frank Spencer	V	233
SMITH, Harold	III	533	SPRIGGS, Frank Spencer	★V	251
SMITH, Horatio Nelson	★V	209	SPRINGER, Baron	V	427
SMITH, Hugh Colin	V	223	SPURRIER, Henry	II	102
SMITH, J H	III	182	SPURRIER, Henry	IV	128
SMITH, Prince	★V	213	SPURRIER, Henry	★V	253
SMITH, Richard	V	205	SPURRIER, Henry	V	349
SMITH, Richard Tilden	III	351	ST DAVIDS, 1st Viscount – see		
SMITH, Richard Tilden	III	906	PHILIPPS, John Wynford		
SMITH, Richard Tilden	★V	216	ST JUST, Lord – see		
SMITH, Richard Tilden	V	719	GRENFELL, Edward Charles		
SMITH, Roland	IV	478	STAFFORD, J H	I	75
SMITH, Rowland	III	168	STAINTON, Ross	V	884
SMITH, Seth	II	427	STAMFORD, Lord	II	484
SMITH, Vivian Hugh	I	617	STAMP, Josiah Charles	I	166
SMITH, Vivian Hugh	IV	456	STAMP, Josiah Charles	I	275
SMITH, Vivian Hugh	★V	223	STAMP, Josiah Charles	I	706
SMITH, W H	III	819	STAMP, Josiah Charles	II	73
SMITH, William Reardon	★V	224	STAMP, Josiah Charles	II	621
SNELUS, George J	V	820	STAMP, Josiah Charles	III	90
SOMERVELL, Arnold Colin	★V	227	STAMP, Josiah Charles	★V	260
SOPWITH, Thomas Octave			STANIER, Francis	III	142
Murdoch	III	237	STANIER, William	II	658
SOPWITH, Thomas Octave			STANIER, William	V	265
Murdoch	IV	931	STANLEY, Albert Henry	I	153
SOPWITH, Thomas Octave			STANLEY, Albert Henry	II	270
Murdoch	V	126	STANLEY, Albert Henry	II	330
SOPWITH, Thomas Octave			STANLEY, Albert Henry	IV	631
Murdoch	★V	231	STANLEY, Albert Henry	IV	678
SOPWITH, Thomas Octave			STANLEY, Albert Henry	IV	785
Murdoch	V	251	STANLEY, Albert Henry	★V	273
SOPWITH, Thomas Octave			STANLEY, Albert Henry	V	511
Murdoch	V	254	STANLEY, Albert Henry	V	631
SOUTHWOOD, Lord	II	263	STANLEY, Charles Orr	IV	787
SPAGNOLETTI, Charles			STANLEY, William Ford		
Ernest Paolo della Diana	★V	236	Robinson	★V	277
SPAIN, H S	III	138	STARLEY, John Kemp	II	207
SPENCER, George	IV	360	STARLEY, John Kemp	III	245
SPENCER, George	★V	239	STARLEY, John Kemp	III	685
SPENCER, Harris	III	251	STARLEY, John Kemp	★V	281
SPENCER, Reuben	IV	1,002	STARLEY, John Kemp	V	498
SPENCER, Thomas	IV	136	STARR, Richard Benjamin	★V	285
SPEYER, Edgar	V	74	STEAD, Charles	III	418
SPEYER, Edgar	V	80	STEAD, Edmund	II	516

Name	Vol	Page	Name	Vol	Page
STEARN, C G	V	408	STOKES, Donald Gresham	IV	128
STEARN, C H	V	471	STOKES, Donald Gresham	V	257
STEDEFORD, Ivan	II	419	STOKES, Donald Gresham	*V	347
STEEL MAITLAND, Arthur	II	357	STOLL, Oswald	*V	355
STEEL, Gerald	III	541	STOLL, Oswald	V	616
STEEL, Gerald	*V	290	STONE, Henry	IV	447
STEEL, Henry	V	290	STONEHAM, Henry	II	666
STEEL, Henry	*V	293	STOREY, Samuel	*V	362
STEEL, Thomas	V	362	STOTHERT, Henry	V	367
STEER, Edward	III	524	STOTHERT, John Lum	*V	367
STEIN, Eric	III	128	STOTT, Philip Sidney	*V	371
STEPHENS, Henry Charles	*V	296	STRAIGHT, Whitney Willard	*V	374
STEPHENS, Holman			STRATHALMOND, Lord –		
Frederick	*V	298	see FRASER, William Milligan		
STEPHENSON, George	III	37	STREAT, Edward Raymond	*V	378
STEPHENSON, Robert	II	597	STREET, Arthur	II	201
STEPHENSON, Robert	III	83	STREET, George	*V	390
STEPHENSON, Robert	V	736	STRIDE, A L	I	4
STEPHENSON, William			STROUDLEY, William	II	181
Haswell	*V	301	STROUDLEY, William	V	66
STEPHENSON, William			STROUDLEY, William	*V	392
Lawrence	*V	303	STURROCK, Archibald	V	339
STERLING, Louis S	I	674	STYLES, Frederick	III	178
STERN, Edward David	*V	309	SUGDEN, Arthur	*V	396
STERN, Herbert	V	25	SUGG, William	V	872
STERN, Herbert	V	310	SUMMERS family	II	480
STEVENS, Harry	III	130	SUMMERS, Henry	III	902
STEVENS, Marshall	*V	312	SUTHERLAND, Arthur		
STEVENSON, James	*V	325	Munro	*V	401
STEVENSON, James Cochran	*V	327	SUTHERLAND, Thomas	IV	30
STEVENSON, W O	II	265	SUTRO, Leopold	III	625
STEWART, Halley	*V	330	SWAN, C S	III	398
STEWART, Percy Malcolm	I	828	SWAN, Joseph Wilson	I	835
STEWART, Percy Malcolm	V	332	SWAN, Joseph Wilson	III	341
STEWART, Percy Malcolm	*V	333	SWAN, Joseph Wilson	*V	404
STEWART-LIBERTY,			SWAYTHLING, Lord – see		
Arthur Ivor	*V	336	MONTAGU, Samuel		
STINNES, Hugo	II	210	SWINBURNE, Robert Walter	IV	518
STINNES, Hugo	II	555	SWINBURNE, Robert Walter	*V	412
STINNES, Hugo	V	219	SWIRE, John Samuel	III	327
STIRLING, James	V	395	SWIRE, John Samuel	*V	414
STIRLING, Patrick	IV	818	SWOPE, Gerard	IV	750
STIRLING, Patrick	*V	339	SYDENHAM, Lord	II	572
STOCKER, Thomas Medland	*V	343	SYKES, Alan John	III	728
STOKER, Kenneth	V	346	SYKES, Alan John	*V	418
STOKER, Robert Burdon	*V	344	SYKES, Charles	II	653
STOKER, R B	V	346	SYKES, William Robert	*V	425
STOKES, Donald Gresham	II	242	SYLVESTER, A Edgar	IV	208
STOKES, Donald Gresham	III	68	SYLVESTER, A Edgar	IV	248

Name	Vol	Page	Name	Vol	Page
SZARVASY, Frederick Alexander	II	513	THOMAS, George Holt	II	49
			THOMAS, George Holt	III	133
SZARVASY, Frederick Alexander	IV	22	THOMAS, George Holt	IV	112
			THOMAS, George Holt	IV	925
SZARVASY, Frederick Alexander	*V	427	THOMAS, George Holt	V	431
			THOMAS, George Holt	*V	480
SZARVASY, Frederick Alexander	V	431	THOMAS, George Holt	V	880
			THOMAS, Herbert John	*V	484
SZARVASY, Frederick Alexander	V	881	THOMAS, Herbert John	V	782
SZLUMPER, James	II	21	THOMAS, John	II	685
TAIT, Andrew Wilson	IV	24	THOMAS, Philip	V	397
TAIT, Andrew Wilson	*V	429	THOMAS, Richard	*V	486
TALBOT, Benjamin	II	447	THOMAS, Sidney Gilchrist	II	136
TALBOT, Benjamin	II	450	THOMAS, Sidney Gilchrist	II	562
TALBOT, Benjamin	*V	433	THOMAS, Sidney Gilchrist	IV	898
TANGYE, Richard	I	448	THOMAS, Sidney Gilchrist	*V	489
TANGYE, Richard	*V	436	THOMAS, Sidney Gilchrist	V	653
TATE, Henry	*V	438	THOMAS, William Miles Webster	II	78
TATTERSALL, John Brown	*V	444			
TAYLEUR, Charles	II	598	THOMAS, William Miles Webster	III	595
TAYLOR, E P	I	761			
TAYLOR, Francis	*V	454	THOMAS, William Miles Webster	IV	338
TAYLOR, George	I	334			
TAYLOR, James Frater	IV	451	THOMAS, William Miles Webster	V	190
TAYLOR, James Frater	IV	561			
TAYLOR, James Frater	*V	458	THOMAS, William Miles Webster	V	376
TAYLOR, Jonas	III	227			
TAYLOR, Theodore Cooke	*V	464	THOMAS, William Miles Webster	*V	496
TEMPLETON, James	I	1	THOMPSON, John	II	318
TEMPLETON, James	V	537	THOMPSON, Joseph Lowes Jr	V	504
TENNANT family	V	327			
TENNANT, Charles	IV	288	THOMPSON, Robert (1819–1910)	*V	501
TENNANT, Charles	IV	403			
TENNANT, Henry	II	543	THOMPSON, Robert (1819–1910)	V	504
TENNANT, Henry	*V	467			
TENNYSON, Charles	IV	466	THOMPSON, Robert (1850–1908)	V	503
TETLEY, Francis William	II	287			
TETLEY, Henry Greenwood	I	803	THOMPSON, Robert (1850–1908)	*V	504
TETLEY, Henry Greenwood	III	508			
TETLEY, Henry Greenwood	III	662	THOMSON, J & G	III	37
TETLEY, Henry Greenwood	*V	470	THOMSON, Roy	I	307
THOMAS, David Alfred	I	322	THOMSON, Roy	I	658
THOMAS, David Alfred	II	679	THORN, Jules	I	735
THOMAS, David Alfred	III	776	THORN, Jules	III	835
THOMAS, David Alfred	III	903	THORN, Jules	*V	507
THOMAS, David Alfred	*V	473	THORNTON, Henry Worth	II	652
THOMAS, Evan	IV	797	THORNTON, Henry Worth	*V	510
THOMAS, George Holt	I	711	THORNTON, Richard	V	356

Name	Vol	Page	Name	Vol	Page
THORNYCROFT, John Edward	V	516	TRINDER, Arthur William	★V	552
THORNYCROFT, John Isaac	★V	513	TRIPPE, Juan T	V	882
THURGOOD, Walter Leonard	III	243	TRITTON, Joseph Herbert	★V	557
THURGOOD, Walter Leonard	★V	520	TROLLOPE, Anthony	V	531
THWAITES, Leslie Basil	★V	523	TROLLOPE, Anthony	V	591
TIARKS, Frank Cyril	IV	530	TROLLOPE, George Howard	I	745
TIARKS, Frank Cyril	V	72	TROLLOPE, George Howard	II	428
TIARKS, Frank Cyril	★V	525	TUKE, Anthony William	II	265
TIARKS, Henry	V	71	TUKE, Anthony William	★V	559
TIARKS, Henry	V	75	TUKE, William Murray	V	559
TILLEY, John	I	350	TURNBULL, Thomas	★V	562
TILLEY, John	★V	531	TURNER, Alfred	V	482
TILLING, Richard	III	149	TURNER, Edward	V	56
TILLING, Thomas	II	478	TURNER, Edward	★V	564
TILLING, Thomas	III	148	TURNER, Edward	V	571
TIMMINS, T S	II	618	TURNER, Eric	II	124
TINDALL, William	III	37	TURNER, Eric	V	58
TIPPETTS, F D	IV	984	TURNER, Eric	V	569
TISDALL, Edmund Charles	★V	534	TURNER, Eric	★V	570
TOMKINSON, Michael	I	1	TURNER, John	I	77
TOMKINSON, Michael	★V	536	TURNER, John	★V	575
TOMPKINS, Granville Richard	I	728	TURNER, N C	V	2
			TURNER, Ronald Mark Cunliffe	II	201
TONGE, G A	III	562	TURNER, Ronald Mark Cunliffe	★V	578
TOOTAL, Edward	III	703			
TOUCHE, George Alexander	V	429	TURQUAND, William	III	33
TOUCHE, George Alexander	★V	539	TURQUAND, William	IV	793
TOZER, Edward	V	294	TURQUAND, William	★V	582
TREE, Herbert Draper Beerbohm	I	148	TURQUAND, William	V	674
			TURQUAND, William	V	767
TREE, Herbert Draper Beerbohm	I	613	TWINING family	II	281
			TWINING, Richard III	II	176
TREE, Herbert Draper Beerbohm	II	341	TWINING, Richard III	★V	585
			TWYMAN, Frank	★V	588
TREE, Herbert Draper Beerbohm	★V	543	TYLER, Henry Whatley	★V	591
			TYRER, Henry	★V	593
TREE, Herbert Draper Beerbohm	V	921	UNWIN, Stanley	IV	77
			UNWIN, Stanley	V	242
TRENCH, Louis	III	424	UNWIN, Stanley	★V	596
TRENCHARD, Hugh	II	143	UNWIN, T Fisher	V	597
TRENCHARD, Hugh	V	39	URWICK, Lyndall Fownes	I	411
TRENCHARD, Hugh	V	232	URWICK, Lyndall Fownes	IV	962
TRENCHARD, Hugh	V	724	URWICK, Lyndall Fownes	V	117
TRENT, Lord – see BOOT, Jesse			URWICK, Lyndall Fownes	V	190
			URWICK, Lyndall Fownes	★V	599
TRESSIDER, Henry	II	276	VAN DEN BERGH, Henry	★V	604
TRICKETT, Henry Whittaker	★V	546	VAN DEN BERGH, Jacob	V	11

Name	Vol	Page	Name	Vol	Page
VAN DEN BERGH, Jacob	*V	604	WALKER, Herbert Ashcombe	II	268
VASSAR-SMITH, Richard			WALKER, Herbert Ashcombe	IV	254
Vassar	IV	467	WALKER, Herbert Ashcombe	V	264
VASSAR-SMITH, Richard			WALKER, Herbert Ashcombe	*V	628
Vassar	IV	595	WALKER, Thomas Andrew	IV	629
VASSAR-SMITH, Richard			WALL, Rolande	III	577
Vassar	IV	916	WALLACE, Charles William	I	590
VASSAR-SMITH, Richard			WALLACE, Charles William	II	639
Vassar	*V	610	WALLACE, Charles William	*V	634
VAUGHAN, John	I	40	WALLENBERG family	II	651
VAUGHAN, John	I	256	WALLIS, Frederick	*V	638
VAUGHAN, John	I	358	WALMSLEY, Benjamin	*V	641
VAUGHAN, John	II	276	WALMSLEY, William	III	891
VAUGHAN, John	IV	898	WALMSLEY, William	*V	641
VAUGHAN, John	V	47	WALTER, Ernest	V	140
VELLACOTT, W E	III	536	WALTER, John III	*V	644
VERDON-ROE, Edwin Alliot			WARD, Harry	*V	647
Verdon	II	118	WARD, J Griffin	II	517
VERDON-ROE, Edwin Alliot			WARD, John	II	517
Verdon	III	237	WARD, William	III	489
VERDON-ROE, Edwin Alliott			WARD, William	*V	649
Verdon	*V	614	WARD, William Humble Eric	*V	655
VERDON-SMITH, Reginald	IV	761	WARDINGTON, Lord – see		
VERULAM, Lord	II	31	PEASE, John William		
VESTEY, Edmund Hoyle	*V	618	Beaumont		
VESTEY, Evelyn	V	621	WARDLE, Thomas	IV	332
VESTEY family	V	318	WARDLE, Thomas	*V	661
VESTEY, William	IV	618	WARING, Arthur Bertram	*V	666
VESTEY, William	*V	618	WARING, Samuel	IV	618
VICKERS, Albert	I	62	WARING, Samuel	V	110
VICKERS, Albert	I	71	WARNER, Frank	*V	668
VICKERS, Albert	I	606	WATERHOUSE, Alfred	II	235
VICKERS, Albert	I	627	WATERHOUSE, Alfred	III	360
VICKERS, Albert	II	34	WATERHOUSE, Alfred	IV	519
VICKERS, Albert	II	365	WATERHOUSE, Alfred	*V	671
VICKERS, Albert	V	137	WATERHOUSE, Alfred	V	674
VICKERS, Albert	*V	622	WATERHOUSE, Edwin	II	103
VICKERS, Douglas	III	252	WATERHOUSE, Edwin	V	582
VICKERS, T	I	627	WATERHOUSE, Edwin	*V	674
VICKERS, Thomas Edward	V	295	WATES, Norman Edward	*V	679
VICKERS, Thomas Edward	*V	622	WATKIN, Edward William	I	627
VIVIAN, Henry	II	617	WATKIN, Edward William	II	338
WADDINGTON, John	V	698	WATKIN, Edward William	II	393
WADE, Charles Henry	II	685	WATKIN, Edward William	II	413
WAITE, John	III	383	WATKIN, Edward William	II	600
WAKEFIELD, Charles	I	711	WATKIN, Edward William	III	153
WALKER, Smith, Robert	II	223	WATKIN, Edward William	III	666
WALKER, Andrew	III	515	WATKIN, Edward William	IV	328
WALKER, Herbert Ashcombe	II	81	WATKIN, Edward William	IV	629

Name	Vol	Page
WATKIN, Edward William	V	106
WATKIN, Edward William	V	591
WATKIN, Edward William	★V	682
WATKINS, Edward	V	66
WATKINS, Francis	III	570
WATKINSON, Harold	III	339
WATSON, George	I	224
WATSON, George	IV	137
WATSON, George	V	15
WATSON, George	V	606
WATSON, J D	II	245
WATSON, James Angus	III	747
WATSON, James Angus	★V	686
WATSON, Joseph	★V	690
WATSON, Robert Irving	I	590
WATSON, Robert Irving	★V	693
WATSON, Victor Hugo	★V	698
WATT, Alexander Pollock	★V	700
WEBB, Arthur	★V	702
WEBB, F W	II	658
WEBB, F W	V	69
WEBB, Weston Fulford Marriott	★V	705
WEDGWOOD, Josiah	★V	707
WEDGWOOD, Ralph Lewis	I	543
WEDGWOOD, Ralph Lewis	II	543
WEDGWOOD, Ralph Lewis	II	659
WEDGWOOD, Ralph Lewis	III	149
WEDGWOOD, Ralph Lewis	IV	244
WEDGWOOD, Ralph Lewis	V	708
WEDGWOOD, Ralph Lewis	★V	712
WEEKS, Ronald Morce	III	619
WEEKS, Ronald Morce	IV	695
WEEKS, Ronald Morce	★V	715
WEINSTOCK, Arnold	II	273
WEINSTOCK, Arnold	III	759
WEINSTOCK, Arnold	IV	425
WEINSTOCK, Arnold	V	508
WEIR, Andrew	V	217
WEIR, Andrew	★V	719
WEIR, George & James	V	721
WEIR, William Douglas	II	332
WEIR, William Douglas	IV	224
WEIR, William Douglas	IV	273
WEIR, William Douglas	IV	281
WEIR, William Douglas	IV	916
WEIR, William Douglas	IV	930
WEIR, William Douglas	IV	974
WEIR, William Douglas	V	202
WEIR, William Douglas	V	266
WEIR, William Douglas	V	713
WEIR, William Douglas	★V	721
WELLCOME, Henry Solomon	IV	635
WELLCOME, Henry Solomon	★V	728
WERNHER, Harold	I	679
WERNHER, Harold	V	740
WERNHER, Julius Carl	I	253
WERNHER, Julius Carl	II	252
WERNHER, Julius Carl	★V	736
WEST, Glynn Hamilton	II	481
WEST, Glynn Hamilton	II	573
WEST, Glynn Hamilton	III	45
WEST, Glynn Hamilton	III	670
WEST, Glynn Hamilton	IV	531
WEST, Glynn Hamilton	IV	1,007
WEST, Glynn Hamilton	V	137
WEST, Glynn Hamilton	★V	742
WEST, John	★V	747
WESTINGHOUSE, George	IV	542
WESTON, Harry	III	176
WESTON, Harry	★V	749
WESTON, Joseph Dodge	III	570
WESTON, Willard Garfield	I	728
WESTON, Willard Garfield	★V	752
WESTON-WEBB, W F M – see WEBB, Weston Fulford Marriott		
WHARNCLIFFE, Lord	III	866
WHEELER, Arthur	III	388
WHEELER, Arthur	★V	759
WHIFFEN, Thomas	★V	763
WHIGHAM, Walter	V	459
WHINNEY, Frederick	III	33
WHINNEY, Frederick	IV	794
WHINNEY, Frederick	V	677
WHINNEY, Frederick	★V	766
WHIPPLE, Robert S	II	16
WHITBREAD, Francis Pelham	I	534
WHITBREAD, Francis Pelham	★V	769
WHITBREAD, Samuel	III	736
WHITE family	II	333
WHITE, Edwin	★V	774
WHITE, George (1840–1912)	I	747
WHITE, George (1840–1912)	★V	776
WHITE, George (1854–1916)	I	516
WHITE, George (1854–1916)	V	484

Name	Vol	Page
WHITE, George (1854–1916)	*V	780
WHITE, George (1854–1916)	V	790
WHITE, James	I	245
WHITE, James	II	192
WHITE, James	II	511
WHITE, James	V	112
WHITE, James	*V	784
WHITE, Stanley	I	516
WHITE-SMITH, Henry	V	782
WHITE-SMITH, Henry	*V	790
WHITEHEAD, Edward	III	337
WHITELEY, William	I	167
WHITELEY, William	I	227
WHITELEY, William	I	510
WHITELEY, William	III	756
WHITELEY, William	III	765
WHITELEY, William	IV	505
WHITELEY, William	*V	792
WHITTAKER, Croyden Meredith	*V	795
WHITTLE, Frank	V	727
WHITTLE, Frank	V	806
WHITTLE, Frank	V	932
WHITWORTH, Benjamin	I	627
WHITWORTH, Joseph	I	58
WHITWORTH, Joseph	I	68
WHITWORTH, Joseph	I	455
WHITWORTH, Joseph	II	218
WHITWORTH, Joseph	II	600
WHITWORTH, Joseph	III	849
WHITWORTH, Joseph	IV	445
WHITWORTH, Joseph	*V	797
WHITWORTH, Joseph	V	854
WICKMAN, Axel Charles	III	176
WILKINSON, Joseph	III	424
WILKINSON, William Boutland	*V	802
WILKS, Spencer Bernau	III	247
WILKS, Spencer Bernau	*V	805
WILLETT, William	IV	103
WILLETT, William	*V	808
WILLEY, Francis Vernon	II	31
WILLEY, Francis Vernon	III	839
WILLEY, Francis Vernon	IV	467
WILLEY, Francis Vernon	*V	810
WILLIAMS, Edmund T	III	603
WILLIAMS, Edward	I	359
WILLIAMS, Edward	IV	897
WILLIAMS, Edward	*V	817
WILLIAMS, Edward Leader	I	9
WILLIAMS, Ernest Hodder	IV	235
WILLIAMS, Evan	III	256
WILLIAMS, Evan	III	824
WILLIAMS, Evan	*V	823
WILLIAMS, George	II	468
WILLIAMS, George	*V	825
WILLIAMS, Robert	II	666
WILLIAMSON family	III	81
WILLIAMSON, Archibald	*V	833
WILLIAMSON, James	*V	837
WILLIAMSON, Stephen	I	119
WILLIS, H R	I	1
WILLOUGHBY, John	II	649
WILLS family	II	255
WILLS family	II	462
WILLS, George Alfred	*V	841
WILLS, Henry Herbert	I	865
WILLS, Henry Herbert	V	841
WILLS, Henry Overton III	V	842
WILLS, Henry Overton III	V	844
WILLS, John Spencer	II	174
WILLS, John Spencer	II	476
WILLS, John Spencer	III	376
WILLS, William Henry	V	841
WILLS, William Henry	*V	843
WILSON, A H	III	565
WILSON, Alan	III	24
WILSON, Arthur	*V	846
WILSON, Charles Henry	II	253
WILSON, Charles Henry	*V	846
WILSON, Charles Rivers	II	474
WILSON, G B H	I	408
WILSON, George	I	577
WILSON, Norman	V	709
WILSON, Peter Cecil	*V	850
WILSON, R J	III	475
WILSON, Stanley J	II	159
WILSON, Walter H	III	39
WILTON, Marie Effie (Marie Bancroft)	I	147
WIMPEY, George	IV	257
WINN, Rowland	*V	852
WINTERBOTTOM, W T	III	104
WINTERSTOKE, Lord – see WILLS, William Henry		
WITHERS, Jackson	III	287

Name	Vol	Page	Name	Vol	Page
WOLFE-BARRY, John	I	865	WOOLTON, Lord – see		
WOLFE-BARRY, Kenneth Alfred	I	196	MARQUIS, Frederick James		
WOLFF, Gustav Wilhelm	III	37	WOOLWORTH, F W	V	303
WOLFF, Gustav Wilhelm	III	456	WOOLWORTH, Fred Moore	V	303
WOLFF, Gustav Wilhelm	IV	703	WORKMAN, Francis	I	683
WOLFF, Gustav Wilhelm	V	195	WORKMAN, Francis	V	857
WOLFF, Gustav Wilhelm	*V	854	WORKMAN, Francis	*V	891
WOLFF, Gustav Wilhelm	V	892	WORSDELL, Thomas	V	436
WOLFSON, Isaac	I	798	WOSTENHOLM, George	IV	994
WOLSELEY, Frederick York	I	79	WOSTENHOLM, George	*V	894
WOLSEY, Walter	II	478	WRIGHT, Barton	I	75
WOLSEY, Walter	III	148	WRIGHT, Charles	III	524
WOLVERTON, Lord	III	670	WRIGHT, Francis	III	125
WOOD, Edward (1839–1917)	II	517	WRIGHT, John Roper	I	117
WOOD, Edward (1839–1917)	IV	459	WRIGHT, John Roper	*V	897
WOOD, Edward (1839–1917)	*V	864	WRIGHT, John Roper	V	904
WOOD, Edward (1846–1930)	*V	860	WRIGHT, Roy	II	203
WOOD, G	I	627	WRIGHT, Whitaker	I	204
WOOD, Hugh Nicholas	*V	867	WRIGHT, Whitaker	II	650
WOOD, Lindsay	V	867	WRIGHT, Whitaker	*V	901
WOOD, Lindsay	*V	870	WRIGHT, William Charles	V	488
WOOD, Whittle	II	385	WRIGHT, William Charles	V	898
WOODALL, Corbet	IV	248	WRIGHT, William Charles	*V	904
WOODALL, Corbet	*V	871	WYATT, Myles Dermot		
WOODALL, Corbet	V	875	Norris	*V	911
WOODALL, Harold W	II	185	WYCHERLEY, John	III	186
WOODALL, Harold W	V	874	WYCHERLEY, Robert Bruce	I	277
WOODALL, William	V	872	WYCHERLEY, Robert Bruce	*V	917
WOODALL, William	*V	875	WYLDBORE-SMITH,		
WOODGER, John	*V	878	Edmund	II	352
WOODROW, Jack	V	455	WYNDHAM SHIRE, L G	II	478
WOODS-HUMPHERY,			WYNDHAM, Charles	*V	920
George Edward	I	424	YAPP, William	I	178
WOODS-HUMPHERY,			YATES, Edward	*V	924
George Edward	V	92	YERKES, Charles Tyson	I	204
WOODS-HUMPHERY,			YERKES, Charles Tyson	I	262
George Edward	*V	880	YERKES, Charles Tyson	IV	630
WOOLF, Charles Moss	I	111	YERKES, Charles Tyson	V	781
WOOLF, Charles Moss	II	89	YOUNG, Alexander Frederick		
WOOLF, Charles Moss	IV	200	Farquhar	*V	926
WOOLF, Charles Moss	IV	493	YOUNG, Arthur Primrose	*V	930
WOOLF, Charles Moss	IV	833	YOUNG, Eric	III	259
WOOLF, Charles Moss	*V	885	YULE, David	I	617
WOOLLARD, F W	III	856	ZAHAROFF, Basil	I	565
WOOLLARD, Frank George	III	65	ZAHAROFF, Basil	V	626
WOOLLARD, Frank George	*V	888	ZEAL, Giles Henry	*V	933

List of members of industry advisory committees

(Including persons consulted for particular industries)
Compiled by Dr Geoffrey Tweedale

INDUSTRIES

Coal and slate mining
William Ashworth, John Goodchild, Graeme Holmes, Jean Lindsay, David Rowe, Arthur Taylor

Food
P J Atkins, Theo Barker, John Burnett, Derek Oddy, Bill Reader, David Richardson

Drink
Tom Corran, Kevin Hawkins, Peter Mathias, Brian Spiller

Tobacco
Bernard Alford

Petroleum
Tony Corley, Ronald W Ferrier, Geoff Jones

Chemicals
Lutz Haber, Bill Reader, Trevor Williams

Iron and steel
Jonathan Boswell, Charlotte Erickson, Steve Tolliday

Non-ferrous metals
Roger Burt, David Rowe

Mechanical and instrument engineering
Alun C Davies, Roderick Floud, David C Phillips, David Rowe

Electrical, electronic and nuclear engineering
Brian Bowers, Margaret Gowing, Leslie Hannah, Patrick Strange, Stephanie Zarach

Railways (manufacture and services)
Theo Barker, Geoffrey Channon, Terry Gourvish, Michael Robbins, Jack Simmons

Motor vehicles (manufacture and services)
Gerald Bloomfield, Roy Church, John Hibbs, Richard Overy, Bill Reader, Aubrey Silberston

Aerospace and air transport
Peter Fearon, Robin Higham, Sir Peter Masefield

Textiles and clothing
Stanley Chapman, Donald Coleman, Douglas Farnie, Tony Howe, John Iredale, David Jenkins, Ken Ponting, Eric Sigsworth, Colin Simmons

Leather and shoes
Bernard Alford, Keith Brooker, G Ronald White, G W Odey

Building materials and construction
Ed Cooney, J B F Earle, Andrew Saint, Sir John Summerson

Timber and furniture
Hew Reid

Paper, printing and publishing
Rachel Lawrence, Bill Reader, Francis Robinson, Philip Sykes

Utilities
Malcolm Falkus, Leslie Hannah, David Roberts, Trevor Williams

Communications
Martin Daunton

Shipping and shipbuilding
Robin Craig, Peter Davies, Robert Greenhill, Gordon Jackson, Sheila Marriner, Alan Pearsall

Distributive trades
Alison Adburgham, P J Atkins, John Beaumont, Lord Briggs, Rosalind Haddon, Bill Philpott

Insurance
Hugh Cockerell, Edwin Green, Oliver Westall

Banking
Edwin Green, Leslie Pressnell, Peter Spiro

Building societies
Esmond J Cleary

Accountants
Dick Edwards, Edgar Jones, Robert H Parker

Financiers and City men
Richard Davenport-Hines

Professional services
Bill Reader

Miscellaneous services
Rachel Low, Robert Murphy, Michael Sanderson

REGIONS

North-East
David Rowe, Stafford Linsley

Birmingham
Roy Hay, A L Minkes, Trevor Raybould, Richard Storey, Jennifer Tann, Rick Trainor

Liverpool
Peter Davies, Gordon Read

Ireland
Leslie Clarkson, David Johnson, Trevor Parkhill

Wales
Colin Baber, Graeme Holmes, L J Williams

Yorkshire
David Jenkins, Eric Sigsworth

List of contributors, showing their entries

A

H W Abbey
William Hill
Margaret Ackrill
Sir Ronald Edwards
Sir Charles Lidbury
R B Adams
Sir Donald Forsyth Anderson
Alison Adburgham
Albert Walter Gamage
Sir Arthur Laseny Liberty
Arthur Stewart-Liberty
Angela Airey
Emerson Muschamp Bainbridge
Geoffrey Alderman
Sir Henry Oakley
B W E Alford
Sir George Alfred Wills
William Henry Wills
   (Lord Winterstoke of Blagdon)
D G C Allan
Sir Norman Longley
Sir Peter Allen
Cecil J T Cronshaw
J K Almond
Sir Thomas Hugh Bell
Henry W F Bolckow
Percy Carlisle Gilchrist
Edward Windsor Richards
Sidney Gilchrist Thomas
Edward Williams
Donald Anderson
Henry B H Blundell
Alfred Hewlett
David A E Lindsay
   (27th Earl of Crawford and Balcarres)
John Armstrong
George Lawson Johnston
   (1st Lord Luke of Pavenham)
John Lawson Johnston
M M Armstrong
Edward Thomas Judge
Peter J Atkins
Arthur Saxby Barham

Sir George Barham
George Titus Barham
Sir Robert R F Butler
Joseph Herbert Maggs
Leonard Maggs
Sir William Price
Edwin White
T Atkins
Sir Henry Montague Hozier
Edmund Charles Tisdall
Jill Austin
Frank Twyman

B

Colin Baber
Alfred Baldwin
William Evans
Louis J B Guéret
Sir Julian S A Hodge
John Lysaght
Philip S Bagwell
John Bell
Sir Francis Henry Dent
Lord Claud John Hamilton
Sir Allen Lanyon Sarle
Hugh Balston
Charles Henry Balston
J H Bamberg
Sir Frank Platt
T C Barker
Sir David Gamble
Sir L Alastair B Pilkington
William H Pilkington
   (1st Lord Pilkington of St Helens)
K A Barlow
Francis William Crossley
Sir William John Crossley
D S M Barrie
David Davies
Sir Basil Bartlett Bt
Sir Herbert Henry Bartlett
James Neville Bartlett
William Adam
Sir Francis Crossley

Michael Tomkinson
Hugh Barty-King
Sir John Pender
Geoffrey Battison
Sir Arthur Ford Hetherington
Sir Henry F H Jones
O A Beckerlegge
Edward Stanley Gibbons
Victor Belcher
William Adams Daw
Francis Radford
Joyce M Bellamy
Dennis Bellamy
C L Bibby
Joseph Bibby
J B Bibby
Joseph Bibby
Clyde Binfield
Sir George Williams
P W Bishop
Alfred E C Shippam
Mona S Black
Thomas Robinson Ferens
R M Black
Sir Thomas Octavius Callender
Janet M Blackman
Henry John Copeman
Katherine Bligh
William Maxwell Aitken
   (1st Lord Beaverbrook)
G T Bloomfield
William Edward Bullock
Sir George William Harriman
Sir Reginald Claud Rootes
William Edward Rootes
   (1st Lord Rootes of Ramsbury)
Michael R Bonavia
Sir Herbert Nigel Gresley
Cyril William Hurcomb
   (Lord Hurcomb of Campden Hill)
Sir Eustace James Missenden
John Booker
Howard Lloyd
John Spencer Phillips
Thomas Salt
Sir Richard V Vassar-Smith
Derek Boothroyd
Theodore Cooke Taylor
Jonathan S Boswell
Sir Arthur John Dorman
Sir Robert Stuart Hilton
Sir Walter Benton Jones

John Boulton
Croyden Meredith Whittaker
Susan Bowden
Sir Charles Blampied Colston
Sir Jules Thorn
Brian Bowers
Rookes E B Crompton
Robert Hammond
Donal William Morphy
Alexander Siemens
Faith Bowers
James Benham
Gordon Boyce
Christopher Furness
   (1st Lord Furness of Grantley)
Marmaduke Furness
   (1st Viscount Furness of Grantley)
Frederick William Lewis
   (1st Lord Essendon)
Benjamin Talbot
Emily Boyle
Sir William Crawford
Sir William Ewart
John Mulholland
   (1st Lord Dunleath of Ballywater, Co Down)
James Nicholson Richardson
Trevor Boyns
Alfred Baldwin
William Evans
Louis J B Guéret
Sir Julian S A Hodge
John Lysaght
Robert Bracegirdle
Charles Bennion
Richard Brewer
Willis Jackson
   (Lord Jackson of Burnley)
Asa Briggs (Lord Briggs)
David Lewis
Frederick James Marquis
   (1st Earl of Woolton)
John C W Reith
   (1st Lord Reith of Stonehaven,
   Kincardineshire)
Harry Gordon Selfridge
John H Y Briggs
William Edward Harrison
Sir Alfred Seale Haslam
Robert Heath II
Robert Heath III
Sir James Heath
Arthur H Heath

P Stanley Briggs
Francis Henry Briggs
J P Bristow
John Cathles Hill
Frank Brittain
Alfred Charles Cossor
David Brooke
Thomas Elliot Harrison
Keith Brooker
Arthur William Barratt
Henry John Bostock
Cecil Colman
Henry Simpson Gee
Sir Moses Philip Manfield
Sir Jonathan North
John George Sears
Sir Arnold Colin Somervell
Sir Edward Wood
Helen Brooks
William Henry Lascelles
Peter W Brooks
Sir Hew Ross Kilner
Edward G W T Knollys
    (2nd Viscount Knollys of Caversham)
Sir Peter Gordon Masefield
Sir Robert McLean
Ronald Morce Weeks
Jonathan Brown
Joseph Rank
R H Bulmer
Edward Frederick Bulmer
David Burgess-Wise
Sir Patrick Hennessy
Percival Lee D Perry
    (Lord Perry of Stock Harvard)
Zuzana Burianova
John Chivers
Kathleen Burk
Robert Henry Brand
    (1st Lord Brand of Eydon)
Edward Charles Grenfell
    (1st Lord St Just)
Vivian Hugh Smith (1st Lord Bicester of
    Tusmore)
Gill Burke
Thomas Bedford Bolitho
Charles Algernon Moreing
John Burnett
Giles Henry Zeal
David Burrage
Sir Richard Rylandes Costain
Hester Bury

Sir Frank Warner
Gordon Bussey
Eric Kirkham Cole
Harold John Pye
William George Pye
Michael F Bywater
Edwin Guthrie
Sir William McLintock
William Quilter
Josiah Charles Stamp
    (Lord Stamp of Shortlands)

C

Michael H Caine
John Middleton Campbell
    (Lord Campbell of Eskan)
W A Campbell
James Crossley Eno
Thomas Hedley
M J Cannons
Albert Eadie
John Cantrell
Holbrook Gaskell
Forrest Capie
Sir Thomas Borthwick
David G Carpenter
Sir George Mowlem Burt
Youssef Cassis
Walter Leaf
Sir Felix Otto Schuster
Philippe Chalmin
Charles E Leonard Lyle
    (1st Lord Lyle of Westbourne)
Anne Channon
Sir Sydney Gordon Russell
Geoffrey Channon
Sir Daniel Gooch
Robert Stevenson Horne
    (Viscount Horne of Slamannan)
Sir James Charles Inglis
Sir James Milne
Sir Felix J C Pole
Stanley D Chapman
Jesse Boot
    (1st Lord Trent of Nottingham)
Charles Paxton Markham
Samuel Morley
Anthony John Mundella
John Player
John Dane Player
William Goodacre Player

Nathan Meyer Rothschild
  (1st Lord Rothschild of Tring)
Martin Chick
William Stuckey Piercy
  (1st Lord Piercy of Burford)
P Chipchase
George Street
Andrew Christie
Sir David Dale
Roy Church
Herbert Austin
  (Lord Austin of Longbridge)
Joe F Clarke
Sir Robert Appleby Bartram
John Thomas Batey
Sir Benjamin Chapman Browne
George Clark
Sir Raylton Dixon
Sir William Theodore Doxford
Sir Ernest John Hunter
Sir George Burton Hunter
Sir James Laing
Andrew Leslie
Sir James Marr
Francis Carr Marshall
The Hon Sir Charles A Parsons
Sir John Priestman
John Wigham Richardson
Sir Herbert Babington Rowell
John Young Short
Robert Thompson (1819-1910)
Robert Thompson (1850-1908)
Helen Clay
Richard Longden Hattersley
Henry Ernest Hollins
Esmond J Cleary
Jabez Spencer Balfour
Sir Charles Harold Bellman
Lewis Coleman Cohen
  (Lord Cohen of Brighton)
James Higham
Sir Enoch Hill
Richard Benjamin Starr
Arthur Webb
Edward Wood
Sir Robert Bruce Wycherley
John B M Coates
John B M Coates
Hugh Cockerell
Swinton Boult
Sir Henry Harben

Thomas A E Layborn
Samuel James Pipkin
Sir Frederick W P Rutter
Thomas Bond Sprague
Arthur G Codd
Sir Thomas Malcolm McAlpine
D C Coleman
Samuel Courtauld III
Samuel Courtauld IV
Henry Dreyfus
Sir John Coldbrook Hanbury-Williams
Henry Johnson
Christopher Frank Kearton
  (Lord Kearton of Whitchurch,
  Buckinghamshire)
Sir Arthur William Knight
Sir Thomas Paul Latham
Henry Greenwood Tetley
Howard Coles
Sir William Mather
Sir Joseph Whitworth
D A Collier
John Galloway
John Hick
John Musgrave
Edward J Connell
Sir Andrew Fairbairn
Joseph Hepworth
E W Cooney
William Higgs
Robert Copeland
Richard R J Copeland
T A B Corley
Sir Joseph Beecham
Thomas Beecham
Wilberforce Bryant
Sir John Traill Cargill
Arthur Carr
Warren de la Rue
Sir Alastair Frederick Down
Philip Ernest Hill
Henry G L Lazell
George Palmer
Frederick Adolphus Simonds
Charles William Wallace
Robert Irving Watson
James White
Tom Corran
Sir Hugh E C Beaver
Sir Henry C O Bonsor
Simon Harvey Combe

Sir Richard Charles Garton
Edward Cecil Guinness
  (1st Earl of Iveagh)
P L Cottrell
William Adams
David Chadwick
Dugald Drummond
Albert Zachariah Grant
Sir Samuel Morton Peto
Sir Herbert Ashcombe Walker
E Course
William Robert Sykes
Robin S Craig
Sir William Gray
Sir Edward Hain
Henry Radcliffe
Sir Robert Ropner
Elizabeth Crittall
Francis Henry Crittall
R F Currie
Siegfried Bettmann
Charles William Wallace

D

M J Daunton
Sir George Evelyn P Murray
David Alfred Thomas
  (1st Viscount Rhondda)
Jenny Davenport
Sir James Bowman
John Scott Hindley
  (Viscount Hyndley)
Sir Edward Roberts Lewis
R P T Davenport-Hines
Sir William Anderson
Clive Latham Baillieu
  (1st Lord Baillieu)
Frederick George Banbury
  (1st Lord Banbury of Southam)
Sir Squire Bancroft
John Wolfe Barry
Lilian Mary Baylis
Gerard Lee Bevan
Sir James F N Birch
Sir George L F Bolton
George Macaulay Booth
Harry S B Brindley
Thomas Sivewright Catto
  (1st Lord Catto of Cairncatto)
Cameron Fromanteel Cobbold
  (1st Lord Cobbold)

Jack Cotton
Charles Birch Crisp
Walter Cunliffe
  (1st Lord Cunliffe)
Sir Hugo V R Cunliffe-Owen
Davison Alexander Dalziel
  (Lord Dalziel of Wooler)
Sir Edmund Gabriel Davis
Guy Payan Dawnay
Sir Arthur Trevor Dawson
Sir Geoffrey de Havilland
Frank Dudley Docker
Charles A T R J J ffrench
  (6th Lord ffrench of Castle ffrench)
Sir Charles Bruce Gardner
Sir Eric Campbell Geddes
Herbert Cokayne Gibbs
  (1st Lord Hunsdon)
Sir Edouard P C Girouard
Sir George D T Goldie
Arthur Morton Grenfell
John Gretton
  (1st Lord Gretton)
Sir John Norton Griffiths
Sir John Sutherland Harmood-Banner
Alexander Henderson
  (1st Lord Faringdon)
William Lionel Hichens
Sir Robert Stuart Hilton
Hugo Hirst
  (Lord Hirst)
Sir Edward Hulton
Godfrey Charles Isaacs
Sir Mark Webster Jenkinson
Sir Harry Jephcott
Sir Herbert Alexander Lawrence
William Heneage Legge
  (6th Earl of Dartmouth)
Sir Guy Harold Locock
Oliver Lyttelton
  (1st Viscount Chandos)
Harry Duncan McGowan
  (1st Lord McGowan of Ardeer)
Sir Harry C Mallaby-Deeley
Sir Edward Manville
Sir Roland Thomas Nugent
Henry Osborne O'Hagan
Frederick Scott Oliver
Albert Samuel Pam
Alan Ian Percy
  (8th Duke of Northumberland)
Arthur J H Pollen

Sir Percy John Pybus
Sir Alexander F P Roger
Sir Hallewell Rogers
Sir William Peter Rylands
Sir David L G S Salomons
John Davenport Siddeley
    (1st Lord Kenilworth)
Andrew Wilson Tait
Sir Glynn Hamilton West
Francis Vernon Willey
    (2nd Lord Barnby)
Whitaker Wright
Rhys David
Cyril Lord
Alun C Davies
Aaron Lufkin Dennison
Thomas Peter Hewitt
Victor Kullberg
Thomas Mercer
P N Davies
Edward Wathen Fyffe
Sir Alfred Lewis Jones
Owen Cosby Philipps
    (Lord Kylsant of Carmarthen)
Henry Tyrer
Martin Davis
Sir Walter Charles Puckey
Roberta A Dayer
Sir Charles Stewart Addis
Susan I Dench
Jonathan Dodgson Carr
Laurie Dennett
Sir Hubert Nutcombe Hume
Stefanie Diaper
Sir Alexander Drake Kleinwort
Ernest Greverus Kleinwort
Francis Dick
George William Malcolm
Mark Dixon
Samuel Leonard Simpson
William Lawrence Stephenson
Tom Donnelly
Stanley Markland
C G Down
Sir Hubert Stanley Houldsworth
Holman Frederick Stephens
Madge Dresser
Sir Francis Nicholas Cowlin
Marguerite W Dupree
Sir Edward Tootal Broadhurst
Sir Edward Raymond Streat
Patricia A Dutton

George Horatio Nelson
    (1st Lord Nelson of Stafford)

E

J B F Earle
John Hadfield
Cecil Martin
David E H Edgerton
Ernest Edgar Blake
Francis Charles Mattison
J R Edwards
Sir Francis D'Arcy Cooper
Sir Arthur Lowes Dickinson
Sir Gilbert Francis Garnsey
William Plender
    (Lord Plender of Sundridge, Kent)
Edwin Waterhouse
Ruth Dudley Edwards
Sir Victor Gollancz
Cyril Ehrlich
John Brinsmead
Dennis Ellam
Sir Robert Ian Bellinger
John R Etor
Theodore Brooke Jones

F

David M Fahey
Sir Sydney Oswald Nevile
Malcolm Falkus
Sir David Milne-Watson
David Fanning
Clarence Charles Hatry
D A Farnie
John Bunting
John Kenworthy Bythell
John Platt
Samuel Radcliffe Platt
John Rylands
Marshall Stevens
Robert Burdon Stoker
Chris Farquharson-Roberts
Sir Alan John Cobham
Susan P Farrant
Henry B W Brand
    (1st Viscount Hampden)
Peter Fearon
Sir Frederick Handley Page
George Holt Thomas
R W Ferrier

Sir Maurice Richard Bridgeman
John Cadman
   (1st Lord Cadman of Silverdale)
William Knox D'Arcy
Sir Arthur E C Drake
William Milligan Fraser
   (1st Lord Strathalmond of Pumpherston)
Charles Greenway
   (Lord Greenway of Stanbridge Earls)
Sir C G Graham Hayman
David Fieldhouse
Frank Samuel
Claude Fivel-Demoret
Albert Eustace Berry
Sidney Flavel
George Pargiter Fuller
Gordon A Fletcher
Lawrence Henry Seccombe
Arthur William Trinder
Roderick C Floud
Arthur Greenwood
Thomas Greenwood
James S Foreman-Peck
John Kemp Starley
Spencer Bernau Wilks
Alan Fowler
Sir Amos Nelson
Katherine A Fricker
Giles Atherton

G

G R M Garratt
Sierd Sint Eriks
Stanley Robert Mullard
S Martin Gaskell
Sir Ernest James Johnson
Sir Albert Lindsay Parkinson
Frank Geary
Sir Edward James Harland
Gustav Wilhelm Wolff
Brian Gee
Sir Horace Darwin
John Ross Griffin
Antony C Gilpin
Sir Edmund Henry Gilpin
Honor Godfrey
Jeremiah James Colman
John Benjamin Sainsbury
John James Sainsbury
Francis Goodall
Sir George Kenning

Sir George Thomas Livesey
Thomas Geoffrey Marriott
Harry Neville Moss
Owen Owen
John Craig Paterson
Sir Ernest Willoughby Petter
Percival Waddams Petter
Robert Harold Posnett
Sir Thomas Boverton Redwood
James Cochran Stevenson
Frederick Alexander Szarvasy
John Goodchild
Emerson Muschamp Bainbridge
Henry Currer Briggs
John C D Charlesworth
Rowland Childe
William T S W Fitzwilliam
   (Earl Fitzwilliam)
Sir William Edward Garforth
Sir Joseph Hewitt
John Grayson Lowood
P J Gooderson
James Williamson
   (Lord Ashton)
Jill L Gosling
Joseph Duveen
   (Lord Duveen of Millbank)
Peter Cecil Wilson
T R Gourvish
Sir James Joseph Allport
Sir Myles Fenton
James Staats Forbes
Sir Edward William Watkin
Margaret Gowing
Christopher Hinton
   (Lord Hinton of Bankside)
Edwin Green
Sir Edward Hopkinson Holden
Robert Bewick Longridge
Sir Edwin Landseer Lutyens
Reginald McKenna
Samuel Montagu
   (1st Lord Swaythling)
George Rae
Sir Charles William Sikes
J Greenacombe
Sir Charles James Freake
Robert G Greenhill
Alexander Balfour
Alfred Booth
Edwin Savory Houlder
Sir Robert Paterson Houston

Sir Ernest Henry Murrant
James Greig
John Hopkinson
C P Griffin
Robert Harrison
Sir John Turner
Carl E R Grundy-Warr
Alick Sydney Dick
C Gulvin
John Cawsey Dennis
Sir Herbert Raymond Dennis
William Foden
Edwin Richard Foden
Sir Henry Spurrier
Donald Gresham Stokes
   (Lord Stokes of Leyland)

H

L F Haber
Ivan Levinstein
A A Hall
John Bowes
James Joicey
   (1st Lord Joicey of Chester-le-Steet, County
   Durham)
Francis Priestman
John Bell Simpson
Sir Lindsay Wood
Kerry Hamilton
Cyril William Hurcomb
   (Lord Hurcomb of Campden Hill)
Leslie Hannah
George Balfour
Sir F H Stanley Brown
Walter McLennan Citrine
William Henry Coates
   (Lord Citrine)
Sir Josiah Eccles
Sir Norman Randall Elliott
Sir John Hacking
Michael Isaac Lipman
Charles Hesterman Merz
Jerry Harris
Sir James Knott
J R Harris
James Harrison
Thomas Harrison
Alfred Holt
A E Harrison
Sir Harold Bowden
Ian Harrison

Sir Cyril Ernest Harrison
Charles E Harvey
Sir John N V Duncan
Sir Charles W E Fielding
Auckland Campbell Geddes
   (1st Lord Geddes)
William Jenkins
Hugh Mackay Matheson
Sir Henry Whittaker Trickett
Sir Ronald M C Turner
Kevin Hawkins
Sir William Waters Butler
Roy Hay
Samuel Allen
Harrison Barrow
Robert Hall Best
Frederick Buck Goodman
R J Hercock
Alfred Hugh Harman
Edward Ball Knobel
John Hibbs
Harold C G Drayton
Sidney Emile Garcke
Sir John Frederick Heaton
Richard Joseph Howley
Martin Higham
Joseph Rowntree
Robin Higham
Sir James Bird
Sir Charles Dennistoun Burney
Sir Gerard J R L d'Erlanger
Sir Roy Hardy Dobson
Sir George Herbert Dowty
Sir George Robert Edwards
Sir Charles Richard Fairey
Sir Alfred H R Fedden
Sir Giles Guthrie
Frank Bernard Halford
Ernest Walter Hives
   (Lord Hives)
Sir Samuel Instone
Sir James Martin
Charles Hubert Scott-Paine
Hugh Oswald Short
John Davenport Siddeley
Sir Arthur Sidgreaves
   (1st Lord Kenilworth)
Sir Basil Smallpeice
Thomas O M Sopwith
Sir Frank Spencer Spriggs
Herbert John Thomas
George Edward Woods-Humphery

Sir George White
Henry White-Smith
Sir Myles D N Wyatt
John O Hitchcock
Sir William Thomas Griffiths
Sir Maurice Hodgson
Sir Stanley Paul Chambers
Len T Holden
Sir Charles John Bartlett
Sir James Reginald Pearson
Jim Holderness
Nathaniel Clayton
J A Holloway
Sir Allan Gordon-Smith
Graeme M Holmes
Henry Seymour Berry
    (1st Lord Buckland of Bwlch)
Francis William Gilbertson
Sir David Richard Llewellyn
Charles B B McLaren
    (1st Lord Aberconway of Bodnant)
Henry Duncan McLaren
    (2nd Lord Aberconway of Bodnant)
Richard Thomas
Sir John Roper Wright
Sir William Charles Wright
Deian Hopkins
George Allardice Riddell
    (Lord Riddell of Walton Heath)
A C Howe
Sir Alfred Herbert Dixon
Edward Hermon
Sir Frank Hollins
Sir William Henry Houldsworth
Henry Lee
Sir Joseph Cocksey Lee
Lennox Bertram Lee
Sir Frederick Thorpe Mappin
Sir Alan John Sykes
Kenneth Hudson
Sir John Keay
Thomas Medland Stocker
L B Hunt
Arthur Blakeney Coussmaker
George Matthey
Sandra Hunt
James Voase Rank
Willard Garfield Weston
H Montgomery Hyde
Sir Edwin Alliott Verdon Verdon-Roe

I

Jane Insley
William F R Stanley
David Iredale
Herman Eugen Falk
John A Iredale
Geoffrey Hill Ambler
Sir Isaac Holden
Samuel Cunliffe Lister
    (1st Lord Masham of Swinton)
George Frederick Raper
R J Irving
Sir Alexander Kaye Butterworth
Sir Eric Campbell Geddes
Sir George Stegmann Gibb
Sir Andrew Noble
Sir Vincent Litchfield Raven
Henry Tennant
Sir Ralph Lewis Wedgwood

J

Gordon Jackson
Arthur Wilson
Charles Wilson
    (Lord Nunburnholme)
Kenneth E Jackson
Halley Stewart
Sir Percy Malcolm Stewart
Russell Jackson
Sir Charles Wyndham
Alan G Jamieson
William Inman
Sir John Isaac Thornycroft
Helen E Jeffries
Sir John Aird
Arthur Perkins Bigelow
Alan Jenkins
Francis Taylor
    (Lord Taylor of Hadfield)
D T Jenkins
Sir John Barran
Sir Jacob Behrens
George Douglas
John Jowitt
Sir Henry Mitchell
Sir Mark Oldroyd
Sir Prince Smith
David J Jeremy

Sir John Anderson
Ernest Bader
Charles J P Ball
Leonard Hugh Bentall
Sir George Mowlem Burt
Sir William H E C Butlin
Alfred Corning Clark
Sir John Edward Cohen
Sir Richard Rylandes Costain
Alfred Cecil Critchley
Julius Charles Drew
John B S Gabriel
Thomas Edmund Gartside
Sir Alexander Gibb
Sir Claude Dixon Gibb
Sir William Pickles Hartley
Philip Sydney Henman
Sir Frederic Collins Hooper
Sir John Jackson
Sir John William Laing
Harold Vincent Mackintosh
   (1st Viscount Mackintosh of Halifax)
John Mackintosh
Gerard N C Mann
Sir Josiah Mason
Bertram Wagstaff Mills
Sir Godfrey Way Mitchell
Sir Robert Ludwig Mond
Anthony John Mundella
George William Odey
Sir Alfred G B Owen
Andrew Pears
Weetman Dickinson Pearson
   (1st Viscount Cowdray)
Sir Ernest Willoughby Petter
Percival Waddams Petter
Robert Harold Posnett
Austin Leonard Reed
The Hon Charles Stewart Rolls
Sir Frederick Henry Royce
Thomas Baron Russell
George Sanger
Thomas O M Sopwith
Sir Albert Spicer
Sir Frank Spencer Spriggs
Sir Edward David Stern
Sir Oswald Stoll
Sir Henry Tate
Sir Henry Whittaker Trickett
Frederick Wallis
Weston F M Webb

Francis Pelham Whitbread
Sir Myles D N Wyatt
David S Johnson
Sir John Milne Barbour
Sir George Smith Clark
Sir Henry Cochrane
Sir Samuel Clement Davidson
Thomas Gallaher
James Mackie
William James Pirrie
   (Viscount Pirrie)
William Holmes Smiles
Francis Workman
Walford Johnson
Arthur Burr
Sir Edward James Harland
Richard Tilden Smith
Gustav Wilhelm Wolff
Aubrey Jones
Sir Andrew Rae Duncan
Charles A Jones
John Morris
Charles Morrison
Edgar Jones
Sir Harold Montague Barton
Henry Alexander Benson
   (Lord Benson)
Raymond Percival Brookes
   (Lord Brookes)
Arthur Cooper
Ernest Cooper
William Welch Deloitte
Sir Robert Palmer Harding
Sir Charles William Hayward
James Hornby Jolly
Arthur Keen
William Royse Lysaght
Sir Basil Edgar Mayhew
Joseph Henry Nettlefold
Sir Kenneth Swift Peacock
John William Sankey
Joseph Sankey
Sir Philip Sidney Stott
William Turquand
Frederick Whinney
Geoffrey G Jones
Sir Arthur Philip Du Cros
William Harvey Du Cros
John Boyd Dunlop
Frederick Lane
Sir Charles Lidbury

Sir Thomas Boverton Redwood
Marcus Samuel
  (1st Viscount Bearsted)
George A Jones
Sir Ivor Philipps
H Kay Jones
Stanley Shaw Bond
Linda Jones
Thomas Avery
Sir James Timmins Chance
Sir Richard Tangye
Stephanie Jones
Thomas Turnbull

K

Ralph A Kaner
George James Harris
Simon Katzenellenbogen
Sir Alfred Chester Beatty
Shirley Keeble
James Alexander Bowie
Sir Robert Robertson Hyde
Sir Charles Garonne Renold
Benjamin Seebohm Rowntree
Harry Ward
Bernard F Keeling
Sir Robert Minshull Shone
David Kenning
Sir George Kenning
Dermot Keogh
William Martin Murphy
H B Kerr
Sir James Carmichael
J Max Keyworth
Sir Arthur Wheeler
Cyril A Kidd
Sir Alfred Chester Beatty
Alexandra Kidner
Charles Reginald Belling
Sir John Tomlinson Brunner
Hamilton Young Castner
Julius Caesar Czarnikow
Harry Neville Moss
John R Killick
Alexander Allan Paton
John Rankin
William Benson Rathbone
John King
Leo F A d'Erlanger
Sir Harold Brewer Hartley
M W Kirby

Joseph Albert Pease
  (1st Lord Gainford of Headlam, County
  Durham)
Sir Evan Williams
P L Kirby
Sir Joseph Wilson Swan
Robert M Kirk
Sir George Bullough
John Bullough
Sir Benjamin Alfred Dobson
Jack Kitchen
Frederic R M de Paula
Derek Knee
David Morgan
Robert Knight
Arthur Baker
David T A Kynaston
Frederick George Banbury
  (1st Lord Banbury of Southam)
Ferdinand Faithfull Begg
Harry Panmure Gordon
Thomas Nickalls
Henry Osborne O'Hagan

L

Joan Lane
Sir Alfred Edward Herbert
Sir William Lyons
Rachel Lawrence
Edward Lloyd
Frank Lloyd
Stephen Lawrence
John Henry Jacques
  (Lord Jacques of Portsea Island)
John T W Mitchell
Sir Arthur Sugden
Joseph Leckey
Sir Benjamin Baker
Charles E Lee
Sir Robert William Perks
Peter J Lee
Arthur William Trinder
Anthony A Letts
Charles John Letts
Wayne Lewchuk
Frank George Woollard
Jonathan M Liebenau
Thomas Holloway
Thomas Morson
Thomas Whiffen
Jean Lindsay

George S G Douglas-Pennant
(2nd Lord Penrhyn)
Stafford M Linsley
William George Armstrong
(1st Lord Armstrong of Cragside)
William C Lister
Alexander Muirhead
Bryan Little
Abraham Laverton
Ian Lloyd
Claude Goodman Johnson
Roger Lloyd-Jones
Harold Marsh Harwood
Sir William Clare Lees
Joan Long
Frank Murphy
Jane Lowe
Charles Vernon Pugh

M

Duncan McDowall
Sir John Hamet Dunn
A H McClelland
Sir William Reardon Smith
Anita McConnell
William F R Stanley
Arthur J McIvor
Sir Charles Wright Macara
John Brown Tattersall
Alan C McKinnon
John Atkins Peacock
Frederick William Rushbrooke
Roger Manvill
Joseph Arthur Rank
(Lord Rank of Sutton Scotney)
Sheila Marriner
William Lidderdale
John Samuel Swire
Peter T Marsh
Joseph Chamberlain
John D Marshall
William Cavendish
(7th Duke of Devonshire)
Sir James Ramsden
Sir Peter Masefield
Herbert George Brackley
Sir Sydney Camm
William Sholto Douglas
(1st Lord Douglas of Kirtleside)
Frank Bernard Halford
John Ronald McCrindle

John Dudley North
Whitney Willard Straight
William Miles Webster Thomas
(Lord Thomas of Remingtham)
Sir George White
John J Mason
Herbert Shepherd Cross
William Henry Holland
(1st Lord Rotherham)
F C Mather
George F S Smith
William M Mathew
Henry Hucks Gibbs
(1st Lord Aldenham)
Derek Matthews
John West
Sir Corbet Woodall
William Woodall
Catherine E Meakin
James Alexander Bowie
T M Megaw
Sir Basil Mott
Ranald C Michie
Samuel Jones Loyd
(Lord Overstone of Overstone and
Fotheringhay)
Rory Miller
Archibald Williamson
(1st Lord Forres of Glenogil)
Rosemary C E Milligan
Sir Michael Willcox Perrin
Sir Henry Solomon Wellcome
A L Minkes
Sir Robert Camm Booth
William Edmund Kenrick
D E Moggridge
John Maynard Keynes
(Lord Keynes of Tilton)
Robert Molesworth Kindersley
(1st Lord Kindersley of West Hoathly)
Charles More
Sir Charles Percy Lister
Robert M Morgan
William Hunter McFadzean
(Lord McFadzean of Woldingham)
J E Morpurgo
Sir Allen Lane
Peter Morris
Alfred Moritz Mond
(1st Lord Melchett of Landford)
Henry Ludwig Mond
(2nd Lord Melchett of Landford)

Ludwig Mond
Sir William Henry Perkin
D John Morton
Sir Henry Doulton
Jocelyn W F Morton
Sir James Morton
Michael S Moss
Sir Frank G C Fison
Montagu Collet Norman
   (Lord Norman of St Clare)
Laurence Richard Philipps
   (1st Lord Milford of Llanstephan)
Sir Frederick Ernest Rebbeck
George Muirhead
Richard Irvin
John Woodger
Lynn Murch
Alexander F F Young
Christopher Murphy
Sir James Horlick
Sir William Capel Slaughter
Robert Murphy
Oscar Deutsch
John Maxwell
Isidore Ostrer
Charles Moss Woolf
Basil G Murray
George Cadbury
Laurence John Cadbury
Paddy Musgrove
Henry Charles Stephens
Norman Mutton
Sir Alfred Bird
William Orme Foster

N

Chris Niblett
Sir Arthur P M Fleming
Ian Nicholson
Stanley Robert Mullard
T R Nevett
Thomas James Barratt
Samuel Herbert Benson
Sir William Smith Crawford
Sir Charles Frederick Higham
Harold Nockolds
Joseph Lucas
Sir Arthur Bertram Waring
Paul Nunn
Charles Cammell

John Devonshire Ellis
Sir William Henry Ellis
Mark Firth

O

Derek Oddy
Sir Thomas Johnstone Lipton
Maurice E Ogborn
Sir William Palin Elderton
G Oldfield
John Player
John Dane Player
William Goodacre Player
E A Olive
Edward James Barford
M John Orbell
John Baring
   (2nd Lord Revelstoke)
Sir Edward Robert Peacock
James Frater Taylor
Richard F Overy
Leonard Percy Lord
   (Lord Lambury of Northfield)
William Richard Morris
   (Viscount Nuffield of Nuffield)

P

R H Parker
John Manger Fells
Sir William Barclay Peat
Michael F Parr
Alfred Waterhouse
Henry W Parris
John A F Aspinall
William Henry Barlow
Sir Henry de Guise Forbes
Sir William Guy Granet
Sir John Hawkshaw
John Ramsbottom
John Saxby
Charles E P D D Spagnoletti
Patrick Stirling
Sir Henry Whatley Tyler
Linda Parry
William Morris
J F Parsons
John Elmes Beale
Peter L Payne
George Spencer

Alan W H Pearsall
Sir Alan Garrett Anderson
James Anderson
Sir Arthur Munro Sutherland
R Peddie
Gerald Steel
Henry Steel
Sir Frederick Pedler
Frank Samuel
Denys C S Pegg
Patrick James Foley
Richard Perren
Sir Edmund Hoyle Vestey
William Vestey
Sir James Angus Watson
Charles R Perry
Sir Stevenson Arthur Blackwood
Frank Ives Scudamore
Sir John Tilley
David C Phillips
Thomas Lake Aveling
Charles Burrell
Nathaniel Clayton
Robert Henry Fowler
James Howard
James Ransome
Robert Charles Ransome
Joseph Ruston
Joseph Shuttleworth
Gordon Phillips
John Walter III
W Philpott
William Whiteley
D W Pittard
Wreford J C Pittard
D C M Platt
James Westlake Platt
K G Ponting
Stephen Moulton
Eric Walter Pasold
M H Port
William Field
Sir George Gilbert Scott
Edward Yates
Andrew N Porter
Sir Donald Currie
Dilwyn Porter
Harry Hananel Marks
Sir Cyril Arthur Pearson
H J Potterton
Henry Curry

R

Stephen Rabson
Sir Donald Forsyth Anderson
John Rackham
Frederick George Creed
Veronica Rady
Frederick Godber
  (Lord Godber of Mayfield, Sussex)
John B Rae
Henry George Ferguson
Joseph Rank
Joseph Arthur Rank
  (Lord Rank of Sutton Scotney)
Trevor Raybould
William Ward (1st Earl of Dudley)
William H E Ward
  (3rd Earl of Dudley)
J Gordon Read
Daniel Adamson
Sir William Bower Forwood
John William Hughes
Thomas Henry Ismay
W J Reader
Sir Robert Barlow
Sir Eric Vansittart Bowater
Sir John Bevan Braithwaite
Joseph Bevan Braithwaite
Selwyn Francis Edge
William Hesketh Lever
  (1st Viscount Leverhulme of the Western
  Isles)
Montagu Stanley Napier
Basil N Reckitt
Sir James Reckitt
M C Reed
Sir George Findlay
Sir Richard Moon
Peter N Reed
John Crosfield
William Gossage
Sir Max Muspratt
Richard H Reed
Rupert Evelyn Beckett
Colin Frederick Campbell
  (1st Lord Colgrain)
Hew F Reid
Louis Bamberger
Lucian Randolph Ercolani
Ebenezer Gomme
Harris Lebus

Hermann Andrew Lebus
Robin Reilly
Josiah Wedgwood V
R W Rennison
Christian A H Allhusen
Utrick Alexander Ritson
Sir William Haswell Stephenson
William Boutland Wilkinson
Jack Reynolds
Ernest Henry Gates
Alfred Illingworth
Sir Titus Salt
D G Rhys
William Hillman
A B Richards
Sir George Alexander Touche
Jeffrey Richards
Sir Michael Elias Balcon
David J Richardson
Montague Gluckstein
Sir Joseph Nathaniel Lyons
Harry Salmon
Kenneth Richardson
Ernest Terah Hooley
Frederick Richard Simms
Margaret Richardson
Ernest Terah Hooley
W Gordon Rimmer
Sir Edwin Airey
William Lawies Jackson
   (1st Lord Allerton of Chapel Allerton)
James Kitson
   (1st Lord Airedale of Gledhow)
Sir Amos Nelson
Joseph Watson
   (1st Lord Manton of Compton Verney)
Victor Hugo Watson
Rowland Winn
Robert H G Ring
John Derby Allcroft
Michael Robbins
Sir John Elliot
Frank Pick
Robert Hope Selbie
Albert Henry Stanley
   (Lord Ashfield of Southwell)
Sir Henry Worth Thornton
David E Roberts
Alfred Colson
Thomas Hawksley
Richard Roberts
Emile Oscar Garcke

Baron Rudolph Bruno Schröder
Frank Cyril Tiarks
Michael Robson
Sir Robert Ropner
Terence Rodgers
Sir Allan MacGregor Smith
E A Rose
Hugh Mason
Mary B Rose
Henry Philips Greg
Catherine M Ross
John Candlish
James Hartley
Ernest Joseph Jobling-Purser
Robert Walter Swinburne
D J Rowe
Edmund Graham Angus
George Angus
William Boyd
Edward Brough
Joseph William Brough
Clive Cookson
Norman Charles Cookson
Roland Antony Cookson
George Crawshay
William Donaldson Cruddas
James Deuchar
John James Fenwick
Alfred James Foster
Sir Percy Llewellyn Hunting
Sir Joseph William Isherwood
Arthur Henry Lancaster
James Leathart
Gerald William Mann
Sir Charles Mark Palmer
Alphonse Constant Reyrolle
Walter Runciman
   (1st Lord Runciman of Shoreston)
Andrew Weir
   (1st Lord Inverforth of Southgate)
Hugh Nicholas Wood
Willliam D Rubinstein
Sir John Reeves Ellerman (1862–1933)
Sir John Reeves Ellerman (1909–1973)
C A Russell
Robert Stirling Newall
Peter E Russell
John F L T Bateman
S P Russell
William Pickersgill
Roger Ryan
John J W Deuchar

S

Leonard Sainer
Sir Charles Clore
Andrew Saint
William Willett
Michael Sanderson
Sir George Alexander
Sir Herbert Beerbohm Tree
Alan J Scarth
Charles Tricks Bowring
Frank Hornby
Christopher J Schmitz
Sir Cecil Lindsay Budd
J W Scott
Harry Clifford-Turner
Frederick Alexander Szarvasy
John P Scott
John Wynford Philipps
    (1st Viscount St Davids of Lydstep Haven)
Cecil Martin Sharp
Francis Trounson Hearle
Christine Shaw
William Maxwell Aitken
William Edward Allen
Bernhard Baron
George Beale
John Bedford
Sir Ernest John P Benn
William Ewert Berry
    (1st Viscount Camrose)
James Gomer Berry
    (1st Viscount Kemsley)
Richard Blackwell
Horatio William Bottomley
Sidney George Brown
Sir Stanley Paul Chambers
Sir Christopher J H Chancellor
Sir Allen George Clark
Sir Charles Blake Cochran
John Cockshut
Douglas Raymond Collins
Simon Harvey Combe
Geoffrey Crowther
    (Lord Crowther of Headingley)
Sir David Dale
Sir David Dale
Joseph Mallaby Dent
Sir John Dewrance
Sir John Evans
Alexander Fleck
    (Lord Fleck of Saltcoats)

William Lionel Fraser
David Gestetner
Alfred C W Harmsworth
    (Viscount Northcliffe)
Harold Sidney Harmsworth
    (1st Viscount Rothermere)
Sir Edward Hulton
Edward Mauger Iliffe
    (1st Lord Iliffe of Yattendon)
Sir Henry Irving
Sir Maxwell Joseph
Edward Levy Lawson
    (1st Lord Burnham of Hall Barn)
Reuben Herbert Ling
Sir Frederick Orridge Macmillan
Michael Marks
Simon Marks
    (1st Lord Marks of Broughton)
Sir Algernon M M Methuen
Charles Edward Mudie
Sir George Newnes
Sir Isaac Pitman
Paul Julius Reuter
    (1st Baron de Reuter)
Alan John Sainsbury
    (Lord Sainsbury of Drury Lane)
John Benjamin Sainsbury
John James Sainsbury
Sir Robert Sainsbury
Israel Moses Sieff
    (Lord Sieff of Brimpton)
Henry Van den Bergh
Jacob Van den Bergh
Alexander Pollock Watt
Eric M Sigsworth
Sir Montague Maurice Burton
William Foster
Sarah Silcox
George Ernest May
    (1st Lord May of Weybridge)
Colin Simmons
Richard Longden Hattersley
Denis Machell Hollins
Henry Ernest Hollins
Jack Simmons
John Mason Cook
Thomas Cook
Sir Samuel Fay
Sir John Fowler
William Stroudley
Judy Slinn
Edwin Freshfield

Sir William Hargreaves Leese
Sir Alfred David McAlpine
William Egerton Mortimer
Sir Leslie Ernest Peppiatt
P Eynon Smart
Francis Augustus Bevan
Sir Frederick C Ellerton
Frederick Crauford Goodenough
Sir William Macnamara Goodenough
John Lubbock
   (1st Lord Avebury of Avebury)
Sir Richard Biddulph Martin
Joseph Herbert Tritton
Anthony William Tuke
Barbara M D Smith
Arthur Chamberlain
Sir Bernard D F Docker
John Young Sangster
Edward Turner
Eric Turner
Michael Stammers
Ralph Brocklebank
Gavin Stamp
Sir Giles Gilbert Scott
Julie G Stark
Hudson Ewbanke Kearley
   (1st Viscount Devonport)
Hew S Stevenson
James Cochran Stevenson
Patricia J Storey
Samuel Storey
Richard A Storey
Sir Stephen France Burman
Henry James Coles
Sidney Smith Flavel
Sir Charles E H Friswell
Cecil Kimber
Henry John Lawson
Sir William Malesbury Letts
Percy Martin
Frederick Richard Simms
Walter Leonard Thurgood
Leslie Basil Thwaites
Harry Weston
Arthur Primrose Young
Geoffrey Stow
James Lyle Mackay
   (1st Earl of Inchcape)
Michael Stratton
James Coster Edwards
Eric E G Street
Geoffrey Marks

J O Stubbs
Sir Joseph Lawrence
Peter Sutcliffe
Sir Humphery Sumner Milford
G Barry Sutton
William Stephens Clark
Philip H Sykes
Albert Edwin Reed
Sir Albert Ralph Reed
Clifford Dommett Sheldon

T

Jennifer Tann
John English
George Kynoch
Sir Joseph Flawith Lockwood
Carole Taylor
Henry Littleton
Dennis Teesdale
Sir Arthur McDougall Duckham
Julian C Temple
Frederick George Miles
Pat M Thane
Sir Ernest Joseph Cassel
Rosamund Thomas
Oliver Sheldon
Lyndall Fownes Urwick
W A Thomas
Edward Rae
F M L Thompson
John Clutton
J C Thompson
Francis Arthur Perkins
David W Thoms
Reginald Walter Maudslay
Lady Elizabeth Thomson
William Douglas Weir
   (1st Viscount Weir of Eastwood)
Robert Thorne
Andrew Handyside
L J Tolly
Sir Charles Garonne Renold
G Tonge
Austin Leonard Reed
Hugh S Torrens
John Lum Stothert
Alistair G Tough
Sir Stephen France Burman
John Howard Colls
Richard H Trainor
John Nock Bagnall

Reuben Farley
Sir Alfred Hickman
Sir Benjamin Hingley
J Malcolm Trickett
Sir Isaac Holden
Samuel Cunliffe Lister
    (1st Lord Masham of Swinton)
Barrie Trinder
Sir Bernhard Samuelson
Frank Trowell
Benjamin Walmsley
William Walmsley
D Gordon Tucker
Gisbert Kapp
Sir William Henry Preece
Gerard L Turnbull
Lloyd Henry Baxendale
John Turner
Sir Vincent H P Caillard
Alison Turton
Sir John Barker
Sir Richard Burbidge
Geoffrey Tweedale
Arthur Balfour
    (1st Lord Riverdale of Sheffield)
Sir Henry Bessemer
Sir John Brown
Albert Arnold Gliksten
James Henry Greathead
Sir Robert Abbott Hadfield
Sir Ambrose Keevil
Sir James Kemnal
Augustus David Klaber
Edward Bryan Latham
John Lewis
John Spedan Lewis
Sir Stuart Sidney Mallinson
Sir William James Mallinson
Sir Holberry Mensforth
Julian E A Mond
    (3rd Lord Melchett of Landford)
Edward Vansittart Neale
Henry George Nelson
    (2nd Lord Nelson of Stafford)
Edwin Noel A Plowden
    (Lord Plowden of Plowden)
Charles F A Portal
    (1st Viscount Portal of Hungerford)
Max John Railing
Sir Harry Railing

Sir Charles William Siemens
Ernest E D Simon
    (1st Lord Simon of Wythenshawe)
Henry Simon
Horatio Nelson Smith
Albert Vickers
Thomas Edward Vickers
Sir Joseph Whitworth
George Wostenholm
S H G Twining
Richard Twining III
A C Twort
Geoffrey Morse Binnie
R E Tyson
William Marcroft

U

Philip Unwin
Sir Stanley Unwin

V

Jean Jacques Van-Helten
Alfred Beit
Julius Carl Wernher
Sean A Vertigan
John Cash
Joseph Cash

W

Lady Gillian Wagner
Joseph Storrs Fry
Kathleen M Wain
Sir Everard Alexander Hambro
David H E Wainwright
Henry Fowler Broadwood
Arthur Brooke
Richard Adam Ellis
Alfred Edward Knight
James Livesey
Herbert Morris
Philip Wallis
Charles James Longman
John Walton
Thomas Routledge
Lee Weatherley
Norman Edward Wates

Ronald B Weir
Thomas Robert Dewar
  (Lord Dewar of Homerstall)
James Stevenson
  (Lord Stevenson of Holmbury)
David Welch
Sir Alexander Korda
Fred Wellings
Sir Halford W L Reddish
Brian West
Sir John Moores
Oliver M Westall
Albert Wellesley Bain
Cuthbert Eden Heath
Sir Edward Mortimer Mountain
Joyce F Wheatley
Frederick John Dove
Raymond R Wile
Alfred Corning Clark
William Barry Owen
L John Williams
George Thomas Clark
William Thomas Lewis
  (1st Lord Merthyr of Senghenydd)
William Menelaus
John Nixon
Charles Wilson
Sir Isaac Lothian Bell
Sir Ellis Hunter
John F Wilson
Sir Gerard V S de Ferranti
Sebastian Ziani de Ferranti
J S G Wilson
Ronald Brodie Gillett
Kevin Wilson
Colin Minton Campbell

R G Wilson
Edward Greene
Ronald Wilson
Sir Anthony Horace Milward
J R Winton
John William B Pease
  (1st Lord Wardington of Alnmouth in the
  County of Northumberland)
Christine Woods
Sir Thomas Wardle
Hugh Woolhouse
Noble Frank Lowndes
Chris Wrigley
James Mortimer Peddie
  (Lord Peddie of the City and County of
  Kingston upon Hull)
Robert J Wyatt
Charles R F Engelbach
Humphrey Wynn
Robert Blackburn

Y

Basil S Yamey
Sir William Samuel Glyn-Jones

Z

Stephanie Zarach
Selchouk Ahmed Ghalib
Walter Patrick Grove
Jonathan H Zeitlin
Henry C S Dyer
Maurice Zinkin
Geoffrey Heyworth
  (Lord Heyworth of Oxton)

List of errata

VOLUME 1

Page no

xx	Line 13	– '1975' should read '1974'.
xxi	Line 10	– 'meridien' should read 'meridiem'.
xxv	Line 5	– 'floreat' should read 'floruit'.
xxviii	Line 18	– 'meridien' should read 'meridiem'.
1	Line 2	– 'MACLAREN' should read 'McLAREN'.
6	Line 16	– 'Godalming' should read 'Sidcup'.
26	Lines 22–24	– Beaverbrook disposed of his holding in the Daily Mail Trust on the open market in 1928–29, and not following his purchase of the Trust's shares in Express Newspapers in 1932–33.
35	Line 6	– *'Victorian Architecture'* should read *'Victorian Architecture in England'*.
57	Line 24	– 'Sharpe' should read 'Sharp'.
68	Lines 16–17	– should read: 'His mother, Ann, was the daughter of William Potter of Walbottle House'.
77	Line 11	– 'Bowden' should read 'Bowdon'.
104	Lines 25–27	– should read: '. . . of Manchester; they had one son and one daughter. After Elizabeth's death in 1892 he married, in 1898, Norah Mossam, daughter of J Compton Merryweather; they had one daughter and one son, whose son inherited Bainbridge's wealth'.
146	Line 32	– 'Newton Abbot: David & Charles' should read 'Batsford'.
155	Line 15	– 'Grantham' should read 'Lingfield'.
172	Line 32	– delete '(qv)'.
197	Line 5	– should read: 'manager of the Royal Institution, FRS, fellow of the Royal Geographical Society. He was chairman of the Royal Society of Arts in 1898–99'.
242	Line 26	– 'director of London Transport' should read 'member of the London Transport Executive'.
261	Line 19	– 'Metroland' should read 'Metro-land'.
272	Lines 7–8	– 'Thomas Cook & Sons' should read 'Thomas Cook & Son'.
280	Line 20	– 'in about 1875' should read 'in 1880'.
295	Line 27	– 'Golborn' should read 'Golborne'.
297	Line 7	– 'Earlstown' should read 'Earlestown'.
322	Line 1	– 'neé Begg' should read 'neé Hogg'.
353	Line 1	– '1879' should read '1897'.
	Line 14	– 'Hitchen' should read 'Hitchin'.
354	Line 21	– 'Hitchen' should read 'Hitchin'.
357	Line 32	– 'Jane Lane' should read 'John Lane'.
363	Line 1	– 'Tredwidden' should read 'Trewidden'.
387	Line 10	– 'Llanwryst' should read 'Llanwrst'.
394	Line 19	– 'Northcliffe' should read 'Rothermere'.
	Line 22	– 'Northcliffe' should read 'Rothermere'.
425	Line 8	– 'Wood-Humphery' should read 'Woods-Humphery'.

VOLUME 1-*continued*

Page no

429	Line 3	– 'Rio de Janiero' should read 'Rio de Janeiro'.
441	Line 11	– 'preserves' should read 'reserves'.
447	Line 8	– 'Christiana' should read 'Christiania'.
450	Line 17	– delete 'PP Report on Woolwich Royal Ordance Factories (1919) Cmd 229'. (Inferior version of preceding title).
491	Last line	– 'Foreag' should read 'Forlag'.
502	Line 33	– delete '(qv)'.
503	Line 15	– 'Stornaway' should read 'Stornoway'.
519	Line 2	– should read 'see LAWSON, Edward Levy'.
528	Last line	– 'Walkenden' should read 'Walkden'.
536	Line 19	– 'Hounsditch' should read 'Houndsditch'.
537		– Picture Caption — 'Auben' should read 'Auburn'.
557	Line 3	– '*News Chronicle*' should read '*Daily News*'.
559	Line 36	– delete '(qv)'; 'Edmund' should read 'Edmond'.
562	Line 18	– delete '(qv)'.
563	Line 2	– 'Institute' should read 'Institution'.
583	Line 11	– delete 's' from 'Railways'.
606	Line 26	– delete '(and later first Lord Shortgrove)' and insert '(created baronet in 1910)'.
607	Line 1	– 'Mordenfeldt' should read 'Nordenfeldt'.
610	Line 18	– 'Farringdon' should read 'Faringdon'.
612	Line 19	– should read 'Mountbatten'.
621	Line 10	– 'Oxford' should read 'Cambridge'.
631	Line 21	– 'Llynri' should read 'Llynvi'.
660	Line 20	– 'Winchelsea' should read 'Winchilsea'.
669	Line 35	– should read 'William Hill'.
700	Line 27	– '£50 million' should read '£123 million'.
709	Line 43	– should read 'GCVO'.
	Line 46	– 'temporary' should read 'acting'.
716	Line 49	– 'reviews' should read 'revues'.
723	Line 38	– should read 'Old Ford business . . .'.
728	Line 28	– 'Heath Government' should read 'Edward Heath, Secretary for Trade and Industry,'.
771	Line 13	– should read 'Brooks's'.
783	Line 10	– should read 'Van den Bergh'.
794	Line 18	– 'Malinde' should read 'Malindi'.
809		– Insert ENTRY CROSS HEADING: COWDRAY, Viscount See PEARSON, Weetman Dickinson.
815	Line 33	– 'KCBE' should read 'KBE'.
860	Line 20	– should read 'Whittle Dene'.

VOLUME 2

Page no

xii	Line 6	– 'Loughborough' should read 'Lanark'.
xix	Line 12	– 'meridien' should read 'meridiem'.
	Line 24	– 'Association' should read 'Corporation'.

VOLUME 2–*continued*

Page no

xxiv	Line 6	– 'floreat' should read 'floruit'.
xxviii	Line 17	– 'meridien' should read 'meridiem'.
xxxi	Line 7	– 'Railway Co' should read 'Railways'.
3	Line 48	– 'Sheldon' should read 'Shildon'.
7	Line 28	'South-West' should read 'South Western'.
9	Line 40	– 'Kirkaldy' should read 'Kirkcaldy'.
24	Line 4	– 'Tuorak' should read 'Toorak'.
	Line 7	– 'Chapstal' should read 'Chaptal'.
58	Line 19	– delete 'in effect'.
63	Line 17	– 'Government Minister' should read 'Controller of Non-Ferrous Metals'.
67	Line 21	– '1921' should read '1920'.
70	Line 27	– 'League of Nations' should read 'League of Nations Union'.
100–103		– insert death date of Alick Sydney Dick: March 1986.
101	Line 42	– 'Adler' should read 'Alder'.
110	Line 21	– 'testament' should read 'testimony'.
121	Line 17	– 'Herbert' should read 'Hebbert'.
	Line 21	– should read 'Metropolitan Amalgamated Railway Carriage & Wagon Co'.
125	Line 18	– '&' should read 'and'.
127	Line 7	– 'East' should read 'Easter'.
	Line 10	– 'Wootton' should read 'Woolton'.
143	Line 43	– 'KGCB' should read 'GCB'.
151	Line 2	– 'Stoney' should read 'Stony'.
164	Line 12	– should read 'Boulton & Paul'.
172	Line 16	– should read 'Pembroke College, Cambridge'.
177	Line 2	– 'Ashhurst' should read 'Ashurst'.
	Line 36	– 'Edward' should read 'Edwin'.
183	Line 42	– 'Staffs' should read 'Staff'.
202	Line 40	– 'Hamersley' should read 'Hammersley'.
211	Line 27	– 'Cunniffe' should read 'Cunliffe'.
212	Line 26	– delete 'and'.
228	Line 40	'Bennet' should read 'Bennett'.
237		Portrait Caption should read '(*courtesy of Clifford Edwards*)'.
238	Line 43	– 'Cassell' should read 'Cassel'.
242	Line 27	'Edwards' should read 'Edwardes'.
243	Line 9	– 'from' should read 'some'.
246	Line 4	'India' should read 'Indian'.
248	Line 2	– 'neé' should read 'né'.
258	Line 20	– 'Errol' should read 'Erroll'.
262	Line 15	– 'School' should read 'College'.
263	Last line	– should read '£500 million'.
265	Line 5	– 'head boy' should read 'prefect'.
265		– This portrait is of Reuben Farley *not* Sir Cecil Ellerton. It should appear on page 323.
266		– Illustration caption should read '. . . *London (former Head Office of the London & South Western Bank)*'.
271		– Under **Writings** – add '"Frank Pick" *DNB 1941–50*'.
276	Line 27	– 'Maine' should read 'Main'.
281	Line 11	– 'London' should read 'Middlesex'.

VOLUME 2-*continued*

Page no

284	Line 18	– should read 'Cartagena, Spain'.
	Line 35	– 'Scotstown' should read 'Scotstoun'.
297	Line 27	– should read 'nv Philips' Gloeilampenfabrieken'.
300	Line 15	– should read 'Oranje'.
301	Line 13	– 'Lincolnshire' should read 'Leicestershire'.
303	Line 13	– 'Fower' should read 'Forrer'.
332	Line 34	– should read 'competition to produce'.
338	Line 41	– '1899' should read '1889'.
354	Line 7	– 'African' should read 'Africanus'.
356	Line 6	– should read 'FIELDING, Sir Charles William Ewing'.
362	Line 12	– 'Edgeware' should read 'Edgware'.
	Line 31	'Phillip' should read 'Phillp'.
367, 368		– add death date of Sir Clavering Fison: 15 April 1985.
370		– Title should read '. . . and 4th Earl Fitzwilliam of Great Britain'.
395	Line 31	– delete '&'.
408	Lines 9–10	– should read 'with the Manchester, Sheffield & Lincolnshire and the Great Northern'.
	Line 16	– delete 'Bradford via'.
	Line 25	– delete 'Lord'.
410	Line 39	– 'Pensnet' should read 'Pensnett'.
412	Line 32	– should read 'first Thames railway bridge'.
426	Line 23	– '55' should read '64'.
439	Line 42	– should read 'Somerdale'.
456	Line 42	– should read 'Britain'.
472	Last line	– should read 'Sir Hubert von Herkomer'.
474	Line 34	– should read 'Magden'.
	Line 43	– should read 'Arnold Forster'.
481	Line 44	– 'this' should read 'his'.
502	Line 2	– should read 'Old Buckenham'.
503	Line 14	– should read 'Freiburg'.
506	Line 19	– delete '*Edinburgh*'.
510	Line 20	– 'First Sea Lord' should read 'First Lord'.
	Line 47	– 'Bill' should read 'Act'.
514	Line 27	– should read 'was a founder member and first president of . . .'.
517	Line 40	– 'Bugworth' should read 'Bagworth'.
519	Line 18	– should read 'Sopron, Hungary'.
522	Line 15	– should read 'Chequer'.
527	Line 26	– should read 'Hinkley'.
531	Line 15	– should read 'Canfield Place'.
532	Line 16	– delete 'London &'.
	Line 22	– should read 'NER' not 'LNER'.
544	Line 3	– delete '&'.
553	Line 31	– should read 'Cokayne'.
557	Line 21	– should read 'Briggens, Stanstead Abbots, Hertfordshire'.
583		– title should read 'GODBER, Frederick, Lord Godber of Mayfield, Sussex'.
585	Line 12	– 'first' should read 'second'.
586	Line 9	– 'Cambridgeshire' should read 'Huntingdonshire'.
590	Line 27	– 'Hansa' should read 'Hausa'.
592	Line 12	– should read 'Collins's'.

VOLUME 2-*continued*

Page no

595	Line 18	– delete '(feller of trees)'.
597	Line 22	– '1763' should read '1783'.
603	Line 12	– should read '2nd ser 3'.
615	Line 20	– should read 'Ingersoll'.
616	Line 10	– should read 'Burgh-le-Marsh'.
626	Lines 7 & 12	– should read 'Kidderminster'.
628	Last Line	– delete line.
629	Line 11	– 'Philmore' should read 'Phillimore'.
	Line 18	– should read 'Depredations'.
635		– Portrait caption should read '*courtesy of Oliver Greene Esq*'.
636		– caption should read '*(copyright Greene King & Sons plc)*'.
637	Line 45	– should read 'neé Brune'.
638	Line 23	– 'Heinemann' should read 'Bodley Head/Jonathan Cape'.
639	Line 36	– 'Surinam' should read 'Syriam'.
640	Line 19	– should read 'HE Nichols'.
641	Line 22	– should read 'Champagne Charlie'.
642		– delete portrait entirely: this is *not* Arthur Greenwood (1845–1910) but Arthur Greenwood the Labour politician.
649		– Picture caption – '*Maldigrave*' should read '*Waldegrave*'.
651	Lines 21–22	– should read 'Algoma Steel Corporation, later controlled by Sir James Dunn (qv). Grenfell's aid was sought to turn it from a near failure into a prosperous business. The reforms . . .'.
656	Line 19	– should read 'Savill'.
666	Line 14	– 'Home' should read 'Horse'.
668	Line 9	– should read 'St John'.
669	Line 17	– 'funds' should read ''[funds]'.
675–678		– add death date of Dr Patrick Grove: April 1986.
683	Lines 23–26	– should read 'In 1905 he was made Viscount Iveagh and received further peerages in 1919, becoming Earl of Iveagh and Viscount Elveden'.
687	Line 19	– '1094' should read '1904'.

VOLUME 3

Page no

xix	Line 12	– '1975' should read '1974'.
xxi	Line 23	– 'Association' should read 'Corporation'.
1	Line 30	– delete '(qv)' after 'Self'.
36	Line 16	– '1890' should read '1980'.
38	Line 8	– insert '(qv)' after 'Wolff'.
47	Line 4	– Title should read 'Viscount Northcliffe of St. Peter in the County of Kent'.
154	Line 42	– delete 'of the responsibility'.
190	Line 22	– should read 'deepest pit at 1,008 yards (to include water at bottom); 1,001 was the depth at which men worked'.
245	Line 21	– William Hillman's life dates should read '1847/48–1921'.
245	Line 27	– 'James Starley' should read 'John K Starley'.
255	Line 25	– Title should read 'Viscount Hyndley of Meads'.
275	Line 2	– Title should read 'Lord Hirst of Witton'.
283	Line 11	– Title should read '1st Lord Hives of Duffield'.
303	Line 14	– Title should read '1st Lord Rotheram of Broughton'.

VOLUME 3–*continued*

Page no

386–387		– should read 'Hulton married first, in November 1900, at Bedford Registry Office, a divorcée five years his senior, Agnes Moir, formerly wife of Henry Bishop Turnball, and daughter of Peter Wood, newspaper proprietor. He married secondly, in February 1916, at Marylebone Registry, Florence Elizabeth Millicent, divorced wife of Thomas Edward Wallen, and daughter of John Warriss'.
571	Line 13	– 'Viscount' should read 'Lord'.
591	Line 26	– 'Nigel' should read 'Noel'; delete '(qv)' after 'Birch'.
687–689		– add death date of T A E Layborn; 17 December 1984.
747	Line 3	– should read –'He had transformed the nature of the British soap trade, he was expanding his business all over the world with factories . . .'.
788	Lines 35–37	– should read 'At the time he was highly praised on all sides and offered honours. He refused a baronetcy because he was afraid that such an honour would put him under pressure to observe the usual custom of leaving the bulk of his money to his heir in order that the title might be maintained in the appropriate style. He accepted . . .'.
788	Lines 46–49	– should read 'He seems to have lost all his capital, for income he relied on three directorships in American railway companies and on his wife's income, derived partly from property settled on her in 1879'.
789	Lines 6–8	– should read '(all educated at Winchester) and three daughters. His son Edward W Lidderdale was appointed to the Branch Banks Service of the Bank of England and served in the Branches at Plymouth, Leeds, London (Western Branch) and Newcastle upon Tyne where he was Agent from 1920 until his retirement in 1934. His . . .'.
792		– This photograph should not have appeared to accompany this entry.
793		– Picture caption should read '(*former Wigan Coal & Iron Co*)'.
845	Line 9	– 'Bertram' should read 'Bircham'.
890–895		– add death date of Sir William Lyons: 8 February 1985.
901		– Illustration caption should read '*transporter bridge*'.

VOLUME 4

Page no

viii		– 'Pasold, Eric Walter': delete 'Sir'.
xix	Line 12	– '1975' should read '1974'.
xxi	Last line	– Association should read 'Corporation'.
211	Line 4	– should read 'MOND, Julian Edward Alfred'.
236		– CROSS REFERENCE required for 'MILFORD, 1st Lord Milford of Llanstephan *see* PHILLIPPS, Laurence Richard'.
		– CROSS REFERENCE should read 'MILLBANK, Lord Duveen of Millbank'
259		– Picture caption should read '"*No Fines*" houses'.
430	Line 36	– 'GKN' should read 'Nettlefolds'.
469		– CROSS REFERENCE required for 'NUNBURNHOLME, Lord – *see* WILSON, Charles Henry'.
473–478		– add death date of George William Odey: 16 October 1985.
498		– Picture caption should read '*Sir Alfred Owen*'.
549–554		– Delete 'Sir' from title, running heads and picture caption.

VOLUME 4–*continued*

Page no

| 649 | Last line | – delete surplus 'the'. |
| 833 | Line 41 | – should read 'CM Woolf (qv)'. |

VOLUME 5

Page no

xix	Line 12	– '1975' should read '1974'.
120	Line 11	– '1964' should read '1974'.
391	Line 42	– should read 'He was twice married'.
411		– delete CROSS REFERENCE to SWANSEA.
489		– title to THOMAS should read 'the Basic process'.
553		– Picture caption should read '(*courtesy of Union Discount Co*)'.
661	Last line	– should read 'Lasenby Liberty'.
700	Line 15	– insert 'He married the sister of the publisher Alexander Strahan, who had founded his publishing firm in Edinburgh and then moved it to London in 1862'.
771	Line 1	– should read 'Whitbreads'.
772	Line 12	– 'Gifford' should read 'Giffard'.
782	Line 1	– delete 'W' from the name of Henry White-Smith.
783	Line 23	– should read '*British Aircraft, 1909–1914*'.
789	Line 29	– '*Clime*' should read '*Chime*'.
793	Line 9	– 'Burbage' should read 'Burbidge'.
797	Line 4	– delete final 'l' of 'Holtzapffell'.
837		– Illustration caption should read '"*Philanthropy*" (*The Rt Hon Lord Ashton*) by *MAC* Mayfair *23 Nov 1911* (*courtesy of Lancaster City Museum*)'.
884	Line 17	– 'Scott-Payne' should read 'Scott-Paine'.
889	Line 50	– should read 'River Rouge'.
902	Line 17	– should read '(qv, under Sir John Wolfe Barry).'.